Culture and Customs of Croatia

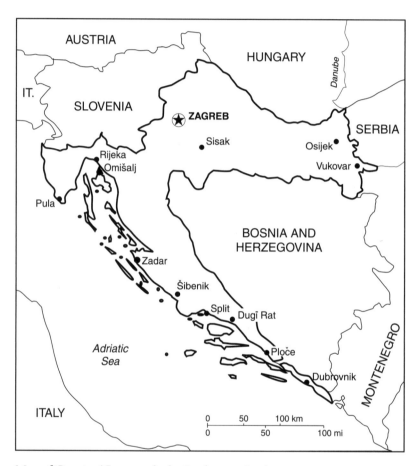

Map of Croatia. (Cartography by Bookcomp, Inc.)

Culture and Customs of Croatia

MARILYN CVITANIC

Culture and Customs of Europe

GREENWOOD

AN IMPRINT OF ABC-CLIO, LLC
Santa Barbara, California • Denver, Colorado • Oxford, England

Library of Congress Cataloging-in-Publication Data
Cvitanic, Marilyn.
  Culture and customs of Croatia / Marilyn Cvitanic.
    p. cm. — (Culture and customs of Europe)
  Includes bibliographical references and index.
    ISBN 978-0-313-35117-4 (hard copy : alk. paper) — ISBN 978-0-313-35118-1 (ebook)
1. Croatia—Civilization.   2. Croatia—Social life and customs.   3. Croatia—Social conditions.
4. Croatia—Intellectual life.   I. Title.
  DR1522.C85 2011
  949.72—dc22   2010037596

ISBN: 978–0–313–35117–4
EISBN: 978–0–313–35118–1

15 14 13 12 11   1 2 3 4 5

This book is also available on the World Wide Web as an eBook.
Visit www.abc-clio.com for details.

Greenwood
An Imprint of ABC-CLIO, LLC

ABC-CLIO, LLC
130 Cremona Drive, P.O. Box 1911
Santa Barbara, California 93116-1911

This book is printed on acid-free paper ∞

Manufactured in the United States of America

Contents

Series Foreword

The Old World and the New World have maintained a fluid exchange of people, ideas, innovations, and styles. Even though the United States became the de facto world leader and economic superpower in the wake of a devastated Europe in World War II, Europe has remained for many the standard-bearer of Western culture.

Millions of Americans can trace their ancestors to Europe. The United States as we know it was built on waves of European immigration, starting with the English, who braved the seas to found the Jamestown Colony in 1607. Bosnian and Albanian immigrants are some of the latest new Americans. In the Gilded Age of one of our great expatriates, the novelist Henry James, the Grand Tour of Europe was de rigueur for young American men of means to prepare them for a life of refinement and taste. In the more recent democratic age, scores of American college students have Eurorailed their way across Great Britain and the Continent, sampling the fabled capitals and burgs in a mad, great adventure, or have benefited from a semester abroad. For other American vacationers and culture vultures, Europe is the prime destination. What is the new post–Cold War, post–Berlin Wall Europe in the new millennium? Even with the different languages, rhythms, and rituals, Europeans have much in common: They are largely well-educated, prosperous, and worldly. They also have similar goals, face common threats, and form alliances. With the advent of the European Union, the open borders, and the Euro, and considering globalization and the prospect of a homogenized Europe, an updated survey of the region is warranted.

Culture and Customs of Europe features individual volumes on the countries most studied for which fresh information is in demand from students and other readers. The Series casts a wide net, including not only the expected countries, such as Spain, France, England, and Germany, but also countries such as Poland and Greece that lie outside Western Europe proper. Each volume is written by a country specialist with intimate knowledge of the contemporary dynamics of a people and culture. Sustained narrative chapters cover the land, the people, and offer a brief history; they also discuss religion, social customs, gender roles, family, marriage, literature and media, performing arts and cinema, and art and architecture. The national character and ongoing popular traditions of each country are framed in a historical context and celebrated along with the latest trends and major cultural figures. A country map, chronology, and evocative photos enhance the text.

The storied and enlightened Europeans will continue to fascinate Americans. Our futures are strongly linked politically, economically, and culturally.

Preface

The Republic of Croatia became a new country in 1991 as a result of the breakup of Yugoslavia through a series of wars that, to this day, remain difficult for many foreigners to understand. The former Yugoslavia was a complicated place with a mix of ethnic groups who spoke similar languages but had historic differences that made the state a volatile and ultimately untenable political entity. Although Croatia is now independent, it inherited the political and sociological complexity of the region. The wars leading to the breakup of Yugoslavia are just the latest in a long series of conflicts, whether economic, cultural, or militaristic in nature.

With a population of barely 4.5 million, Croatia's remarkably diverse landscape and culture make it a fascinating place to visit, and a surprisingly challenging country to study. Historians are quick to note that the country's most significant border approximates the 1,500-year-old division between the Eastern and Western Roman Empire, straddling the cultural divide between Europe and the Balkans. Over the centuries, its territory has been controlled by a procession of foreign monarchs and invading armies, many of which have left their mark on the religious and political thought of the region, as well as the psychology of its people.

Generalizations about a country and its people are convenient, and sometimes unavoidable. Croatia's diversity, however, makes sweeping statements particularly deceptive. In attempting to create an accurate picture, I have been as specific as possible with respect to regional differences as well as the historic events that have shaped contemporary Croatia. My hope is that readers will come to appreciate the unique convergence that this point in history represents. For the first time in approximately 900 years, Croatians living along the Adriatic coast, from the arid, rocky Dalmatian hinterland to the flat Pannonian plains, all belong to one sovereign state that is finally in a position to establish itself as part of the larger European community.

As a result of independence, the arts—including cinema, literature, and music—now offer a new, fresh perspective. Constitutionally, Croatian artists enjoy more freedom of expression than ever before. And while influenced by the former Yugoslavia, Europe, and the United States, the Croatian cultural scene is no longer just a subtext to a larger, overwhelming artistic agenda. In the years since independence, significant works of art, particularly films, have reflected the domestic experience, thereby legitimizing a uniquely Croatian viewpoint and reducing tendencies to mimic creative movements elsewhere in the world. In some cases, this self-awareness has unfortunately but predictably degenerated into blind expressions of nationalism, but those instances are becoming fewer as time goes on.

One can read (or write) about a country extensively but to understand it, ultimately, one must visit. My hope is that whatever knowledge I have acquired through my repeated trips to Croatia over the years is reflected in these pages and, in turn, inspires the reader to experience Croatia firsthand.

Acknowledgments

Many thanks to John Kruth for infinite support, patience, proofreading skills, and musical knowledge. Also to my parents Matilda and Niksa Cvitanic for making Croatia my second home and instilling in me an appreciation of its culture and people. And thanks again (and again) to my editor Kaitlin Ciarmiello.

Chronology

8000–4000 BCE	Neolithic farming settlements develop throughout Slavonia, particularly in the vicinity of Vukovar, as well as along the Adriatic coast, on the islands of Korcula and Hvar.
2500 BCE	Coastal communities involved in shipping and trade exist.
Fourth Century BCE	Celts arrive in the latter part of the fourth century BCE and introduce the potter's wheel to the local culture. Greek settlers arrive at approximately the same time and influence the cultural landscape of the Adriatic region where they establish small colonies, the most significant of which is at Starigrad on the Dalmatian island of Hvar and on the nearby island of Vis.
229–219 BCE	Romans and Illyrians fight wars primarily in the coastal regions of Dalmatia.
End of Third Century CE	Roman Emperor Diocletian builds his palace in Split.
Fourth and Fifth Centuries	Huns and Germanic tribes invade.
Sixth Century	Byzantium controls Dalmatia.
Seventh Century	Slavic tribes, including Croats, migrate to territory in and around present-day Croatia.
Ninth Century	Croats convert to Christianity.

910–928	King Tomislav reigns.
1066	King Kresimir IV founds Sibenik, the first large city established by native Croats as opposed to their Romans or Illyrian predecessors.
1102	Croatia loses independence through union with Hungary.
1202	During the Fourth Crusade, Venetians use crusaders to conquer Zadar.
1242	Mongols sack Zagreb.
1526	Following the defeat of Hungary by the Ottoman Turks at the Battle of Mohacs, Croatia (along with Hungary) pledges allegiance to Austrian Archduke Ferdinand of Hapsburg as king.
1528	Creation of the Military Frontier prevents Ottoman incursions.
1593	Croatia defeats the Ottoman army at Sisak.
1797	Venice loses control of Dalmatia and Istria to the Hapsburg Empire.
1805	Dalmatia comes under French rule as a result of Napoleon's victories against Austria.
1814	Hapsburgs regain control of Dalmatia and most of Croatia.
1830s	A group of Croatian writers founded the Illyrian movement (also known as the Croatian Revival), marking the first major step forward in the development of a modern Croatian identity.
1847	Croatian language replaces Latin as official language of the Sabor.
1848	Ban Josip Jelacic leads successful military effort to suppress Hungarian nationalist rebels.
1905	Stjepan Radic founds Croatian People's Peasant Party.
1914–1918	Croatia sides with Austria-Hungary during World War I.
1918	Croatian Sabor declares that the unified lands of Croatia, Dalmatia, and Slavonia will join the South Slav state, which became known as the Kingdom of Serbs, Croats, and Slovenes.
1928	Montenegrin politician Punisa Pacic assassinates Stjepan Radic in Belgrade at meeting of Parliament.
1929	Serbian King Alexander I establishes a royal dictatorship and the country is renamed Yugoslavia.
1934	Exiled members of an early Ustashe movement, with help from Macedonian radicals, assassinate King Alexander.

April 1941	Germany invades Greece and Yugoslavia. Italy declares war on Yugoslavia. The Ustashe quickly fills the leadership vacuum and, with the support of the German occupiers, establishes the Independent State of Croatia.
June 1941	Partisan resistance begins civil war against the Ustashe regime.
1945	World War II ends and Croatia becomes part of the Socialist Federal People's Republic of Yugoslavia.
1945–1948	Soon after World War II, much of the economy is nationalized and subject to centralized control by the Federal Planning Office in Belgrade, following the Soviet model.
1948	Josip Broz Tito does not follow policy dictates from Stalin and ultimately breaks with the Soviet Union.
1965	Economic weaknesses lead to introduction of some free market elements and liberalization.
1968–1971	The movement for greater Croatian autonomy, referred to as the Croatian Spring, culminates in 1971 when members of the Communist Party, along with students from the University of Zagreb, take to the streets in protest.
May 4, 1980	Josip Broz Tito dies.
1980s	Yugoslav economy stagnates. Communist authorities are unable to motivate workers, and production declines. Republics begin to assert independence.
1989	Communism collapses in Eastern Europe.
May 1990	Ultranationalist Franjo Tudjman leads the *Hrvatska demokratska zajednica* (HDZ), or Croatian Democratic Union, to victory in the first free multiparty elections in decades.
June 25, 1991	Croatia declares independence.
July 3, 1991	Homeland War begins. *Jena Nomina Anatomica* (JNA), or Yugoslav People's Army, occupies part of Slavonia.
April 8, 1992	The United States recognizes Croatia as an independent state.
May 1992	Croatia enters the United Nations.
August 4–August 8, 1995	Operation Storm, a large-scale military effort to retake parts of Croatia that had been occupied by ethnic Serbs, succeeds after four days.
November 21, 1995	Dayton Peace Accords end the Homeland War.
1997	Croatia reelects Tudjman prime minister but faces criticism regarding HDZ authoritarian policies and tolerance for corrupt business practices by well-connected "tycoons."
1998	East Slavonia, the last occupied part of the country, is peacefully integrated.

December 16, 1999	Prime Minister Tudjman dies.
January 2000	Social Democratic Party wins parliamentary elections. Ivica Racan becomes prime minister.
September 2001	The Hague tribunal on war crimes and crimes against humanity indicts Yugoslav President Slobodan Milosevic for crimes committed during the Homeland War.
February 2003	Croatia applies for European Union (EU) membership.
November 2003	Ivo Sanader of the HDZ becomes prime minister.
December 2005	The arrest of fugitive Croatian General Ante Gotovina, who is wanted by the Hague tribunal on war crimes, allows EU accession talks to begin in earnest.
November 2008	Croatia is on track to join the EU by 2011, but EU officials demand additional action against corruption and organized crime.
April 2009	Croatia joins North Atlantic Treaty Organization (NATO).
July 2009	Prime Minister Sanader resigns. Sanader's deputy, Jadranka Kosor, becomes prime minister.
January 2010	Ivo Josipovic, of the Social Democrats, wins the presidential election.

1

Geography and History

One only need look at the crescent shape of Croatia to recognize that its borders were not created according to natural geographic barriers or human convenience. An overview of Croatian history illustrates the fluctuating nature of those perimeters, which most recently have been determined by the Homeland War of the 1990s. The conflict and resulting treaties established Croatia's borders with Serbia and Bosnia and Herzegovina[1], but some issues still remain unresolved. As of August 2010, Croatia has been engaged in a border dispute with neighboring Slovenia, which originated in 1991 when both states left Yugoslavia. This disagreement is of particular importance to Croatia because it has delayed Croatia's entry into the European Union. The most pressing issue is the border that extends through Piran Bay, also known as Savudrija Bay. At present, its exact location is in doubt, resulting in problems for naval police patrols and confusion over fishing rights.

Croatia is located in southeastern Europe and shares borders with Bosnia and Herzegovina, Slovenia, Serbia, and Montenegro, and has a coastline of 1,104 miles (1,777 kilometers) along the Adriatic Sea. It has a total area of 21,831 square miles (56,542 square kilometers) making Croatia approximately the size of West Virginia and the 133rd largest country in the world.[2]

Its landscape varies dramatically, as anyone who has driven throughout the country can attest. More than 1,000 islands are spread throughout the coastal waters and dramatic mountain ranges contrast with flat plains in the interior of the country.

Geographically, Croatia can be divided into three regions: the north and northeastern part, the central mountainous highlands, and the coastal area.

The north and northeastern part of Croatia encompasses the territory in the vicinity of Zagreb as well as Slavonia to the east, including the Pannonian and para-Pannonian plains. To the north of Zagreb are the Zagorje Hills, which extend to the Slovenian border and are on the fringes of the Julian Alps. This beautiful region is covered with lush vegetation, small vineyards, and orchards.

In contrast, Slavonia is largely flat and includes some of Croatia's most fertile farmland. The Sava and Drava rivers both flow through this region and over the centuries have deposited rich soil contributing to the high quality of the land for farming. The lush, wild vegetation that grows along the riverbanks creates a welcome contrast to the fields and cultivated farmland that characterizes this region. Both of these rivers are navigable and therefore relevant for transportation. The Sava is the longest river in Croatia, beginning in Slovenia, running through Zagreb and providing approximately 373 miles (600 kilometers) of navigable waterways. Rivers also form Croatia's international borders along the northern crescent of the country with the Sava delineating a large part of the border with Bosnia and Herzegovina and the Drava defining a bit of the border with Hungary but then joining the Danube, which creates the Croatian border with Vojovdina, a province of Serbia.

The climate of this region is characterized as continental, meaning that the summers are hot and the winters are cold. In the Pannonian plains, the average temperatures as calculated from data collected between 1961 and 1991 range from 32°F (0.4°C) in the winter to 68°F (20.3°C) in the summer.[3,4] Scientists have projected that temperatures may increase in Pannonia approximately four degrees within the next hundred years due to global climate change.

The central mountainous highland region is part of the Dinaric Alps and runs northwest to southeast. This mountain range is linked to Europe's main Alpine mountain range by the Julian Alps which stretch from northeastern Italy through Slovenia. The Dinaric Alps run to the coastline and into the Adriatic where, partially submerged, they form the islands off of the Croatian coast. The largest of the Dinaric peaks is called Mount Troglav, which has an elevation of 6,276 feet (1,913 meters). Just as well known is the Biokovo range, which is closest to the shoreline and provides for breathtaking views as one drives along the main coastal highway tracing the edge of the mountain range.

The Biokovo range rising above the Dalmatian town of Makarska. (Courtesy of the author.)

These mountains form a barrier between the Adriatic Sea and the interior region of the country. Natural passes do not exist.[5] Travelers must drive across treacherous mountain roads that trace ancient trails along which, for centuries, sure-footed mules carried goods between inland and coastal towns. Typically, the peaks are jagged, dramatic, and barren, providing a striking contrast to the heavy vegetation at lower elevations. The mountains are sparsely populated and agriculture is minimal.

The rough terrain of the Dinaric Alps is characteristic of a karst landscape. This sort of topography is created by the dissolution of soluble stone, such as limestone or dolomite, and while this topography is also found in other regions of Croatia, the Dinaric Alps are a particularly good example of this geological phenomenon. Like most karst landscapes, Croatia has a significant number of underground springs, most of which have not yet been tapped for commercial purposes. Caves and sinkholes also typify karst landscapes. According to the Speleological Committee of the Croatian Mountaineering Association, 49 caves in Croatia have a depth exceeding 1,706 feet (250 meters) The deepest of these caves is located in the vicinity of Mount Velebit and extends 4,567 feet (1,392 meters) underground.[6]

Cold winters and warm summers are typical for this mountainous region, although temperatures are milder at lower elevations, especially in the winter.

The higher peaks generally are covered with snow during the winter months and rainfall can be significant during the fall and spring. The average temperature range is from 60–68°F (16–20°C) in June to 21–36°F (–6–2°C) in January.

Coastal Croatia includes the Istrian Peninsula to the north and the Dalmatian coast farther south. The Istrian Peninsula is the northernmost coastal part of Croatia located between the Gulf of Trieste and the Bay of Kvarner. The beaches are popular with tourists, but the interior is compelling in its own right with a green hilly landscape covered by vineyards, orchards, and fields situated between lush forests. Istria's tallest peak is Mount Ucka with an elevation of 4,580 feet (1,396 meters). It is part of the Cicarija mountain range, which divides the Kvarner region from central Istria. The terrain does not lend itself to large-scale agriculture; smaller farms and vineyards abound, as do picturesque hilltop villages.

The Lim Fjord, also known as Lim Bay, is one of the most dramatic coastal features of the Istrian Peninsula. The Lim Valley follows the Pazincica River for 22 miles (35 kilometers), until descending into the Adriatic, creating the a deep turquoise fjord. Lined by steep cliffs on both sides, legend has it that the fjord was a favorite hiding place for pirates waiting to attack Venetian merchant ships. Today it is a popular tourist attraction and also is used to cultivate mussels and oysters.

Upon heading southward to the Dalmatian coast, the green hills of Istria give way to a drier, more barren, but equally beautiful landscape. The Dalmatian coast begins with the island of Rab and extends southward to include the coastal cities of Zadar, Sibenik, Split, and Dubrovnik. The scenery along this stretch of coast is among the most dramatic in Europe with the jagged Dinaric Alps descending into clear blue Adriatic waters to create a shoreline full of idyllic inlets, some of which have served as harbors for centuries. Standing anywhere along the Dalmatian coast, one can see islands along the horizon, making for a dramatic panorama. The mountainous terrain coupled with a dry climate have made large-scale agriculture difficult in most of Dalmatia, although olives have been cultivated for centuries along with vineyards for wine production.

The Dalmatian coast and Istria have a Mediterranean climate that ranges from 36–46°F (2–8°C) in January to 64–75°F (18–24°C) in June. July and August can get quite a bit hotter with temperatures topping 104°F (40°C). As in Pannonia, scientists expect these temperatures to rise between three and almost five degrees in the next 100 years because of global climate change.[7]

The coastal region is subject to distinct winds, known as the Bura, the Jugo, and the Mistral. The Bura has attained legendary status in Croatia. It is a dry wind that blows from the Dinaric Alps to the sea and can reach dangerous speeds of 50 meters per second or more than 100 miles per hour.[8] The dramatic geography of the coastal mountains leads to the creation of wind tunnels through which air rushes to the coast resulting in the Bura, which is strongest at the Velebit Kanal (near Krk) and in the Gulf of Trieste, but affects the entire coast south of the Istrian Peninsula and Dalmatia. Known to overturn boats and cars, a strong Bura will force the closing of ferry crossings and even some bridges. This potentially violent wind poses a particular concern for sailors, because it can start abruptly. Seas that were calm a moment before are suddenly treacherous, making it especially dangerous for vacationers who are unfamiliar with local conditions. In the summer, the Bura lasts a few days at most, and often provides welcome relief from the hot and somewhat hazy and humid air that accumulates along the coast. Particularly in larger seaside cities such as Split, it cleanses the atmosphere and reduces particulate air pollution. During the winter months, it can be quite unpleasant, lasting for weeks at a time bringing a biting cold along with it, and often rain and snow.

The Jugo, also known as the Sirocco, comes from the Sahara in Africa and brings the warmth and moisture that often precedes a summer storm. It is found throughout the Mediterranean, and unlike the Bura, which can begin suddenly, the Jugo develops more slowly and is rarely as powerful. It typically is found in the southern areas of the Adriatic coast where it tends to be strongest; however, in the spring, the Jugo also blows in the northern coastal regions. Locals often complain that this wind causes health problems, including headaches, fatigue, and joint pain because of the increase in humidity.

Finally, the Mistral is a refreshing summer breeze that blows in from the relatively cool sea across the warmer land and brings much-needed relief from the heat in the summer. It is milder than the Bura and generally is considered good for sailing and outdoor summer sports, and is especially ideal for windsurfing.

The coastal region also includes the largest archipelago in the Adriatic with 698 islands, 389 islets, 78 reefs, and approximately 2,500 miles (4,023 kilometers) of shoreline.[9] Although reports vary, somewhere between 47 and 66 islands are inhabited.[10] The economy of most islands centers around tourism so during the winter months the population declines. In spite of this, the islands still export some traditional products, such as wine and olive oil, to mainland Croatia, and in some cases internationally.

The Croatian archipelago extends along the entire length of the coastline. The Kvarner Bay, located in the Northern Adriatic between the Istrian Peninsula and the Northern Dalmatian coast is home to the largest islands, Cres and Krk, each approximately 154 square miles (400 square kilometers). In central and southern Dalmatian, the islands are the product of Dinaric Alpine peaks that are partially submerged in the Adriatic. As a result, they have the same karst landscape as the mainland, are generally hilly with curvaceous coastlines, and support only minimal agriculture. Some larger islands, however, have significant mountain peaks, the largest of these being Vidova Gora (2,559 feet, 780 meters) on the island of Brac, which is the third largest island at 153 square miles (396 square kilometers). Although it is technically not an island, the Peljesac Peninsula is attached to the mainland by such a small strip of land that it seems like one. The peninsula covers a substantial area just north of Dubrovnik and is famous for the red wine that has been produced there for many years.

HISTORY

The earliest evidence of the Croats as a unique people begins in the fourth century. It generally is believed that the earliest Croats were a Slavic tribe living in the region north of the Carpathian Mountains. Apparently these tribal societies were not influenced by Roman civilization, living hundreds of miles from the borders of the Empire.

The Croats arrived in the Balkans with other Slavic tribes in the seventh century. The reason and precise date of their slow migration is unclear, but eventually they found themselves in the Roman province of Illyricum, whose defenses were severely weakened by successive attacks of invading barbarian tribes. While some Croats remained in Pannonia, a northern region of 21st-century Croatia, others continued on to Dalmatia and the Adriatic Sea where they eventually settled cities and dominated the coastal region. Unlike earlier Slavic tribes, the Croats did not invade or attack the cities and towns they came across; rather they settled in the area and soon adopted the indigenous Roman culture.

Although these early Croatians were largely self-governing, with seven or eight clans wielding power over a kingdom organized into districts governed by a series of local princes, they could not remain entirely independent of the Byzantine Empire, which by the sixth century had regained its strength under the reign of Emperor Justinian. By the end of the seventh century, they had accepted Byzantine authority over both the interior of the country as well as the Dalmatian coast. This authority was partially shifted to Charlemagne in the ninth century as the Frankish ruler took control over Dalmatia, with the exception of a handful of cities and islands that made up a Byzantine province governed by locally stationed representatives.

The Introduction of Christianity and the First Croatian State

Thanks to Charlemagne's efforts, Christianity spread through Dalmatia. While Croats certainly were exposed to Christianity through their Roman neighbors and perhaps some converted earlier, the mass baptisms of the ninth century represented a permanent shift toward Christianity, and ultimately Catholicism, which is a trademark of Croatian culture to this day.

This ninth-century conversion also led to the development of the first Croatian bishopric in the city of Nin, led by the charismatic bishop Grgur Ninski (Gregory of Nin), who made history by challenging the authority of the Roman church. He conducted services in the Croatian language as opposed to Latin, which few Croatians had studied. Aside from its practical implications, this move marked the beginning of a conflict between those favoring an independent Croatian church and those willing to yield to the pope in Rome. It has also guaranteed Grgur Ninski a permanent place in Croatian history as one of first to take a stand for Croatian autonomy.

Ivan Mestrovic's statue of Grgur Ninski, currently located in Split near the Golden Gate of the Diocletian Palace. (Courtesy of the author.)

In the 10th century, with the ongoing struggle between the bishopric of Nin and papal authorities as a backdrop, Tomislav I, then the duke of Dalmatian Croatia, fended off separate waves of Hungarian and Bulgarian invaders. Having defeated his enemies, Tomislav united Dalamatia with Pannonian Croatia, creating one large Croatian state extending to the Drava River and including the string of cities along the Adriatic. With the pope's permission, Tomislav was crowned king of Croatia in 925. According to prevailing scholarship, Tomislav's kingdom, the first independent Croatian state, included modern Croatia, parts of Bosnia and the coastal region of Montenegro. According to legend, King Tomislav could field an army of 100,000 foot soldiers, on par with the Byzantine Empire. Although this may be an exaggeration, Tomislav's newly united Croatia was nevertheless regarded as a significant power in medieval Europe.

Croatia's military strength made the conflict between Grgur Ninski and the papal authorities based in the Dalmatian city of Split all the more relevant. The bishop wanted to weaken ties to Rome by establishing a church governed primarily by local Croatian bishops, thereby giving Nin independence from the pope and papal representatives based in the archbishopric of Split. Grgur, along with other Croat clergy, wanted to deviate from Church tradition in a number of ways. He not only delivered the Mass in the local language, but also advocated married clergy and opposed the Latin alphabet, favoring instead the use of Glagolica, the local alphabet.

Rome took this conflict seriously and officially put an end to the efforts of the renegade bishop through two papal synods held in Split in the years 925 and 928. Synods were meetings held by high-ranking church officials in which the issues at hand were debated and votes were cast. Little is known of King Tomislav's final position in this debate, although it is clear he was in a delicate spot. While on good terms with Rome, having sworn allegiance to the pope, the king could not deny the influence of Grgur among the local population. Both synods were guaranteed to affirm the authority of the archbishopric of Split over Nin since papal representatives outnumbered the lone Grgur. The second synod was held only to quell local protests that erupted after the results of the first meeting. When these synods repeatedly sided with Rome, the bishopric of Nin was dismantled and Grgur was offered the bishopric of Sisak, a backwoods ruin at the time, and therefore considered unacceptable. Little was heard from the bishop after that and King Tomislav's name eventually vanished from historical records.

In his comprehensive history of Croatia, Marcus Tanner noted that the conflict between Grgur of Nin and papal authorities represented a crucial moment in Croatian history.[11] Had King Tomislav actively defended Grgur, perhaps Rome would not have pressed their point in defending the archbishopric of Split against Nin. In that case, the bishopric of Nin could have become the single preeminent ecclesiastical authority in Croatia, lessening Rome's influence and placing even more power in the hands of the Croatian king.

Grgur's efforts were not entirely unsuccessful. Although use of the old Croatian language at Mass was forbidden, it was never completely abolished. The persistence of this practice can be attributed, at least in part, to an independent streak within the Croatian clergy, but on an even more practical level, to the fact that few local priests and even fewer members of the lay population had ever studied Latin. Finally in the 15th century, Rome officially allowed the celebration of the Mass in Croatian and use of Glagolitic script for the liturgy. This rule eventually applied to the rest of Croatia and became a long-standing tradition in many coastal cities.[12] Notably, Croatia was the first and only European country given this privilege.

Invasions and Loss of Sovereignty

In the meantime, King Tomislav's suppression of the Hungarian invaders was only temporary. By the end of his reign, Croatia covered a large amount of territory and wielded substantial military power. Unfortunately, however, it lacked a centralized place of political, economic, and religious authority. After Tomislav's death, infighting among various religious and secular authorities weakened the state and culminated in the assassination of Tomislav's successor, an act that precipitated violence and anarchy, making Croatia a vulnerable target for European powers, most notably the Venetians, looking to gain territory and influence.

By the beginning of the 11th century, Venice had invaded and conquered coastal Dalmatia. Approximately 50 years later, King Kresimir IV regained this territory for the Croatian Crown and, in 1066, founded the city of Sibenik on the Dalmatian coast. Thus, Sibenik, still sometimes referred to as "Kresimirovgrad" (Kresimir's City) holds the unique honor of being the first large city founded by native Croats rather than their Roman or Illyrian predecessors.

Although Kresimir certainly strengthened Croatia by regaining territory from the Venetians, the state was still fragile and its future uncertain. In 1076, Kresimir's successor, Zvonimir, accepted papal sovereignty to provide stability to the otherwise vulnerable Croatian state.

King Zvonimir staved off foreign aggression until his death, but soon afterward the Hungarians invaded again. In 1102, Croatia lost its independence and would remain subject to control by foreign powers for nearly 900 years. Initially, the Hungarian king, Kalman, allowed Croatia substantial autonomy by agreeing to preserve the local culture and, to a great extent, local control, by refraining from populating Croatian cities with Hungarians.

This was just one condition of an agreement called the Pacta Conveta between King Kalman and the local noble families. The Pacta Conveta stated that Croatia and Hungary exist as two separate states governed by the same ruler, namely, the Hungarian King Kalman and his successors. It is doubtful that Croatia entered into this union voluntarily. Although the Croatians hoped their alliance with Hungary would protect coastal cities from Venetian aggression, the Pacta Conveta did not provide for an even balance of power. It left Croatia with an independent feudal parliament called the Sabor but gave the Hungarian king the right to collect taxes, appoint local governing authorities, and most important, control the Croatian military.

Despite the threat of Venetian invasion and Hungarian domination, Croatian culture continued to evolve, reflecting trends taking place on a larger scale in other more stable European states. With the exception of the higher echelons of clergy, the population of Croatia, as well as the rest of Europe, was largely illiterate. In the 12th century, however, a new social order based on legal documents and the written word began to emerge. Historical records reveal that along the Dalmatian coast notaries engaged in the practice of certifying public documents. The city of Korcula, appears to have been the first to employ written statutes as law in 1214.[13] Literacy slowly increased, as did the publishing of books. Perhaps the most famous text of this period is the *Historia Salonitana,* a history of the city of Split from antiquity through the Middle Ages written in the 13th century by the Archdeacon Thomas of Split. Historians have noted that this text not only is one of the best of its kind, but also reflects the priority that the Split bishopric placed on educating its clergy.[14] Most clergy, including Archdeacon Thomas, were educated abroad and later returned to Croatia.

The cultural progress of this period occurred within the context of political instability. Croatian hopes of defending their coastal cities were dashed in a series of Venetian invasions after Kalman's death in 1116. Control of the Adriatic was critical for Venetian trade with Byzantium, which was still an important economic and political entity. The Hungarians also valued access to the coast, but they were at a geographic disadvantage, trying to control an area so far away from their base in Pannonia. The Venetians' initial invasions did not yield permanent territorial gains but did lead to the destruction of the coastal city of Biograd, until that point a major economic and political center. Biograd never regained its prior status, and for centuries, has existed in the shadow of its powerful neighbor, Zadar.

Ultimately, the Venetians set their sights on Zadar, whose fortifications included an impressive seawall. After a series of failed attempts by the Venetian military to capture the city, including an unproductive 10-year siege, they sought a different approach. The Fourth Crusade, a particularly bloody chapter of Venetian history, provided just the opportunity they were looking for.

To compensate the city of Venice for providing ships and trained crews for the crusade, which was supposed to invade Jerusalem by way of Egypt, the crusaders conquered Zadar for the Venetians. The attack, which took place in 1202, was particularly vicious as it violated the papal order forbidding aggression toward Christians. The citizens of Zadar were caught off guard and hung banners bearing crosses over the city walls thinking that surely the crusaders had made a mistake. The banners were ignored and the city was destroyed. In response, the pope proceeded to excommunicate the crusaders and ordered Venice to pay Zadar for damages. In the end, Zadar was never compensated. Although the ruined city eventually recovered, its character had changed forever. In 1358, Zadar was returned to the Croat-Hungarian state, though it was eventually "sold" to Venice along with much of the Dalmatian coast in the early 15th century and remained under Venetian control until the Napoleonic wars in the late 18th century.

Meanwhile, by the mid-13th century, Slavonia, located in the interior of Croatia, faced a different threat—Mongol invaders. Their reputation as fierce and ruthless fighters preceded them, inspiring terror throughout the countryside as they approached. Expert horsemen, the Mongols traveled quickly raiding villages and small towns in their path. Having already defeated large armies in Russia, they easily subdued the Hungarian military. Before they were finished with Europe, the Mongols slaughtered at least 70,000 European soldiers, many of whom were knights and members of the noble classes.[15] The defeat of the armies in the Eastern European region made the Mongol goal of conquering Western Europe much more of a realistic possibility.

Regarding Croatia, the Mongols eventually would destroy Zagreb, which had temporarily served as a sanctuary for the exiled King Bela and members of his court until they were forced to flee to the Dalmatian coast. Through a lucky twist of fate, the Mongols never conquered Split or Trogir. As they prepared to lay siege to Trogir, the invaders apparently were informed of the death of the Mongol Khan (their king). Sparing the cities along the Adriatic, the nomadic army suddenly packed up and headed home in preparation for the battle over the succession of the Mongol throne. Although the invasions had weakened the authority of King Bela, Zagreb was quickly rebuilt.

In the meantime, feudalism was prevalent in Slavonia and feudal lords expanded their estates, building fortified castles and private armies. The death of King Bela in 1270 allowed the most powerful of the feudal families, the Subics of Bribir and the Frankopans of Krk, to assert their independence. They installed Pavao Subic as an independent monarch, giving him the title "Ban Subic," Ban being a term for viceroy, or one who governs a region as the representative of the monarchy. He controlled the coastal cities of Split, Trogir, and Sibenik as well as some interior territories. Unfortunately, Ban Subic, at the insistence of the pope, attacked Zadar in an attempt to free the city from Venetian control. Not only was Subic killed in the debacle, but Split and Trogir allied themselves with Venice to defeat Subic's forces. While the Hungarians ruled the Croatian interior, Dalmatia was a different story. By rebelling against the Hungarian crown, the Croat nobility gave Venice the opening it needed to expand its Dalmatian conquests over Split, Trogir, Sibenk, and Nin by 1329.

Ultimately, Dalmatia returned to Hungarian control in 1358, when King Louis I pressured the Venetians to give up their conquests peacefully. The local nobility also submitted to the Hungarian king, placing the coastal territory from Istria to Albania under the Hungarian crown. By all accounts, this was a relatively peaceful period of cultural and economic growth. Trade between the coastal and interior regions led to the spread of Glagolitic script and the first vernacular literature in the form of texts describing the lives of saints and early church figures.

The death of King Louis I in 1382 began a period of civil war and lawlessness culminating, with the help of a group of Croatian nobles, in the crowning of Ladislas of Naples, as ruler of southern Croatia in 1408. That Ladislas's claim to central Dalmatia was questionable did not stop him from selling control of Zadar and its surroundings to the Venetians for a small fee. Exhausted by war, the Dalmatian people finally accepted the Venetian protectorate, which by 1420 extended down the entire coastline from Zadar to Dubrovnik. This situation had numerous pros and cons. The economy of coastal Dalmatia had declined under Venetian control. Coastal cities were of vital importance under Hungary, with Croatia facilitating maritime links with the rest of the world. Because Venice already had established its own trading routes, it viewed these cities as potential competitors for trade and production of goods similar to those already controlled by the Venetians. Living in the shadow of Venice, the Dalmatian coast never reached its full economic potential. The population, however, both inland as well as on the islands was well aware of the impending threat of invasion by Ottoman Turks. Lacking any means of defending themselves from an enemy that already had conquered Bulgaria and Serbia, the Croatians needed the protection Venice offered. The area remained under Venetian control until the fall of the Venetian Republic in 1797.

Development along the Adriatic

Although feudalism was prevalent inland, the peasants living along the coast enjoyed considerable freedom, could lease land, and legally retained the right to at least part of the harvest. Coastal cities were well positioned for trade and grew wealthier, developing shipbuilding industries as well as trade in olive oil, salt, and fish. Split outgrew its city walls and suburbs began to develop.

Urban development along the coast was encouraged by the arrival of monastic orders, primarily the Franciscans and Dominicans. Unlike their predecessors, who built monasteries in rural areas, these orders settled in the cities and became an integral part of urban life. They spread throughout Europe, bringing increased attention to cities and contributing to the cultural and economic development that set the stage for the building of large Gothic cathedrals throughout the continent. The prosperous cities of the Dalmatian coast were not left behind. Between the 12th and 14th centuries, cathedral construction was begun in Trogir and Sibenik while the older cathedral in Dubrovnik was rebuilt in the Romanesque style.

Dubrovnik stood in contrast to other major cities along the Adriatic, which were victims of repeated periods of turmoil between the Venetians, the Croatian-Hungarian state, and the Croat nobility. The other major Adriatic cities of Split, Trogir, Sibenik, and Zadar lagged behind Dubrovnik both culturally and economically.

Since its founding in the 7th century, Dubrovnik (called Ragusa until 1909) managed to avoid the foreign attacks that other coastal cities experienced. Political dexterity must be credited because potential enemies, which included Byzantium and Venice as well as Serbian and Bosnian warlords living in the interior, surrounded Dubrovnik. Dubrovnik never fully ceded political independence, although it did proclaim sovereignty to various governments from time to time according to political expediency. Most significant, the city maintained some Byzantine connections until 1205 when it accepted Venetian sovereignty. Dubrovnik managed to avoid strong connections to the Hungarian-Croatian state for as long as possible. Historians have noted that, once it emerged from a period of Venetian sovereignty in 1358, it did not require new citizens to proclaim allegiance to Hungary-Croatia. Instead, they pledged allegiance only to Dubrovnik, allowing the city to use the split with Venice to further assert its independence.

By the mid-14th century, Dubrovnik reached near complete independence from Hungary-Croatia. It was in an ideal position to thrive both economically and culturally and needed little outside help. Its location made it an essential stop for maritime trade between the Balkan interior and the Western Mediterranean and Europe. The adjacent Bosnian and Serbian territory was rich in natural resources, including silver, but few outsiders dared venture into this lawless wilderness. Merchants from Dubrovnik knew the countryside and profited significantly by acting as middlemen between the tribal kings and warlords of the hinterland and European merchants. Eventually

Dubrovnik bought land in Bosnia and Serbia, establishing small but profitable trading colonies, primarily in coastal regions.

As a result of its long history of peace and prosperity, Dubrovnik not only rivaled Venice for the control of maritime trade, but its citizens also enjoyed a higher standard of living than elsewhere in Croatia. Like other major European cities, Dubrovnik's streets were paved, and it had a system for water supply and sewage disposal, and in certain ways, it was ahead of its European counterparts. It boasted the first pharmacy in Europe as well as a lazaretto, part of a system of quarantine for visitors who might possibly spread communicable diseases, such as bubonic plague. An orphanage and home for the elderly also were included within the city walls.

Ottoman Invasions and the Military Frontier

The Ottoman Turks were descendants of one of many nomadic Turkish tribes, which, after migrating from the central Asian steppe, converted to Islam. They were skilled warriors who fought for the expansion of Islam and managed to conquer substantial territory and get rich in the process. The Ottoman forces, composed largely of highly motivated, quick-moving cavalry with strong unity of command, easily conquered much of the Balkans by the beginning of the 15th century. By contrast, European armies often were manned by untrained peasants commanded by independent noblemen who were motivated chiefly by their personal interests. To make matters worse, the Balkan states frequently suffered regional conflicts making Serbia, Bosnia, Bulgaria, and Croatia vulnerable targets. While the Turks were on Croatia's doorstep, having defeated the Serbs in 1392, the country was still fragmented over issues of succession after the death of Hungarian King Louis I in 1382. In the meantime, by 1396 Dubrovnik's business community had seized the moment and negotiated a treaty and trade agreement with the Ottomans.

The Ottoman Turks first entered Croatia through Slavonia. They had a standardized but effective strategy of making successive raids on an area, avoiding major military confrontation but weakening the population both economically and psychologically. Eventually, even the nobility and their armies could not put up much resistance. Often those who could leave did so, creating significant migrations of refugees, many of whom headed to the Adriatic coast and islands, others leaving the country all together.

The most significant battle for Croatia took place in 1493 at Krbava Valley near Lika, southwest of Zagreb. The Croats were soundly defeated and heads of the noble families killed. Generally, the territory could not be defended effectively, there had been too many invasions, too much devastation, and much of the population had already fled or been taken into Ottoman slavery. Poised to conquer Croatia and having taken part of Slavonia, the

Ottomans made their way to the coast and captured the port city of Makarska in 1500. With the exception of Northern Dalmatia, which was still largely under Venetian control, the remaining Croatian territory was part of the Hungarian-Croatian state. Rather than defend Croat land, Hungary occupied itself with internal tensions between the nobility and the crown. Ultimately, the monarchy was weakened significantly, leaving the country without a strong central government and either unable or unwilling to protect vulnerable regions, including most of Croatia, from Ottoman forces.

The Croatians did not give up territory without a fight, however. Clearly, war against the Ottomans was different from previous conflicts that occurred around royal succession or acceptance of the sovereignty of one or another Christian state. Croatians, along with the rest of Europe, saw the Islamic Ottoman forces as a threat to Christianity, and therefore a threat to the essence of their civilization. By virtue of its relative proximity to the east and west, Croatia acted as a buffer between the Ottomans and much of Western Europe. By 1519, Pope Leo X called Croatia the bulwark of Christendom. With the loss of Knin to the Turks in 1522, coupled with the absence of Hungarian defenses, Croatia looked to the Hapsburg Emperor Charles V for assistance as well as to the pope. Should Croatia fall to the Ottomans, little would stop the Turks from invading Western Europe. Even so, help did not arrive, and the conditions in Croatia deteriorated. Ottoman raids were catastrophic for the general population with villages burned, livestock stolen, prisoners taken into slavery, and the economy of the rural regions of the country severely jeopardized.

The decisive 1526 victory of the Turks over the poorly organized and ill-equipped Hungarian army in the field of Mohacs, presently located in southern Hungary near the Croatian border, opened Europe to Ottoman advances quickly leading to the capture of Buda (present-day Budapest). At this point, the Croatian nobility pledged allegiance to the Austrian Archduke Ferdinand Hapsburg with the hope of assistance in fending off Ottoman advances. Once again, help was not forthcoming, and more Croatian territory continued to fall to the Turks. By 1540, the last of the Christian outposts in Bosnia fell and the Ottomans continued their conquest of Slavonian territory, claiming the towns of Osijek, Bihac, and Vitrovica.

The town of Sisak became vulnerable and with it the integrity of the Croatian state. Should Sisak fall, the Ottomans easily could progress to Zagreb and split the state in two. At this point, Croatia had been reduced to a fraction of its pre-Ottoman size, and its economy was severely damaged. The precarious nature of the situation forced the Hapsburgs to act decisively.

The Vienna-based Hapsburg leadership decided to step up defenses in the region. Most significantly, in 1538 the Croatians, with support from

Vienna, organized a military frontier along the border of Ottoman territory. This defensive network was composed of a string of castles that are still referred to by their Croatian name, *Vojna Krajina,* which translates into the Military Frontier. The frontier extended from the Drava River to the Kupna River and from the Kupna to the Adriatic. The town of Karlovac, near Zagreb, was the headquarters of the Military Frontier command and built specifically to suit this purpose. It was a garrison city, designed within massive walls in the shape of a six-pointed star. Some historians have called Karlovac a model of Renaissance city planning,[16] but others have noted that since the town was built on damp marshland, it was an undesirable place to live and had trouble attracting residents.

By 1570, the entire Military Frontier was manned by about 3,000 poorly armed men spread across a series of crumbling forts. The Croatian Sabor was disappointed in the poor way the region was administered but could do little as the Hapsburgs funded the endeavor and viewed *Vojna Krajna* as Austrian territory.

The situation was further complicated when the Hapsburgs invited the Vlachs to settle and defend the area. These were mountain people of Orthodox faith whose ethnicity has been debated by contemporary Croatian and Serbian scholars in light of the recent Homeland War of the 1990s in which Croatia and Serbia fought over possession of the Military Frontier. Whether the Vlachs are ethnic Serbs or simply identified as such because of later political pressure is unknown. However, in the early 17th century, they populated, worked, and defended the war-torn region.

Once the Hapsburgs placed the region under direct control of the Austrian military, they also instituted the Vlach Statutes of 1630, which, in exchange for a commitment of lifelong military service in defense of the Military Frontier, the Vlachs were freed of any feudal obligations the Croatian nobility or Church might impose and gave them ownership of the land they cultivated.

The frontier was strengthened, but the privileges of the Croatian nobility were severely compromised. Although feudalism had declined in much of Europe by the 16th century, it was still quite common in inland Croatia. Few people outside of the nobility were free, thus the freedom of those living in the Military Frontier provided inspiration to those still living in feudal bondage on large estates. The extent of this threat to the nobility is illustrated by comparing the size of Croatia, about 4,093 square miles (10,600 square kilometers) to that of the Military Frontier at 3,088 miles (8,000 square kilometers).[17]

By the end of the 16th century, the Turkish offensive slowed somewhat, partly due to two failed attempts to conquer Vienna in which Croatian forces played an important role. The first attempt in 1529 ended in a siege lasting approximately two months, ultimately forcing Suleiman, the legendary Ottoman ruler, to retreat and regroup only to return again in 1566. The second Ottoman incursion was blocked at a fortress at Szigetvar, Hungary, which was defended by Hapsburg forces led by Croatian Ban Subic Zrinski. About a month into the siege of the city, the 72-year-old Suleiman died, forcing the army to attack Szigetvar quickly, because they soon would have to return to Istanbul for the succession of the new Sultan. The courage of Zrinski's defending army in the face of an impending attack is legendary. Although greatly outnumbered, Zrinski repeatedly refused offers to surrender, thereby forcing the aggressors to expend valuable time and military resources to finally conquer Szigetvar. Zrinski and most of his soldiers were killed defending their position, but they managed to successfully delay the Ottoman assault on Vienna and, ultimately, Zrinski was credited with saving Vienna. He became a national hero, recognized to this day in the popular Croatian opera *Nikola Subic Zrinski*.

Although they were weakened, in 1593, the Ottomans managed yet again to launch a campaign against Croat territory, this time opting to attack Sisak directly rather than the seemingly impregnable Karlovac. Initially they were defeated and tried again, unsuccessfully, the following year. Although they were unable to progress further, their persistence initiated a long period of bloody guerilla warfare, which accomplished little for either side.

In 1683, the allied Hapsburg, German, and Polish army dealt the Ottoman army a decisive blow at Vienna. The tide had turned, giving the locals the upper hand in the conflict. Over the next several years, the Turks lost ground in the region and in 1699 signed another peace treaty forcing the return of all Croatian and Slavonian land except for part of Srijem, presently located on the border between Croatia and Serbia. The Ottoman threat was diminished, but skirmishes continued during the first half of the 18th century and, finally, the borders of the country were fixed on the Una-Sava line.

At this point, Croatian Catholics living in Bosnia, which remained under Ottoman control, migrated to newly freed Croatia lands (Dalmatia was still under Venetian control). To replace those leaving Bosnia came people from other Balkan regions of the Ottoman Empire who eventually adopted the Serbian Orthodox faith as well as the Serbian ethnic identity. This group ultimately formed the Serbian minority in Bosnia, which became a source of political tension and ethnic conflict through the present day.

By the 18th century, Croatia was largely a military state under Hapsburg control amounting to 15,500 square miles (40,300 square kilometers), of which only 3,700 square miles (9,620 square kilometers) were outside of the Military Frontier.

The Military Frontier served to protect Europe from diseases that spread from the east. In 1710, a "Plague Edict" was established. If plague or other contagious disease appeared in Turkey, a quarantine period was enforced. All travelers and goods coming from the East would be held at the border for anywhere from three to six weeks before entering Croatia and the rest of Western Europe.

By the middle of the 16th century, Venetian territory in Dalmatia was stripped down to a narrow stretch of the coast, isolated from the rest of Croatia by Ottoman lands. Zagreb and its surroundings were emerging as political and economic centers, which they still are in the 21st century. Simultaneously, northern Adriatic towns such as Rijeka grew more important, providing safe access to the sea, which Dalmatia could no longer offer.

As usual, Dubrovnik proved to be the exception. Realizing that they could not defend themselves from Ottoman invaders, Dubrovnik broke with the defeated Hungarian-Croatian state and accepted Ottoman protection, all the while maintaining as much independence as possible. The city's trading links with both the Balkans and Mediterranean allowed them to act as middlemen between east and west as well as pursuing direct trading interests. The city retained its economic standing until April 6, 1667, when an earthquake and subsequent fire devastated the town, killing nearly half of the population of 7,000. Dubrovnik managed to hold on to its independence during this difficult time, but its economy was permanently damaged.

Declining Power of the Nobility

With the waning Ottoman threat, Croatia finally was able to develop both economically and culturally. Generally, the Croatian population did not enjoy the same standard of living experienced in more prosperous parts of Western Europe, but wealth did accumulate. The nobility and growing bourgeoisie built large mansions in their hometowns as well as lush vacation homes along the Dalmatian coast.

The inland state of Croatia was not given the kind of support it was hoping for, from either the Austrians or Hungarians.[18] The Croatian Sabor appealed for as much sovereignty as possible but ultimately had little influence because both Austria and Hungary were actively vying for control over various parts of the country. In short, the Hapsburgs governed the Military Frontier while much of the rest of the country was still dominated by a traditional feudal system. Immigration and resettlement further complicated the situation. When Slavonia was relinquished by the Ottomans, it was resettled by Catholic Croats and Orthodox Serbs, who returned to the old villages that they abandoned during the years of heaviest fighting. In the meantime, the Hapsburgs encouraged peasant immigration to Croatian lands. The Germans

and Hungarians moving to Slavonia created a large population of free peasants, thereby destabilizing the existing feudal system. To preserve the power
of the nobility, the Hapsburg government made a point of selling or granting
Croatian territory to German or Hungarian nobles. The Catholic and Orthodox churches also were granted substantial parcels of land.

A great deal of the territory recovered from the Ottomans was considered
part of the Military Frontier. The Hapsburgs in Vienna controlled the
Frontier, and its population still enjoyed their freedom from the feudal
system that was the norm in the rest of civil Croatia. Although the Coatian
Sabor, with its strong ties to the noble class, was determined to govern the area,
their claim to it was fragile at best. Many of the Frontier soldiers were
motivated to push the Ottomans back because they wanted to increase the
territory they eventually could control. Being freemen, the land was theirs
to cultivate, they were not bound to the demands of an aristocratic overlord.
Generally, the Sabor's power eroded between the pressures of the Austrians,
the Hungarians, and in the Military Frontier, the Orthodox Serbs.

It was only a matter of time before the Croatian peasants outside the
Military Frontier revolted against the feudal lords who continued to tax and
exploit them. By the middle of the 18th century, a series of uprisings led to the
establishment of laws limiting the degree to which serfs could be exploited.
Although this signaled greater freedom for the individual peasant class, the
state of Croatia was still caught between Vienna and Hungary, each attempting to exercise as much control as possible. By the end of the 18th century,
any hope of substantially increasing Croatian sovereignty was suspended for
the foreseeable future.

In 1790, the Hapsburg King Joseph II tried to centralize power in Vienna.
Along with his plan came a series of reforms that challenged the traditional
privileges of the Catholic Church and noble classes. Joseph II focused on
the abolition of feudalism, the establishment of tax reforms to alleviate the
burdens placed on the peasant and middle classes, freedom of worship for
Protestants, and, finally, the establishment of German as the official language.
These reforms did not sit well with the Croat nobility. Hoping to retain some
autonomy and authority, members of the Croatian Sabor aligned themselves
with Hungary. The plan backfired: the Sabor was dissolved, and rather than
fostering a more independent Croatia, the Hungarian Parliament did their
best to create a permanent Hungarian identity in Croatia by enforcing the use
of the Hungarian language and annexing Slavonia.

Dalmatia and the End of Venetian Rule

In the meantime, Dalmatia was still under Venetian rule, which had
expanded to cover land seceded by the Ottomans in the 17th century. While

the population had grown to include Christians who fled from Ottoman occupied areas of Bosnia, the region's economy did not grow. Dalmatia's fortunes declined substantially under the Venetians. By the time the Venetian Republic fell in 1797, Dalmatia was in deep economic trouble. The Venetians repressed development by forcing the region to import as much as possible from Venice. Dalmatia could export raw materials to the Venetians such as lumber, olives, salt, and wine, but Venice set the prices it paid for these exports, thereby keeping Dalmatia impoverished while denying any real support for development of industry or public works.[19] Once prosperous, Dalmatians found themselves destitute, with reports of starvation coming from the interior. A major outbreak of plague hit in 1783 setting the region into a decline from which it would not emerge for decades.

In 1797, the Venetian Republic crumbled as Napoleon invaded Italy. Initially Dalmatia and Istria were given to the Hapsburgs but soon war broke out again and, in 1805, after Napoleon's victories against Austria, Dalmatia fell into French hands. While Dubrovnik was not included in treaties between the Austrians and French, the independent republic had grown weak and vulnerable. Mediterranean and Balkan trade routes had slowed, leading to an economic decline that eroded the authority of the governing nobility which proved increasingly ineffectual in maintaining the Republic's independence. In 1808 the French, who had entered the city peacefully, effectively ended Dubrovnik's centuries as a sovereign republic by replacing the traditional governing senate with French rule. Auguste Frédéric Louis Viesse de Marmont, a French general, having already been named governor of Dalmatia, was given the title duke of Ragusa (Dubrovnik) and, for the first time, Dubrovnik was governed by a foreign power.

This period was characterized by a number of wars, but Dalmatia generally benefited from French rule. New roads were constructed and old ones refurbished. The first newspaper, *King's Dalmatian*, was published in both Croatian and Italian, the Italian language being an artifact of Venetian rule and preferred by the nobility. The French also did away with the remaining vestiges of feudalism and built new schools for both boys and girls, and demanded by law that at least one child in every family be educated. French reforms were ambitious and expensive enough that Napoleon criticized Marmont for excessive spending. The period of French rule was short, ending in 1813 with Napoleon's ill-planned campaign against Russia. Dalmatia was then awarded to Austria with the British given control of the islands of Vis and Korcula. At this point, in 1815, the Austrians took control of Dubrovnik and included it in the Kingdom of Dalmatia without differentiation from the rest of the state. The French reforms were quickly forgotten as Austria abolished all earlier laws and an attempt was made to turn back the clock to a Croatia that existed before French control. However, freedom from Venetian rule, coupled with advances made during the short period of French occupation, had planted the seeds of a national Croatian identity in Dalmatia that would influence events into the 21st century.

The Illyrian Movement

Croatia was fragmented both territorially as well as by regional differences in culture and language. It also was caught between two powers, Austria and Hungary. In 1790, when Hapsburg King Joseph II tried to strengthen his monarchy and expand his control over the region, the Croatian nobility responded by strengthening their ties to Hungary. Their hope was that Hungary would preserve the Sabor, thereby at least keeping some power in the hands of the Croatian nobility, who lived in the northern regions of the state. Meanwhile, administration of the coast was in transition. After the French left, Dalmatia initially was controlled by Vienna for a short while, but in 1813, the Austrians turned over administration of Dalmatia to the Italian minority which had controlled the region under Venice. With the departure of the French in 1813, no further attempts were made to increase literacy or otherwise improve conditions in Dalmatia.

The notion of a cohesive Croatian language was at the foundation of the early nationalist movements that began to surface in Croatia as well as elsewhere in Europe. Given the fragmentation and occupation of Croat territory by other countries, it not surprising that this nascent nationalism was counterbalanced by a strong regionalism, characterized by, among other things, a multitude of dialects spoken throughout Croatia. The introduction of a common language was critical in unifying the country. In this sense, Croatia was in step with much of the rest of Europe; the use of vernacular language for civic affairs was a trend that was gaining popularity in Europe along with a general nationalistic consciousness that swelled in Croatia.

During the first half of the 19th century, an increasing pressure to force a Hungarian identity on Croatia led to a backlash, with Croats asserting their own culture through the revitalization of their heritage, and most importantly, the definition of a Croatian mother tongue. Although the importance of a common Croatian language was acknowledged in Zagreb's intellectual circles, it was not until the early 1830s that a viable nationalist Slav movement was born. Ljudevit Gaj is credited as the founder of the Illyrian movement, which began with a group of like-minded young intellectuals in Zagreb interested in developing and promoting Slavic identity in response to the pressures of increasing Hungarian nationalism.

Gaj was born just north of Zagreb in 1809 and was fascinated by Croatian history and folklore from an early age. Before studying in Vienna, he attended school in Varazdin, where, to his disappointment, he found his education lacking in reference to Croatian identity. Classes were held in Latin and the overall emphasis was Hungarian—contemporary Croatia was nowhere to be found. Gaj's experience was not unique—throughout Croatia, the native culture and language was relegated to the peasant classes. The growth of a young bourgeois class in the early 19th century served Gaj's interests well. Many of the early members of the Illyrian movement were business people and professionals as well as intellectuals who had roots in the peasant class and historically had never identified with the local nobility, whose deep ties to Hungary were still apparent.

By identifying itself as "Illyrian," Gaj's movement aspired to include all South Slavs, and reflected the notion that Slavs living under the Hungarian umbrella were descendants of the ancient Illyrian tribe. Although it began in Zagreb, the Illyrian movement was not conceptualized as a vehicle for Croatian nationalism per se. Their selection of the *Stovaski* dialect, spoken by Serbs as well as Croats, reflects this broader notion of Slavic identity. Ivo Goldstein and Nikolina Jovanovic[20] note that by selecting the term "Illyrian," Gaj promoted the idea that Slavs were indigenous to the region, a theory dismissed by later historians but that was functional for Gaj's goal of combating regionalism and the pressures of Hungarian nationalism. In the end, however, the movement remained primarily Croatian with the Slovenes and Serbs actively pursuing their own national identities.

The Illyrian movement marks a major step forward in the development of a modern Croatian identity, but substantial obstacles remained. Croatia was divided administratively between Austrian and Hungarian control with the majority of the populace identifying regionally rather than with Croatia as a single entity. As the Illyrian movement progressed, it became known as the Croatian National Revival and is associated with Gaj's 1835 publication of *Novine Horvatske* (Croatian News) and its literary supplement, *Danica Horvatska*. The paper was written in the *Stovaski* dialect and included patriotic political editorials, poems, and fiction. Gaj's personal contribution to the Croatian Revival included his popular poem known by its first line, "Croatia is not finished yet." By 1841, the movement was large enough to form the Illyrian Party, a political party whose objective was the formation of a unified Croatian state within the current Hungarian system.

The Illyrians sparked a countermovement among the nobility who still were aligned with Hungary, thus forcing Vienna to act to maintain the stability of the region. Vienna, viewing the Hungarian threat as the greater of the two, placated the Hungarian nobility by temporarily banning use of the term "Illyrian," while simultaneously supporting the standardization of a Croatian language. The Illyrian Party continued along its course, simply changing its name to the National Party and going on to found *Matica hrvatska* (Croatian Queen Bee), a cultural institution dedicated to the further development of a standard Croatian language and unified Croat identity.

Croatian links to Hungary were weakened because of external as well as internal events. In 1848 Hungarian nationalists rebelled against Hapsburg rule. By this time Hungarian nationalism and an independent Hungary was more threatening to Croatia than Hapsburg rule. The Hungarian nationalist movement had little regard for Croatia and proposed to reduce Croatian territory and reinstate Latin as the official language. The Sabor, in turn, declared war against Hungary and supplied the Hapsburgs with military assistance to suppress the Hungarian revolt. Josip Jelacic, for whom the main square in Zagreb is named, was a dedicated Austrian officer and Croat, and had been elected to the office of Ban by the Sabor. He led the military effort and, alongside Austrian forces, suppressed the nationalist Hungarian revolt. Jelacic sympathized with Illyrian ideals and quickly became a national hero.

During the spring of 1848, a meeting of the nationalist movement in Croatia met in Zagreb to craft and adopt the "Demands of the People" (*Narodna Zahtijevanja*). This document outlined a delicate balance between Hungary, Austria, and the notion of Croatian independence, and called for the unification of the "Slav People of the Triune Kingdom" (referring to Austria, Hungary, and Slav lands) into an autonomous state while remaining loyal to the Hapsburg monarchy and maintaining some administrative ties to Hungary. Most significant, the document called for the abolition of serfdom, a call heeded by Jelacic, who issued a proclamation freeing serfs from their obligatory labor on feudal estates. By the summer of 1848, the Croatian Sabor took the related and equally unprecedented step of making the nobility and clergy liable to taxation for the first time.

Ultimately, the revolutionary movements in Croatia and Hungary led to political instability and forced the Hapsburg monarchy to tighten control over Croatia, abolishing Croatian autonomy, reducing Jelacic's political significance, and effectively placing Croatia under Hapsburg rule.

Jelacic continued to serve as *Ban* until his death in 1859, although this period of Hapsburg rule must have been frustrating. His dreams of an independent Croatia with a strong and unique cultural identity were crushed, and he was rendered powerless. Despite his failures, Jelacic remained dear to the hearts of Croat people. In 1866, a statue of the *Ban* on horseback was erected in the main square in Zagreb, which was renamed in his honor. Jelacic's legacy was questioned in the mid-20th century when Communist leaders of Croatia labeled him a tool of the Hapsburgs for having fought in the name of an oppressive monarchy rather than being the leader of a progressive political movement. In 1945, his statue was removed, and Zagreb's main square was renamed Square of the Republic. Jelacic's legacy was revived in 1991 when Croatia declared independence from Yugoslavia. His statue was dusted off and placed once again in its original location and the square renamed in his honor.

Hapsburg Rule and Croatian Nationalism

Hapsburg rule was not entirely negative for Croatia, modernization certainly occurred, but Croatian nationalist sentiments were oppressed. In 1851, the Hapsburgs dissolved the Croatian Sabor, removing any pretense of self-government. Freedom of the press was abolished, the Croatian flag was banned, and German became the official language. In the meantime, the Austrian program of reform generated an environment conducive to free enterprise and the development of a market economy. Generally, these reforms were based on the creation of a modern administrative bureaucracy, fiscal system of taxation, and judiciary. Additionally, improvements were made in infrastructure, such as the building and maintenance of roads and construction of a railway. The Hapsburgs initiated a modern postal system and for the first time stamps were used in Croatia. The entire Hapsburg state became a single market, eliminating all internal customs and other obstacles to commerce.

Unfortunately, much of Croatia was barely beyond feudalism and unable to fully take advantage of the new market opportunities. Historians have noted[21] that more than 90 percent of the population paid the lowest tax rate because they still lived in homes with thatched roofs. Most peasants, as well as lords, were having trouble adjusting to the postfeudal economy. Peasants had few resources to begin producing anything on their own and the land-owning classes were angered by the fact that provisions were not made to ease the transition from a feudal to a market-based economy. In the meantime, a modernization program began to yield positive results in education. Many new four-year elementary schools were opened throughout Croatia. A large proportion of peasant children did not attend these schools and illiteracy remained high, but at least a system of basic public education was established. In the high schools, German was emphasized and Croatian was portrayed as an inferior language.

In spite of Austria's best efforts to obliterate Croatian nationalism, strong feelings remained throughout the 1850s. The notion of Yugoslavia, a unified state of Southern Slavs, took hold by projecting the idea that Croatians were part of a family of Slavic peoples. Simultaneously, as Croatian nationalism continued to grow, its proponents rejected the pan-Slavic philosophy of the Illyrian movement. Ultimately, these nationalistic sentiments evolved into an opposition to Austrian control of Croatia and pushed toward the development of a uniquely Croatian culture within a Southern Slav or Yugoslav framework.

On this scene of Slavic nationalist consciousness came Joseph Georg Strossmayer, a Roman Catholic bishop who delved deeply into affairs of politics as well as religion. Like Jelacic, Strossmayer believed in the unity of Orthodox and Catholic Slavs and felt that the divisions between the two groups were emphasized by Vienna and Hungary to more easily control the Croatians and Serbs.[22]

Early on, Strossmayer established his reputation as an independent thinker. When he received his degree in theology from the University of Pest in 1837, his examining board predicted that he would either become the "greatest heretic of the nineteenth century or the strongest pillar of the Catholic Church."[23] While still in his 30s, Strossmayer was appointed bishop of his home diocese of Djakovo, located in Slavonia. In addition to building schools and libraries, in 1866, he initiated construction of the local cathedral, which remains the most significant architectural landmark of the region. While attending to his ecclesiastical duties, Strossmayer displayed a clear commitment to *Jugoslavenstvo,* or south Slavism, which called for the unification of all Southern Slavs currently under Austrian and Ottoman rule. This grand notion was the central theme of the National Party (as the Illyrians were now known), but from a practical standpoint, Strossmayer and his colleagues focused on alliances between Croats and the state of Serbia.

While Strossmayer's Nationalist Party aroused patriotic sentiments, it did little to further Croatian sovereignty. In 1867, the Austro-Hungarian dual monarchy was created leaving inland Croatia under Hungarian control while Dalmatia remained Austrian. The Hungarians granted Croatia the right to use the Croatian language in official contexts, but despite Strossmayer's best efforts, they severely limited any reforms that promoted sovereignty or national identity, including allocating 55 percent of Croatia's revenue toward a joint treasury, leaving only 45 percent for domestic projects.[24]

Strossmayer eventually retreated from the political frontline but continued his cultural efforts, including the founding of the Academy of Arts and Sciences and the development of the University of Zagreb into a European-caliber institution. He never abandoned the notion of *Jugoslavenstvo,* and in his later years, he focused on the reconciliation of Catholic and Orthodox churches as a means of unifying Croatians, who are primarily Catholic, and Serbs, who are largely Orthodox. Although these efforts were futile, Strossmayer's contributions to Croatian national identity and culture were substantial and earned him a permanent place in Croatian history.

In addition to Strossmayer, other significant figures emerged from the Illyrian movement. Of these, Ante Starcevic was the most influential, although ultimately his philosophy differed significantly from Strossmayer's. Rather than promote the unification of Croats and Serbs, by the 1850s, Starcevic adopted a vehemently anti-Serbian position, a reaction based on Serbia's complete lack of interest in the Illyrian movement. The Serbs had a semiautonomous nation, which presented a foreign policy more oriented toward the expansion of Serbian territory than any concept of South Slavic unity. Leading Serbian intellectuals espoused the view that the majority of the Croatian population of Slavonia, Bosnia, and even most of Dalmatia were actually Serbian, based on the perception that the dialect spoken in these areas was of Serbian origin. The Catholic population of Croatia had little interest in such theories, but the Orthodox minority, lead by the clergy, identified with this view to the extent that their loyalty to Austria-Hungary and Croatia eventually was compromised by a desire for recognition of a Serbian nation within Croatia.

In 1861, Starcevic was elected to the Croatian Sabor where he continually pushed for weakening ties with Austria-Hungary and eventually founded the Croatian Party of Rights (HSP) based on the demand for Croatian autonomy.

Starcevic's call for an independent and uniquely Croatian state was, at the very least, a pragmatic reaction to Serbia's position. He is credited with giving rise to the concept of a Croatian national identity and generally is viewed as a patriot. His legacy, however, is complicated by his vehemently anti-Serbian language, which has been used over the decades to fuel ethnic tensions between Serbs and Croats.

Toward the end of the 19th century, mutual opposition to Austro-Hungarian control quelled animosities between Serbs and Croatians. Political tensions between Austria-Hungary and Croatia and Serbia led to the formation of a Croat-Serb coalition. The Military Frontier officially became part of Croatia in 1881, increasing the Serbian population within Croatia and making a unified South Slav state a practical necessity, whether Croatia ultimately remained under Austro-Hungarian control or not. In 1906, a Croat-Serb coalition party swept elections in both Croatia and Dalmatia and took control of local government throughout the region. At the same time, Croatian politics began to expand beyond theoretical debates about the nature of a Croatian state and focused on improving the standard of living for the general population composed mostly of peasants. Stjepan Radic, the most influential Croatian politician at the turn of the century, founded the Croatian People's Peasant Party on a platform of Croatian autonomy as well as peasants' rights and land reform, all of which stood to undermine Austro-Hungarian authority.

World War I and the Kingdom of Serbs, Croats, and Slovenes

The dissolution of Austria-Hungary in World War I did not result in Croatian sovereignty, but it did lead to the creation of a new country based on the unity of the South Slavs. In 1918, the Croatian Sabor declared that the unified lands of Croatia, Dalmatia, and Slavonia would join the South Slav state, which became known as the Kingdom of Serbs, Croats, and Slovenes. Stjepan Radic and his Croatian People's Peasant Party objected to this union fearing that Croat rights would be subordinated to the interests of the more powerful Serbia. Over the next 10 years, Radic's party gained popularity as Serbian leaders dominated the new state at the expense of Croat interests. He continually called for an independent Croatian state, but by 1921 a highly centralized government was formed further compromising Croatian prospects for self-rule. Radic was assassinated on the floor of the Sabor in 1928 by a Montenegrin extremist. His People's Peasant Party had succeeded in establishing some land reforms for peasants and continued to function as a force for Croatian independence in the increasingly chaotic political environment of the new South Slav state.

Dalmatia, which was not prosperous to begin with, received another setback with the dissolution of Austria-Hungary. The region had provided the large Austro-Hungarian state with an outlet to the sea and benefited accordingly. The Dalmatian economy also relied on its shipbuilding industry that specialized in construction of commercial wooden sailing ships, a fragile business at best because steamships rapidly were replacing wooden vessels. Fishing and agriculture were important industries that gradually began to decline at this time.

Using the threat of civil war as justification, a dictatorship was established in 1929 under Serbian King Alexander I. The state was renamed Yugoslavia and under the pretense of ethnic unity, internal provincial borders were redrawn based on geography rather than history, thereby dividing Croatia into several parts. Radical elements in the Croatian nationalist movement were hardened by the assassination of Radic, and after the parliamentary government was suspended, Ante Pavelic, a leading Croatian nationalist, founded the Ustashe Croatian Liberation Movement. The Ustashe, as they became known, believed in the creation of a free, self-governing Croatian state, independent of foreign rule, and they declared their willingness to fight for it. Although most Croats believed that their problems could be solved within the framework of the unified state of Yugoslavia, the Ustashe argued for its destruction. The Yugoslav leadership, based in the Serbian capital city of Belgrade, tried to imprison Pavelic. He and his followers went into exile, eventually finding refuge and support in Italy under Fascist leader Benito Mussolini. The Ustashe, with help from Macedonian radicals, successfully planned and executed the assassination of King Alexander in 1934. Prince Paul, the late king's cousin, became acting regent while the king, Peter II, was underage. Prince Paul initially did little to address Croat grievances. In 1939, faced with growing pressure from the Croatian Peasant Party, Prince Paul was forced to allow the creation of a self-governing Croatian province within Yugoslavia. This solution to growing tensions between Croats and Serbs might have worked had World War II not broken out.

World War II

Yugoslavia's initial declaration of neutrality in World War II did little to protect it from German and Italian aggression. The country itself was divided. The Serbian regent, Prince Paul, harbored strong ties to England where he was educated and lived for a number of years, and Serbia itself leaned toward France and Great Britain. Some Croats harbored sympathies toward Germany, which was quick to exploit divisions between Croats and Serbs by promising to satisfy the Ustashe's demand for an independent state of Croatia, whose borders would expand to include parts of Bosnia and Herzegovina.

In April 1941, Germany declared war on Yugoslavia. The country's leadership was in chaos and the Yugoslav army offered little resistance. The Croatian Peasant Party declined to take a clear stand against the Germans. Roman Catholic archbishop Cardinal Alojzije Stepinac also remained passive. The Ustashe quickly filled the leadership vacuum and, with the support of the German occupiers, proclaimed the establishment of the Independent State of Croatia, also known as the *Nezavisna Drzava Hrvatska* (NDH), with Pavelic as head of state.

Pavelic's new government did not enjoy popular support. The Ustashe leadership had spent years in exile and never developed a strong following among either intellectuals in Zagreb or the peasant class. Their leadership of the NDH did little to build enthusiasm, as the new state was independent in name only. The coastal region was controlled by Italy while the Germans controlled the area around Zagreb as well as Slavonia and part of Bosnia. In reality, the NDH was little more than a Nazi puppet state based on a dictatorship that mercilessly persecuted Jews, Serbs, Gypsies, and Croats who opposed the Ustashe agenda.

A resistance movement, known as the Partisans, soon began under the leadership of Josip Broz, better known as "Tito."[25] Of Croatian and Slovenian descent, Tito was the secretary general of the Communist Party of Yugoslavia. He emerged as leader of the multiethnic Partisan movement, and he had little trouble finding recruits. In addition to the Serbian population, which was clearly threatened, the Ustashe had alienated Croats from a variety of backgrounds and geographic regions. The population of Dalmatia never identified with the Ustashe movement in the first place and certainly felt betrayed by the apparent ease with which the NDH leadership allowed Italian annexation. The Ustashe's persecution of left-wing intellectuals and Jews offended many in Zagreb's more cosmopolitan circles, and while some joined Partisan forces in the countryside, others remained in the city planning and undertaking terrorist activities, including the assassination of Ustashe and German soldiers. Croatia, like the rest of Yugoslavia, became increasingly sympathetic to the Partisan cause, especially once the United States entered the war on the side of the Allies. The defeat of the Nazi regime and the end of the Ustashe's grip on Croatia was now only a matter of time. By 1943, Tito's Partisans defeated the Ustashe and Serbian royalist forces (known as Chetniks) in a bloody civil war, which took place under the umbrella of the larger conflict of World War II.

The Ustashe's ruthless suppression of ethnic minorities created an atmosphere of terror throughout the territory of the NDH. In an effort to create an ethnically pure Croatian state, the Ustashe adopted the Nazi's methods of ethnic cleansing, which included widespread atrocities throughout Croatia as well as the parts of Bosnia and Herzegovina with large Serbian populations. Orthodox Serbs sometimes were spared if they converted to Catholicism and occasionally Jews were given the option of buying "honorary" Aryan status.[26] Many Jews were sent to concentration camps, along with Gypsies, Communists, and other political prisoners. The largest of these camps was located along the Croatian-Bosnian border at Jasenovac. Historians have debated how many people perished at the hands of the Ustashe. Recent studies estimate the death toll at the concentration camps at 120,000 with numerous others killed in massacres throughout the region.

In the final days of the war, the Partisans captured Belgrade with help from the Soviet Red Army. They marched onward to Zagreb while the Ustashe and their sympathizers fled to Austria. Pavelic managed to escape and ended up living in exile in Argentina. The majority of the Ustashe army along with civilian refugees crossed the Austrian border and surrendered to British forces at the village of Bleiburg. Initially, the British viewed the Ustashe as prisoners of war, but the British policy soon changed, and they were loaded into trains and shipped back to the Yugoslav side of the border. The trains were met by the Partisans, who indiscriminately slaughtered both civilians and soldiers. Survivors were forced to endure long marches to prison camps, where many were killed. An estimated 40,000 to 100,000[27] Croatians perished as a result of the Bleiburg episode, the final horrific chapter of Croatia's involvement in World War II.

Socialist Federal Republic of Yugoslavia

In 1945, Croatia became part of the Socialist Federal Republic of Yugoslavia, which consisted of six republics: Croatia, Serbia, Montenegro, Slovenia, Bosnia and Herzegovina, and Macedonia. Tito emerged as premier (and in 1953 adopted the title of president) of the postwar government, and the Croatian Communist Party soon suppressed all political opposition, including those calling for a sovereign Croatian state. Tito's Yugoslavia initially was modeled after the Soviet Union and based on the concept of an ethnically diverse but unified state with a strong central government. Because many Serbs served in the Partisan forces during the war and were, by far, the most numerous ethnic group, they were rewarded with a substantial number of important posts in the federal government and army. The strong Serbian influence in the central government eventually led to a less than equitable status for Croatia and the exploitation of Croatia's economic resources, which were used to bolster the economies of other less prosperous Yugoslav republics.

At this time, the borders of the Republic of Croatia were set, mostly according to historic precedent. A commission using ethnic standards fixed the border with Serbia. Areas with a larger Serbian population became part of Serbia, while border areas in which the Serbian population was not a majority remained in Croatia. These borders are of particular relevance because they later would be the focus of fierce fighting during the Homeland War of the 1990s.[28]

At the end of World War II, Croatia's economy was largely agricultural and an effort was made to follow the Soviet model by establishing a land reform program of collective farms. Although stubborn resistance by the peasantry forced authorities to moderate their initial approach, the government set limits on the amount of land individuals could own and larger estates were redistributed to landless peasant families. A number of larger state-run farms also were created. Peasants could keep a fixed amount of farm products for their own use, but all else was sold either to the government or at local markets at set prices. In general, this system proved inefficient and agricultural production stagnated.

Soon after the war, the rest of the economy was nationalized and subject to centralized control by the Federal Planning Office in Belgrade, once again following the Soviet model. Unlike other Communist states in Europe, however, Yugoslavia resisted becoming a Soviet satellite. Tito was not inclined to follow policy dictates from Stalin and ultimately broke with the Soviet Union in 1948. Stalin's threats, including military invasion, only strengthened Tito's position at home. Tito's independence allowed him flexibility in determining Yugoslavia's economic policies leading to less central planning and the gradual introduction of market-oriented reforms that were uniquely Yugoslav and clearly experimental. For example, "workers' councils" were elected by the workers to govern larger enterprises. Although Communist Party members typically dominated these councils, they provided a sense of self-determination.

The outcome of Tito's reforms included more autonomy for the republics and greater contact with the Western Hemisphere as well as an awakening of nationalist sentiments in Croatia. The loosening of economic restrictions led to Croatia's relative prosperity and exploitation by the Yugoslav federal authorities was obvious and widely resented. For example, by the mid-1960s, Yugoslavia's economic policies were liberal enough for Croatia to develop a tourist industry. With tourism came a substantial amount of foreign currency, primarily through hotels. All of this currency had to be transferred to the Yugoslav authorities in Belgrade, leading to feelings of resentment and exploitation. These funds were not used to improve conditions in Croatia. Furthermore, Croatians claimed, little of this wealth was devoted to economic development at all. Rather, they said, it was wasted on politically motivated projects, which did little for the common good.

Whatever the case, this perception contributed to nationalist sentiments, which were further fueled by the impression that the Yugoslav authorities actively suppressed distinctions between Serbian and Croatian culture, particularly in the area of language. Cultural organizations such as the Croatian Writers Union and *Matica hrvatska* protested a new "Serbo-Croat" dictionary featuring a preference for Serbian terms, relegating Croatian to a dialect rather than a distinct language.

The movement for greater Croatian autonomy, referred to as the Croatian Spring, culminated in 1971 when members of the Communist Party along with students from the University of Zagreb took to the streets in protest. Although the protests were quickly broken up by federal authorities and some participants jailed, Tito eventually met some of their demands, including the right of Croatia to keep more foreign currency earnings. At this time, constitutional amendments were introduced allowing increased autonomy for all of the republics.

Initially the Croatian economy responded positively to these reforms; however, by the 1980s the Yugoslavian economy as a whole began to stagnate. Tito died in 1980 and Communist authorities were unable to motivate workers. Production declined and it became clear that the federal authorities had borrowed a substantial amount of money from international sources, including the United States. The relative progress made in the previous decade was fueled by foreign debt that the state eventually was unable to repay. Economic problems were met by increased nationalist sentiments throughout Yugoslavia as well as disillusionment with the socialist system. In 1987 Slobodan Milosevic, then head of the League of Communists, promoted his intentions to create a "Greater Serbia" that would encompass all regions of Yugoslavia with a significant Serbian population. This concept threatened Croatia, which had a substantial Serbian population in the Krajina region (part of the old Military Frontier), as well as Bosnia and Kosovo which were also home to many Serbs.

An Independent Croatia and the Homeland War

Like much of Eastern Europe, the breakup of the Soviet Union in 1989 brought change to Yugoslavia. As it was, the state could not withstand much more ethnic or nationalistic tension. Tito had downplayed separatist ambitions whenever possible, going so far as to replace the names of streets and squares commemorating patriotic figures from either Croatian or Serbian history with new names reflective of the Yugoslav state as a whole. But the combination of a stagnant economy and growing nationalism on the part of Croatia, Serbia, and Slovenia doomed Yugoslavia.

In 1989, Ivica Racan, the elected leader of the League of Communists, initiated the first democratic elections in decades. This prospect led to the creation of a multitude of political parties and brought up the inevitable question of whether Croatia should seek independence. Among the newly formed political parties was the Croatian Democratic Union also known as the HDZ (*Hrvatska democratska zajednica*) led by Franjo Tudjman (1922–1999). A successful Partisan general who quickly rose to military prominence in Yugoslavia, Tudjman was expelled from the Communist Party in 1967[29] and sentenced to jail for antigovernment activities, which included accusing the Yugoslav government of exaggerating the crimes committed by the Ustashe during World War II. Tudjman's HDZ appealed to nationalist sentiments when he promoted a realignment of power between Serbs and Croatians, which meant, simply, the removal of Serbs from influential positions in Croatia. The HDZ also took a stand against the ruling Yugoslav regime, thus drawing support from émigré communities abroad, particularly in the United States and Canada, which espoused strong anti-Communist beliefs. Among those joining the HDZ was Stjepan ("Stipe") Mesic, future prime minister and president of Croatia, who was jailed for dissident activities during the Croatian Spring of 1971 and became politically active again in 1989.

Multiparty elections were held in the spring of 1990. In addition to the HDZ, other significant political parties participated. Ivica Racan changed the name of the dominant Communist Party in Croatia to the Party of Democratic Change (also known as the SDP, *Stranka demokratskih promjena*) in the hope of separating the party from Serbian Communists. In the meantime, Serbs in the Krajina region organized the Serbian Democratic Party, also known as the SDS (*Srpska demokratska stranka*), which promoted the establishment of autonomous Serbian regions within Croatia. Serbian nationalists in Belgrade led by Slobodan Milosevic supported this effort, as it potentially would draw the Croatian Krajina region into a new Greater Serbian state. The threat of

Serbian hegemony and the shrinking of Croatia's border mobilized support for the HDZ and the party won a solid victory in the 1990 elections.

But Croatia was still part of Yugoslavia, and while Croatian leaders initially proposed a new constitution to turn Yugoslavia into a confederation of independent states, Belgrade had other plans. Serbian President Milosevic hoped to create a more centralized Yugoslavia with an expanded Serbian republic at the helm.[30] In the meantime, the new HDZ government, with Franjo Tudjman as president and Stipe Mesic as prime minister drafted a new constitution that proclaimed Croatia's sovereignty and right to secede from Yugoslavia. Serbs living in Croatia began to feel increasingly alienated as the government began to remove them from important posts in the judiciary and police. Furthermore, the HDZ rhetoric failed to acknowledge the rights of Serbs living in Croatia. Even streets named after prominent Serbs were given new names steeped in Croatian history and symbolism. In response, Belgrade filled the national media with anti-Croatian propaganda, likening the new leadership to the Ustashe of World War II. The end result was a deepening separation between the Serbian and Croatian population, setting the mood for the violence that would soon take place.

In early 1991, Slovenia took steps to separate from Yugoslavia. Croatia did the same, but while Milosevic was willing to part with Slovenia, Croatia was a different story. Violence was first triggered in Croatia within the predominantly Serbian region of Krajina, in the vicinity of the city of Knin. Leaders of the local Serbian population declared the region the "Autonomous Province of Serbian Krajina" in an attempt to remove the area from the jurisdiction of the Croatian government. Serbia's secret police, the SDB (*Sluzba drzavne bezbednosti*) got involved, taking direction from Milosevic who calculated that a Serb separatist movement could appropriate enough territory to divide Croatia in two and destroy any plans for an independent Croatian state. The SDB distributed arms to the Serbian population with the help of the Yugoslav Army (JNA) which was also taking orders from Milosevic in Belgrade. Fighting soon began between Croatia's police force and JNA-backed Serbian rebels.

On May 19, 1991, a referendum was held in Croatia in which the voters supported the creation of an independent Croatian state. Turnout was more than 80 percent and more than 90 percent voted in favor of separation from Yugoslavia. Independence was declared on June 25, 1991, and armed clashes in Serbian-dominated regions soon followed. The JNA was Serbia's primary fighting force and, in response, Croatia created the Croatian National Guard. Serious fighting that characterized the Homeland War[31] (also known as the Croatian War of Independence) began with the JNA launching a major offensive in eastern Slavonia. During the course of the war, the major coastal cities of Dubrovnik, Split, Sibenik, and Zadar were shelled and the inland the cities of Vukovar, Sisak, Osijek, Slavonski Brod, and Vincovci were attacked. In October 1991, President Tudjman called for all Croatians to mobilize against the "greater Serbian imperialism" that Milosevic was promoting through military force, which included the JNA as well as Serbian paramilitary organizations.

The bloodiest battle of the war was fought in the town of Vukovar. The JNA, which by now was a primarily Serbian army, surrounded the town for more than two months during which time a poorly armed Croatian National Guard brigade defended Vukovar against the far better equipped army. By the time the JNA captured Vukovar in November 1991, constant shelling had destroyed the town. Many civilians had fled, and the fate of those who remained was dire. Journalists entering the town immediately after JNA occupation reported seeing bodies of dead civilians in the streets. At least 500 patients remained in the city hospital; many of these were men who

Dubrovnik in 1996. New roofs illustrate the extent of immediate postwar reconstruction. (Courtesy of the author.)

were injured while defending the town. More than 300 of these patients, all non-Serbian, were taken to a nearby field and massacred. For Croats, the atrocities at Vukovar came to symbolize Serbian brutality and continue to fuel anti-Serbian sentiment into the 21st century. The massacre was also the focus of war crimes tribunals in the Hague, the Netherlands, which yielded prison sentences for several high-ranking JNA officers.

While the siege of Vukovar was certainly one of the most brutal events of the war, the international media focused on Dubrovnik, which was also besieged by JNA forces in late 1991. Once again, Croatian defenders were severely outnumbered by the JNA. Water and electricity were cut at the beginning of the siege, making conditions especially difficult because the city was already crowded with refugees from other parts of Croatia who thought they had found a safe haven in Dubrovnik. Because of its international reputation as a popular tourist spot and cultural status as a UNESCO (United Nations Educational, Scientific, and Cultural Organization) World Heritage Site, Dubrovnik seemed an unlikely target for Serbian military aggression. For these reasons, the siege also drew plenty of media attention, which only increased when it became apparent that civilian targets were constantly being shelled. A United Nations–sponsored ceasefire was negotiated and shelling ended by early 1992, but the siege continued until May when a successful Croatian offensive broke the blockade.

Under pressure from the European Union, Tudjman and Milosevic negotiated a peace agreement allowing Croatia to officially be recognized by the European community on January 15, 1992. The agreement also stipulated that JNA forces leave Croatia and that the UN security force known as UNPROFOR patrol Serbian-controlled areas of Slavonia and Krajina, which became known as UN Protected Areas. For the most part, the ceasefire held, although the UN Protected Areas were never actually demilitarized. UNPROFOR allowed Serbian paramilitary organizations to continue operating. By the end of 1992, Croatia lost nearly one-third of its territory to the breakaway Krajina Serb Republic. Croatia was effectively partitioned by this peace treaty, which divided the country in two at its narrowest point, legitimized Serbian claims to Krajina, and undermined Croatia's sovereignty. At the same time, the JNA shifted its focus to military efforts in Bosnia where war was just beginning.

The declaration of independence by both Slovenia and Croatia signaled the end of Yugoslavia and the beginning of military conflict in the Republic of Bosnia and Herzegovina as well as in Croatia. Milosevic's goal of transforming Yugoslavia into a Serbian state involved claiming a substantial amount of territory in the Republic of Bosnia and Herzegovina. In January 1992, the Serbian members of the parliament of Bosnia and Herzegovina established

the Serbian Republic of Bosnia and Herzegovina. In the meantime, nationalist Croats living on the Bosnian side of their mutual border founded the
Croatian Community of Herzeg-Bosnia, as a separate political, cultural, and
economic entity in the territory of Bosnia and Herzegovina. Finally, in March
1992, the Republic of Bosnia and Herzegovina declared independence from
Yugoslavia leading to the outbreak of war in April when the JNA attacked the
capital city of Sarajevo.

While the Croats were sympathetic to the struggle against Serbian aggression, Tudjman and the HDZ also saw an opportunity to expand Croatia's
borders and initiated an ill-conceived plan, beginning with the establishment
of the aforementioned Croatian Community of Herzeg-Bosnia in the region
of Herzegovina with a large Croatian population, and its corresponding military branch, the Croatian Defense Council (HVO). The idea was to expand
Croatia's borders to include Herzegovina, with little regard for the Bosniaks
(Bosnians of Muslim descent) living in the region. As the self-proclaimed
Croat leadership of Herzeg-Bosnia tried to dismantle all preexisting institutions and remove Bosniaks from positions of authority, local resistance grew.
Soon military conflict broke out between the HVO and the Bosnian Territorial Defense (TO), a military organization formed in response to the HVO.
By late 1992, Croat forces had taken much of Central Bosnia, but the HVO
tactics were brutal, eventually leading to accusations of war crimes and ethnic
cleansing, including indiscriminate terrorizing and killing of civilians.

The Croat-Bosniak conflict ended in 1994 with the signing of a peace
treaty known as the Washington Agreement because it was mediated by the
United States and signed in Washington, D.C., and Vienna. Tensions between
the Bosniaks (Bosnian Muslims) and Croats subsided, but the situation in the
former Yugoslavia still had not stabilized.

Croatia was determined to regain territory it had lost, including the
breakaway Autonomous Province of Serb Krajina. In May 1995, the Croatian
military conducted Operation Flash, an offensive that successfully captured
Serbian-occupied territory in western Slavonia. UN peacekeepers did little
to stop the military action because the UN Security Council already had
declared that these UN Protected Areas belonged to Croatia. Operation Flash
was a precursor to a larger military action called Operation Storm, which
reclaimed all of the Serbian-controlled Krajina region and made Croatia a
contiguous country again. Croats celebrated this action as a legitimate effort
to take back territory that was rightfully theirs. International response was
less enthusiastic as Operation Storm involved the invasion of UN Protected
Areas. But, ultimately, the success of Operation Storm was generally considered a turning point in the war by peace negotiators as well as military
experts. The terms of the Dayton Agreement finally put an end to military

conflict in the former Yugoslavia. Operation Storm, (along with NATO bombardment of Serbian forces in Bosnia) shifted the military balance of power in the region to the point at which Serbian leaders were willing to abandon the notion of a expanding their borders to include Krajina and, finally, a lasting peace became possible.

The success of Operation Storm was not without a human price. The Croatian armed forces reported 473 troops killed and 2,017 injured with at least as many civilian casualties.[32] Human Rights Watch reports 526 Serbs killed, 116 of whom were reportedly civilians.[33] Casualty figures vary, however, especially with respect to civilians. Officially, the Croatian government invited the Serbs living in the region to remain, but most fled to Bosnia and Herzegovina and to Serbia. According to Serbian sources, an estimated 200,000 Krajina Serbs were displaced,[34] furthering accusations of ethnic cleansing and, after several years, the indictment of a number of Croatian military leaders with war crimes. The accusations reflected actions that took place up to three months after Croatia had secured the region and included the harassment and killing of civilians, burning and looting of Serb villages, and theft of property. As of 2010, trials were under way at the International Criminal Tribunal for the former Yugoslavia (ICTY) located in the Hague, the Netherlands.

The war years also produced a refugee crisis throughout the former Yugoslavia. The actual number of refugees was hard to determine. The United Nations High Commissioner for Refugees (UNHCR) determined that between 1991 and 1997 approximately 950,000 prewar Croatian citizens left their homes due to fear of persecution or simply because their homes were, or might be, destroyed as a result of fighting. While some of these refugees originally lived within Croatia, many lived in Serbia and other regions of Yugoslavia. Formally called internally displaced persons (IDPs), about 550,000[35] of the 950,000 were citizens of Croatian ethnicity and approximately 400,000 were ethnic Serbians. Some scholars suggest that this number is exaggerated,[36] perhaps because some people were counted twice. In any case, the number of IDPs in Croatia decreased significantly after 1991, from 500,000 to 260,705 in 1992. While some were able to move in with family and friends, or return to their homes relatively quickly, others remained homeless and relied on government assistance for food and shelter.

The IDP population has decreased substantially since the war, down to only approximately 2,400 people as of June 2009, with 1,600 of those being ethnic Serbs. Overall, Croatian refugees had an easier time resettling than their Serbian counterparts, although many members of both groups discussed here originally resided in Croatia. Almost half of the Serbians who returned did not manage to stay. Both Croatian and Serbian refugees faced issues of poverty, but Serbs were burdened with discrimination, both in terms of finding housing and employment. Since the war, the Croatian government has made efforts to facilitate the return of ethnic Serbs in accordance with requirements established for EU membership. The number of IDPs has remained steady over the last three years, however, indicating that further efforts must be made to resolve the situation.[37]

The Aftermath of the Homeland War and Croatian Independence

Croatia had finally achieved independence, for the first time since the beginning of the 12th century. Once the celebrating was over, the hard work of reinventing the country had to begin. Croatia's physical infrastructure and economy had been ravaged by war. Homes and factories were destroyed. Men who had served in the military were now free to pursue civilian jobs only to face the disappointments of unemployment. And, finally, the transition from socialism to capitalism would have to be achieved in the midst of this complicated and uncertain environment.

Tudjman's legacy is forever bound to the fulfillment of the dream of an independent Croatia. Within a year of the success of Operation Storm, rumors about the president's poor health began to circulate. If the obstacles facing Croatia were not already difficult enough, the leader of the HDZ and first president of the country would begin the process of rebuilding Croatia while suffering from a terminal illness.

To attract the necessary foreign capital and begin the postwar economic recovery, the HDZ began to privatize Croatian industries, which were public property until that time. This process of "privatization" was not always successful as many valuable enterprises ended up in the hands of politically connected individuals who did not always have the necessary business acumen to manage the assets they suddenly controlled. Many of these "tycoons," as they became known, were unscrupulous political operators motivated by self-interest and short-term gains. They maximized their personal profits by selling whatever assets they could and closing otherwise viable businesses down entirely. Most of the tycoons' connections to the HDZ were tight enough to prevent the government from reining them in, even when they drove businesses into bankruptcy and, on occasion, engaged in illegal activities such as money laundering. As a result, the economy floundered, unemployment grew, and foreign investment dwindled while a small class of wealthy families emerged.

By the time President Tudjman succumbed to cancer in December 1999, Croats were ready for change. In parliamentary elections held in January 2000, the HDZ lost a significant number of seats to a coalition of opposition parties. Later that year, Stipe Mesic, who had broken with Tudjman in 1994 over his aggressive policies in Bosnia, was elected president and Ivica Racan of the Social Democratic Party was elected prime minister. By all accounts this marked a shift in political direction for Croatia. A coalition government was formed and Mesic vowed to reduce the powers of the presidency, eliminate corruption in the privatization process, improve international relations, and steer Croatia toward EU membership. Although Mesic and Racan reached out to the Western Hemisphere countries by meeting conditions necessary to begin the long process of EU membership, including cooperating with the war crimes tribunal in the Hague, unemployment continued to grow and economic policy stagnated.

Dissatisfaction with domestic conditions brought the reemergence of the HDZ in 2003. The party had distanced itself from the policies of Tudjman's era and reestablished itself as a significant political force under the leadership of moderate Ivo Sanader, who was named prime minister at the end of 2003. Along with President Mesic, he continued to bring Croatia closer to EU admission by taking a strong stand against corruption and continued cooperation with the war crimes tribunal. (See Chapter 3 for more detail on Sanader and his unexpected resignation in 2009.)

Croatia's progress toward EU membership continues, but some major issues still need to be addressed. For example, as of 2007,[38] the European Parliament stated that an "open competitive market economy" is essential to membership, which implies that Croatia must meet EU standards for the sale of state-owned assets. In other words, when state property is transferred to the private sector, it must be sold in a fair and open manner, rather than exclusively ending up in the hands of the politically well connected. The issue of state subsidies must be addressed, particularly with reference to the shipbuilding industry, which is still heavily subsidized. Judicial reform has been a long-standing issue in terms of EU membership. The European Parliament insists that reforms create a "professional and independent judiciary." Croatian courts must be free of political favoritism and a "persisting bias amongst some judicial staff against non-Croatian nationals." Finally, the return of ethnic Serbian refugees to Croatia is also a political precondition for EU membership.[39] This condition not only includes the integration of minorities into the daily life of Croatian communities but also the potential payment of pensions covering the years worked by people who lived in the Republic of Serbian Krajina during the Homeland War.

Although the aforementioned criteria for EU accession are politically charged and potentially controversial, the previously mentioned issue of border disputes with Slovenia is perhaps the most persistent obstacle to progress. The border disputes deal with both maritime and land borders and date back to 1993 when Slovenia claimed that the original borders between the republics under Yugoslavia were erroneous. With respect to the maritime border, Croatia claims that the border extends through the middle of the Piran Bay, while Slovenia has declared sovereignty over the entire bay. Slovenia argues that its police controlled the entire gulf between 1954 and 1991,[40] thereby providing historical precedent for their sovereignty. Valuable fishing rights, as well as other options for economic use of the bay, hinge on the outcome of this dispute. Slovenia has also argued that certain pieces of Croatian territory along the land border formed by the Dragonja River are rightfully Slovenian.

As of September 2010, both Croatia and Slovenia have agreed to accept the results of an arbitration agreement thereby removing a major obstacle to Croatia's entry into the EU. In the meantime, recent concerns about the euro's stability as well as pending domestic judicial reforms and ongoing reports of high-level corruption continue to slow Croatia's progress. While many Croatians expected to join the EU by 2011, it appears that the country will need at least one additional year to meet accession criteria, making 2012 the year that Croatia becomes a full-fledged member of the European Union.

NOTES

1. Bosnia and Herzegovina is one country. For expediency, it is sometimes simply referred to as Bosnia in this and other texts.

2. Central Intelligence Agency, "The World Factbook: Croatia." https://www .cia.gov/library/publications/the-world-factbook/geos/hr.html (retrieved October 10, 2009).

3. United Nations Development Programme (UNDP), "A Climate for Change: Climate Change and Its Impacts on Society and Economy in Croatia," *Human Development Report, Croatia, 2008.* http://europeandcis.undp.org/home/show/ A006D9DC-F203-1EE9-B2EDE14ABB69E2E9 (retrieved April 18, 2009).

4. *Encyclopaedia Britannica Online,* s.v."Croatia," http://www.britannica.com/ EBchecked/topic/143561/Croatia (retrieved April 16, 2009).

5. *Columbia Encyclopedia,* s.v. "Dinaric Alps," http://www.answers.com/topic/ dinaric-alps (retrieved March 20, 2009).

6. "Caves in Croatia," Speleological Committee of the Croatian Mountaineering Association. http://public.carnet.hr/speleo/karta.html (retrieved August 22, 2008).

7. UNDP, "A Climate for Change."

8. Francis H. Eterovich and Christopher Spalatin, eds., *Croati:, Land, People and Culture,* Vol. 1 (Toronto: University of Toronto Press, 1964).

9. "Geographical and Meteorological Data," *Statistical Yearbook for 2005* (Zagreb: Central Bureau of Statistics of Republic of Croatia, 2005).

10. Josip Faricic, "Hrvatski pseudo-otoci" (in Croatian). http://www.geografija .hr/clanci/853/hrvatski-pseudo-otoci (retrieved February 23, 2003).

11. Marcus Tanner, *Croatia: A Nation Forged in War* (New Haven, CT: Yale Nota Bene, 2001), 10–11.

12. Andrew Shipman, "Glagolitic," *Catholic Encyclopedia*, Vol. 6 (New York: Robert Appleton Company, 1909). http://www.newadvent.org/cathen/06575b.htm (retrieved June 15, 2010).

13. Ivo Goldstein and Nikolina Jovanovic, *Croatia: A History* (London: C. Hurst and Co. Ltd 1999), 25.

14. Goldstein and Jovanovic, *Croatia*, 25.

15. Robert Guisepi, "The Mongols: The Last Great Nomadic Challenges: From Chinggis Khan to Timur," 1992. http://history-world.org/mongol_empire.htm (retrieved May 3, 2010).

16. Goldstein and Jovanovic, *Croatia*, 39.

17. Ibid., 41.

18. At this time Croatia was still a distinct state that was part of Hungary as per the Pacta Conveta of 1102. However, once the Ottomans were defeated, much of Hungary fell under the auspices of the Austrian Hapsburgs, thereby creating a powerful Austrian influence in Croatia.

19. Tanner, *Croatia: A Nation Forged in War*, 62.

20. Goldstein and Jovanovic, *Croatia*, 60.

21. Ibid., 73.

22. Tanner, *Croatia*, 95.

23. Branka Magas, *Croatia Through History: the Making of a European State* (London: Saqi Books, 2007), 310.

24. Tanner, *Croatia*, 99.

25. Josip Broz, also known by his nickname "Tito," held a number of different titles between 1943 and his death in 1980. He was the leader of Yugoslavia during this period and held the offices of secretary general of the Communist Party from 1939 onward and president from 1953 until his death. He was also frequently referred to as Marshal Tito, a title that originated from his position as supreme commander of the armed forces. In this text, he will be referred to simply as Tito or President Tito as this title best reflects his position in the Yugoslav government.

26. William Bartlett, *Croatia: Between Europe and the Balkans* (New York: Routledge, 2003), 20.

27. Bartlett, *Croatia*, 24.

28. Goldstein and Jovanovic, *Croatia*, 159.

29. *Encyclopaedia Britannica Online*, s.v. "Tudjman, Franjo," http://search.eb.com/eb/article-9389236 (retrieved January 29, 2009).

30. Bartlett, *Croatia*, 35.

31. The term "Homeland War" will be used because that is what the war is called in Croatia. The war is also sometimes called the "Croatian Civil War" and also is included under the broader term the "Balkan War."

32. "President Makes State of the Nation Address to Parliament," Croatian Radio, Zagreb, in Serbo-Croat, January 15, 1996, BBC Summary of World Broadcasts, January 17, 1996.

33. Human Rights Watch, "Impunity for Abuses Committed During 'Operation Storm' and the Denial of the Right of Refugees to Return to the Krajina," August 1, 1996. http://www.unhcr.org/refworld/docid/3ae6a7d70.html (retrieved June 15, 2010).

34. Ibid.

35. Organization for Security and Cooperation in Europe (OSCE), "A Study on Access to Pertaining Rights and (Re)integration of Displaced Persons in Croatia, Bosnia and Herzegovina, and Serbia in 2006," March 2007. http://www.osce.org/publications/srb/2007/02/23473_805_en.pdf (retrieved June 2, 2010).

36. Paul Stubbs, "Croatia," in *Internally Displaced People: A Global Survey*, ed. Janie Hampton (London: Earthscan, 1998).

37. Internal Placement Monitoring Centre, *Croatia: Housing Rights and Employment Still Preventing Durable Solutions; A Profile of the Internal Displacement Situation,* September 1, 2009). http://www.internal-displacement.org (retrieved September 20, 2010).

38. "Croatia: Good Progress towards Accession and Some Issues Remain" (press release, European Parliament, April 25, 2007).

39. See EU-Croatia Relations page at http://www.euractiv.com/en/enlargement/eu-croatia-relations/article-129605 (retrieved November 8, 2009).

40. Jernej Letnar Cernic and Matej Avbelj, "The Conundrum of the Piran Bay: Slovenia v. Croatia: The Case of Maritime Delimitation," *Journal of International Law & Policy* 5, no. 2 (2007):1–19.

2

Religion

According to the 2001 census, approximately 87.8 percent of Croatians identify themselves as Roman Catholic. Serbian Orthodox Christians make up another 4.4 percent of the population, while Islam and Judaism have a following of about 1 percent each. Another 5.2 percent of the population does not have any religious affiliation.[1] Other active religious groups include Baptists, Evangelical Christians (Seventh-day Adventists, Jehovah's Witnesses, and Pentecostals), Mormons, and the Hindu Hare Krishna sect.

Traditionally, religion has played a large role in Croatian life, from the personal to the political. When Croatia was part of Yugoslavia, religious practice was discouraged, even though it never completely disappeared. In their book on Croatian culture published in the 1960s, Francis Eterovich and Christopher Spalatin characterized the relationship between the Communist regime and the Catholic Church as an "apparent truce" under which a constant battle for the hearts and minds of Croatians continued beneath the surface.[2] While Catholicism survived under Communism, the combination of decades of religious repression and the Homeland War, during which the mostly Orthodox Serbian forces made a point of destroying Catholic churches, inextricably tied Catholicism to Croatian national identity and patriotism. Once Croatia achieved independence, the public immediately engaged in outward displays of religious devotion and enthusiasm for their faith. In the years since independence, the Catholic Church remains a highly respected and influential institution and even Croatians who do not attend Mass or observe religious holidays self-identify as Catholics.

Although church and state technically are separate, sermons often contain political content and political leaders are expected to attend Mass and religious celebrations. The media enhances the substantial influence that priests enjoy in Croatian society. Contractual agreements between the Church and the state-run Croatian State Radio and Television guarantee that the Roman Catholic Church gets up to 10 hours a month of broadcast time compared with 10 minutes or less for other religious groups.[3] Not surprisingly, many Croatians side with the Vatican on social issues and oppose capital punishment and euthanasia. Although the Church considers abortion a sin, the practice remains legal, but only until the 12th week of pregnancy.

Pope John Paul II rewarded Croatia's devotion to Roman Catholicism with repeated visits (in 1994, 1998, and 2003) and the 1998 beatification

Saint Mark's Church in Zagreb, featuring a tile roof displaying the coats of arms of Croatia, Dalmatia, Slavonia, and the city of Zagreb. (Courtesy of the author.)

of Cardinal Alojzije Stepinac, the archbishop of Zagreb and leader of the Catholic Church in Croatia during World War II. Cardinal Stepinac, who died in 1960, is the focus of both a large, devoted following and lingering controversy. In 1946 the Yugoslav government accused the cardinal of collaborating with the Ustashe during World War II and sentenced him to a long prison term. Church leaders, however, considered him a martyr and secretly began the beatification process during the Communist era. It is generally acknowledged that the trial against Stepinac was a propaganda stunt by Communist officials with an inevitable guilty verdict. It also is well known, however, that some Catholic priests sympathized with the Ustashe regime. According to historian Ivo Goldstein's account,[4] Stepinac initially expressed support for the new Croatian state established during World War II by the Ustashe in collaboration with the Nazis. However, he and other church officials openly protested the violence and racial intolerance perpetrated by this regime. He is remembered for having saved numerous Jews from the Holocaust and, with the help of the Vatican, protected other members of

Baroque altar in Christ Our Savior Church located in Koprivnica. (Courtesy of the author.)

persecuted minorities. His critics claim that he could have done more to undermine the Nazi cause, but it appears that Stepinac had to walk a fine line between the Ustashe and their opponents, the Communist partisans who clearly opposed the Catholic Church.

FREEDOM OF RELIGION AND NON-CATHOLIC FAITHS

The Croatian Constitution protects freedom of religious thought and public displays of religious practice. Although the Catholic Church maintains close ties to the government and may seem like the official state religion, it is not. The government allows groups with 500 members or more to register as officially recognized religious communities, thus conferring legal standing and tax-exempt status.

The religious tolerance expressed in the Constitution is manifested in the existence of religious groups other than Roman Catholics. While communities of Serbian Orthodox Christians, Jews, and Muslims traditionally have lived in Croatia, new religious groups have emerged, including Evangelical Christians and various Eastern faiths.

Evangelical churches, which first appeared in Croatia in the 1920s in the form of Baptist and Pentecostal movements, expanded substantially in the years since independence.[5] By the year 2000, several new independent churches were founded in Croatia, including the Full Gospel Church in Zagreb (1989), Christian Prophetic Church "Maranatha" in Split (1992), the Good News Church in Zagreb (1993), the Christian Center "Bethezda" in Zadar (1995), the Evangelical Methodist Church in Split (1995), and the Christian Prophetic Church in Zagreb (1997). Much of this expansion began through efforts of missionaries, primarily from the United States.

Buddhist and Hindu groups also are attracting attention, particularly among young people. Buddhism first appeared in Zagreb in the 1980s and has expanded since then with a variety of sects, including traditions originating in Tibet, Japan, and China. Like the Evangelical movement, interest in Buddhism increased with religious tolerance after independence. The popularity of yoga also contributed to the spread of Eastern philosophy in Croatia, making it hard to find statistics that accurately describe the true interest level among the general population. Many Croatians study Eastern philosophy and diligently practice yoga and meditation but still identify primarily with the Catholic Church.

The International Society for Krishna Consciousness (ISKCON), also known as the Hare Krishna movement, is the only officially recognized Hindu organization in Croatia. Currently, the ISKCON movement has nine centers in Croatia and the government has recently donated 5,382 square feet

(500 square meters) of space in Zagreb for the organization's humanitarian work.[6] While ISKCON's popularity is a relatively recent phenomenon, the study of Hinduism in Croatia has a long tradition dating back to the 18th century when a monk named Filip Vesdin traveled to India as a missionary and researched Indian religions extensively. He returned to write several books on the subject of Hinduism as well as a text on Sanskrit grammar, the first published in Europe.[7]

While Croatia never has had a large Jewish population, evidence of Jewish settlements dates back to Roman times with larger communities developing along the Dalmatian coast by the 14th century. Jews are mentioned in the municipal records of Zadar (1303), Dubrovnik (1326), and Split (1397), and, later, in Sibenik (1432) and Rijeka (1436).[8] With the exception of expulsion from Hapsburg territories in the Croatian interior during the 16th century, Jewish communities generally were stable and prosperous, especially in larger cities along the coast such as Dubrovnik and Split. As in the rest of Europe, these communities did not fare well during World War II. Of the 25,000 Jews living in Croatia at the start of the war, only 5,000 survived the Holocaust. After the war, the Yugoslav government recognized Jews as an official ethnic and religious community, but at the same time, the Communist leadership discouraged religious practice. Only one rabbi served the entire country. As the years progressed, most Jews in Croatia assimilated into the general population and lost touch with their religious heritage. Few of the 2,000 Jews living in Croatia by 1990 were observant. After the Homeland War, the Croatian government, in the interest of showing the world that the anti-Semitism of the Ustashe era was a thing of the past, tried to make Jews feel secure and welcome. The government granted Jewish groups legal recognition and provided funding for the rebuilding of a Jewish center in Zagreb that was destroyed by a bomb in 1991. Many Jews left the country anyway, but those who remained have created new organizations that, while not religious per ser, revolve around a shared cultural heritage. For example, in addition to religious services, the Jewish community in Zagreb offers Hebrew classes, a youth club, a Klezmer group, a women's club, and a senior citizens' club. Also located in Zagreb is the Lavoslav Sik Library, the largest Jewish library in the Balkans with a collection of 2,000 bound periodicals, 6,000 documents, and other materials.

In 1998 an Orthodox rabbi took up residence in Zagreb and provided what was for most local Jews their first introduction to traditional concepts such as a Kosher kitchen. Many Croatian Jews live in mixed marriages, and the notion of changing one's daily life to meet the demands of the Jewish faith was more than they cared to do, especially since the rabbi requested that non-Jewish spouses convert.[9] While many are reluctant to fully embrace a religious lifestyle, Croatian Jews are committed to maintaining their Jewish identity and heritage, which includes the development and preservation of cultural sites. The Zagreb Jewish community's long-term goals include the construction of a cultural center at the site of the city's first synagogue, which was destroyed in late 1941 by the Ustashe regime.

With the help of international aid organizations such as UNESCO (United Nations Educational, Scientific, and Cultural Organization), Jewish cultural sites, including a number of cemeteries, are being preserved. Only three synagogues, located in Split, Rijeka, and Dubrovnik, were not destroyed or converted for other uses since World War II. The Split synagogue, founded in 1500, was fully restored and reopened in 1996. The Dubrovnik synagogue, which was founded in 1408, making it the second oldest synagogue in Europe, was heavily damaged in the Homeland War. It was restored and rededicated in 1997 and includes an exhibition space where rare ritual objects as well as Torah scrolls from the 13th and 14th centuries are on display. The Rijeka synagogue is newer, built in 1928, and has received protective status as a cultural monument.

Perhaps more than any other religious minority in recent years, Croatia's Serbian Orthodox population has faced dwindling numbers and discrimination. Political struggles between Croatians and Serbians often were couched in religious terms as Croatians are traditionally Catholic and Serbians are Orthodox. Relations between these two groups have been repeatedly strained by war during the 20th century, and although World Wars I and II had broader repercussions, neither was as divisive as the recent Homeland War, which pitted Serb and Croat directly against one another. Churches became military targets as they symbolized cultural as well as national identity for both groups. Thus, antagonism toward the Serbian Orthodox Church has lingered after the war in Croatia, even though the Constitution guarantees freedom of religion.

The central government has repeatedly emphasized the importance of religious tolerance for Croatia to create a post-Communist identity befitting a modern European state. Local officials, including police and members of the judiciary, do not always share this sentiment, however, and Serbian Orthodox churches and congregations became targets for vandalism and harassment. To make matters worse, Serbian Orthodox clergy arriving from Serbia, Bosnia and Herzegovina, and Montenegro have difficulty getting the long-term residency status that guarantees such benefits as health care and pensions. Foreigners can remain in the country only for six months at a time and the law does not allow exceptions for Orthodox clergy. On the positive side, with the passage of time, complaints of discrimination and vandalism of Orthodox Church property have declined, indicating a trend of greater acceptance and tolerance on the part of the Croatian population and the limitation of this sort of illegal behavior to fringe members of society.

Islam was introduced to Croatia as early as the 15th century by invading Ottoman Turks. The Ottomans did not directly pressure conquered populations into converting to Islam, and they displayed some religious tolerance, especially toward Orthodox Christianity. Because the Catholic Church had a history of crusades against Islam, the Turks viewed the Vatican as an untrustworthy political enemy. Mistrust still exists between Muslims and Catholics in many parts of the world and has fueled prejudices that have only gotten worse with the political events and violence stemming from the September 11 attacks in New York City. Throughout Croatia the historical tension between the two faiths lingers. Islam is still considered a foreign religion by many, even though a small Muslim population has lived peacefully in Croatia for centuries. Croatian aggression during the Bosnian War (1992–1995), which often is symbolized by the destruction of the famous bridge in the Bosnian city of Mostar, exacerbated tensions between Muslims and Christians.

According to 2001 census figures, Muslims account for 1.3 percent (57,687) of Croatia's population. Within this group are approximately 20,000 people who declare themselves as Muslim by nationality, and another 20,000 who identify themselves as Bosniaks (Bosnian Muslims). About 10,000 people consider themselves Croats of Islamic faith. As with other religious groups, Islam was repressed during the Communist era, but today many of Croatia's Muslims actively practice their faith. Zagreb is home to a large modernist mosque that was completed in the late 1980s, representing the culmination of decades of effort. A new mosque is slated for construction in Rijeka and was designed by ADB Zagreb Company using the ideas of Dusan Dzamonja, a contemporary Croatian sculptor. As with the Zagreb mosque, this €8 million project was financed by donations from abroad, which were needed to supplement domestic funds. The final design includes a café, a restaurant, and a 75-foot (23-meter)-high minaret. The mosque will be used for educational and cultural purposes as well as religious services.

Notes

1. Central Intelligence Agency, "The World Factbook, Croatia," https://www.cia.gov/library/publications/the-world-factbook/geos/hr.html (retrieved September 26, 2009).

2. Francis H. Eterovich and Christopher Spalatin, eds., *Croatia: Land, People and Culture,* Vol. 1 (Toronto: University of Toronto Press, 1964).

3. World Trade Press, *Croatia Religion* (Best Country Reports, 2007), www.bestcountryreports.com.

4. Ivo Goldstein, *Croatia: A History* (London: C. Hurst & Co., 1999), 136–139.

5. Stanko Jambrek, "The Great Commission in the Context of the Evangelical Churches of Croatia in the Second Part of the Twentieth Century," *KAIROS: Evangelical Journal of Theology* 2, no. 2 (2008): 153–179.

6. Branko Bjelajac, "Serbia: Religious Freedom Survey, August 2004," *World Wide Religious News,* Forum 18, August 5, 2004, http://www.wwrn.org/article (retrieved February 17, 2010).

7. See "India–Croatia Relations," Embassy of India, Zagreb, Croatia, http://www.indianembassy.hr/bilateral-relations.html.

8. U.S. Commission for the Preservation of America's Heritage Abroad, *Jewish Heritage Sites in Croatia: Preliminary Report, 2005.* http://www.heritageabroad.gov/reports/doc/CROATIA_Report_2006.pdf (retrieved February 17, 2010).

9. Nila Ginger Hofman, *Renewed Survival: Jewish Community Life in Croatia* (Lanham, MD: Lexington Books, 2005).

3

Civic Values and Political Thought

Upon achieving independence in the 1990s, Croatia was finally free to develop a system of government that served its own values and interests. This chapter discusses Croatian domestic political and governance issues with respect to the attitudes and priorities reflected in the policy-making process. A country at the crossroads of East and West, Croatia looks clearly to Western European models of government and political thought. As part of the former Yugoslavia, one of the most liberal and progressive countries in Eastern Europe, Croatia initially had an advantage over many of its Eastern European counterparts that also achieved sovereignty in the post-Soviet 1990s. Many Croatians had some experience, albeit indirectly through travel and media, with democratic institutions and capitalism as well as contact with the large diaspora in Germany, Canada, and the United States. Much of that advantage was eliminated by the Homeland War, which ushered in an era of ethnic nationalism and corruption under the rule of authoritarian and corrupt political leadership. Croatia has since tried to regain its economic footing and direct its policies toward the pragmatic goal of European Union (EU) membership, which has not proven easy. Croatians are steadfast in their commitment to democracy and the free market, but the EU membership process has required painful self-examination. Xenophobic right-wing nationalism, political favoritism and corruption, and discrimination against minorities are all issues that the government and citizenry have had to face head-on in the past several years to gain EU membership and respect in the international community.

System of Government[1]

In the 21st century, the government of the Republic of Croatia is a parliamentary democracy, like most countries in Western and Central Europe. The government, headed by the prime minister, is politically responsible only to the Croatian Parliament (Sabor), which has 153 members who are elected by direct vote to serve four-year terms. The country is divided into 14 districts, each with 10 representatives. A certain number of seats are reserved for national minorities, as well as Croatians living abroad without a fixed residence in Croatia (the Croatian diaspora). The majority of these voters live in Bosnia and Herzegovina. As of the 2007 parliamentary elections, the diaspora held five seats. The Sabor meets twice per year and has authority to amend the Constitution, pass laws and budgets, declare war, and appoint officers to specified positions.

After the 2000 elections and the death of President Tudjman, the constitution was amended to reduce the power of the president and enhance that of the Sabor and prime minister. The president is elected by popular vote for a five-year term with a limit of two terms. He or she still appoints the prime minister and cabinet officers, but the Sabor must approve the nominees. The president is also commander in chief of the Armed Forces, and represents the Republic of Croatia abroad. Stipe Mesic was elected president in 2000 and again in 2005. He is known for his level-headedness and relaxed attitude, making him one of the most popular politicians in Croatia.[2] At the end of his second term in 2010, Mesic stepped down and Ivo Josipovic of the SDP (Social Democratic Party of Croatia, *Socijaldemokratska partija Hrvatske*) was elected on an anticorruption platform. Before becoming president, Josipovic enjoyed a distinguished academic career as a professor on the faculty of law at the University of Zagreb and also made a name for himself as a composer of classical music and director of Zagreb's prestigious music Biennale (*see* Chapter 9, Music and Performing Arts).

The office of prime minister is the most influential in Croatian government, and while a presidential nominee fills the office, he or she only assumes office after a vote of confidence by the Sabor. In the parliamentary elections held in November 2007, the HDZ (the Croatian Democratic Union, *Hrvatska demokratska zajednica*) took 36.6 percent of the votes, followed by the SDP with 31.2 percent. After several weeks of negotiations, Ivo Sanader of the HDZ was appointed prime minister for the second time and his government took office in January 2008 after forming a coalition between the HDZ and other significant political parties. His 2009 resignation and replacement by Jadranka Kosor are discussed later in this chapter.

NATIONALISM AND THE POLITICAL LANDSCAPE

Since the Homeland War, Croatia's political landscape has reflected a combination of devotion to national identity and a desire for respect and engagement in the broader European community. During President Franjo Tudjman's years in office (1990–1999), which included the Homeland War and the period immediately afterward, Tudjman promoted a nationalistic view of the Croat state summed up by the phrase "Croatia for Croatians." This philosophy was embraced by the political right and effectively made Serbs and other ethnic minorities feel unwelcome.

Croatian nationalism as represented by Tudjman and the HDZ political party, which he helped found in 1989, was a response to the years of Communist rule under the Yugoslav government in Belgrade. From an economic standpoint, the HDZ represented a shift away from a state-run economic system and toward private enterprise and capitalism. From a broader philosophical perspective, the HDZ ideology was considered right wing, in support of the preservation of conservative values and traditional Croatian culture, and the exclusion of Serbian or other ethnic influences. By contrast, in the former Yugoslavia, Communist rhetoric preached equality among all ethnic groups, thereby leaving little room for openly pro-Croat (or pro-Serb) nationalist thinking. All positive references toward an independent Croatian state were banned in the media. Croatian nationalism was immediately associated with the atrocities committed by the Ustashe's Nazi puppet government established during World War II, certainly a shameful chapter in Croatian history.

After the breakup of Yugoslavia in the early 1990s, some members Tudjman's HDZ party, in their effort to blindly extol all things Croatian, openly embraced elements of the bygone Ustashe era. This attempt by right-wing politicians to transform the Ustashe legacy into an inspirational and patriotic moment in Croatian history did not go unnoticed. The HDZ's historical revisionism was criticized in the European and American press, most forcefully in a 1997 editorial in the *New York Times* in which A. M. Rosenthal likened the Tudjman era to the "rebirth of Croatian Fascism."[3] Meanwhile, domestic political opposition to the HDZ led to the formation of opposing political parties, which distanced themselves from hard-line nationalism while also criticizing Tudjman's involvement in the war in Bosnia and discrimination against the Serbian minority.

A debate between right and left has been ongoing since the Homeland War. Although the colorful and simplistic nature of right-wing rhetoric always attracts attention, the opposition, composed of centrist and left wing political parties, have also voiced their opinions clearly. In the elections of 2000,[4] held only a month after Tudjman's death, moderate Stipe Mesic was elected president and Ivica Racan of the SDP (formerly the League of Communists of Croatia) was named prime minister, removing the HDZ from power, at least for a few years. Racan began the process of integrating Croatia into the European community, something his predecessors were only marginally concerned with. He was in the unenviable position of answering to international demands that were unpopular at home, including the return of Serbian refugees to Croatia and the arrest of prominent Croatian military figures accused of war crimes during the 1990s. Racan took measures to hasten refugee repatriation and redirected Croatia's foreign policy toward the goal of EU membership.

Domestically, Racan had to appease hard-line nationalists by allowing them to keep the influential positions they acquired in the military, the judiciary, and intelligence services during the Tudjman era. As a result, much-needed reforms in these areas were stalled, weakening Racan's support among his base, which included anti-HDZ voters. As the HDZ continued to oppose Racan, his government also faced increasing pressure by the International Criminal Tribunal for the former Yugoslavia (ICTY) to arrest Croatian generals indicted for war crimes. The question of war crimes and ICTY cooperation is still particularly sensitive as many Croatians view their military actions as a legitimate defensive response against Serbian aggression. In February 2002, five government ministers resigned over issues surrounding ICTY cooperation, beginning a domestic debate that would continue for years.

In spite of Racan's best efforts to reform government and move toward a more progressive Croatian state, the HDZ regained power in the 2003 elections and Sanader was appointed prime minister. By this time, however, the HDZ had separated from the Tudjman legacy and presented itself in a more moderate light, as a party ready to bring Croatia into the European community. Sanader went so far as to offer an official apology to those who suffered "under HDZ rule" and made significant efforts to facilitate the return of Serbian refugees to Croatia. Early in Sanader's administration, Croatia began the North Atlantic Treaty Organization (NATO) membership process and formally applied to join the European Union. Croatia was formally welcomed as a NATO member in April 2009, but the EU accession process has progressed more slowly.

The domestic controversy regarding war crimes extradition was heightened early in Sanader's administration, as ICTY cooperation became a stumbling block in Croatia's EU membership process. In recent years, however, officials with the ICTY acknowledge that Croatia has increasingly cooperated with their demands and cite the 2005 arrest of Gen. Ante Gotovina in

Spain as a major step forward. Gotovina's arrest was not without domestic controversy. Many Croatians who live in the Krajina region, an area that was occupied by separatist Serbs in the early 1990s, consider Gotovina a hero. The Croatian military liberated Krajina during Operation Storm, a four-day military effort in which between 150,000 and 200,000 Serbs fled the area and hundreds of civilians were killed. The ICTY accused Gotovina of both personal and command responsibility for the murder of civilians and the destruction of property, making it nearly impossible for Serbian residents to ever return home. The general went into hiding after his 2001 indictment and traveled abroad under an assumed name.

When he was finally arrested in Spain in 2005, veterans of the Homeland War organized rallies and, according to a Reuters estimate, the largest attracted more than 40,000 protesters in Split.[5] Meanwhile, only about 500 people gathered in Zagreb in support of Gen. Gotovina, serving as a reminder that public opinion regarding his arrest was mixed. Many Croats felt that he should turn himself in for the sake of Croatia's international standing and EU prospects, while others regarded Gotovina as a folk hero who defied both international and domestic authorities for the sake of principle. Before his arrest, posters and billboards depicting the general as a war hero were seen throughout the country, but most frequently in Dalmatia. At least two prominent right-wing Croatian pop singers, Marko Perkovic (who performs under the name Thompson) and Miroslav Skoro wrote hit songs celebrating Gotovina. A biography on the general's life was published under the romantic title *Warrior, Adventurer and General, a Biography of Ante Gotovina*. The most interesting artistic project inspired by the general's saga was the 2005 black comedy *Two Players on the Bench* by Croatian filmmaker Dejdan Sorak. The film does not take sides regarding Gotovina's indictment, but creates a complex plot revolving around an inspired attempt to exonerate a Croatian general wanted by an international war crimes tribunal.

Gotovina has pled "not guilty" to all charges against him, which range from looting to murder. Whether or not he is guilty, Gotovina's arrest removed a major obstacle to Croatia's progress toward EU membership. In the meantime, the Croatian press and the public closely followed his trial, which concluded in early September 2010, with a judgment expected shortly thereafter.

In recent years, many Croatians have lost patience with the politics of nationalism and want to disassociate themselves from symbols of right-wing fanaticism. For example, in 2005 a small group of right-wing reactionaries posted an unauthorized plaque commemorating Mile Budak, a minister in Croatia's World War II Ustashe government. A public outcry ensued and the government ordered the plaque destroyed along with at least one other monument dedicated to an Ustashe official.[6] At the same time, scholars note that the Tudjman years have instilled a xenophobic mentality in a generation of young people who exhibit intolerance for anyone they do not consider prototypically Croatian, including homosexuals, black people, Muslims, and especially Serbs. This mentality is decreasing over time, and while fringe elements always exist in politics, the Croatian public has become more centrist over time and primarily is focused on issues having an immediate effect on their lives, such as unemployment, inflation, and crime.

Of recent interest is the unexplained resignation of prime minister Sanader on July 1, 2009. While he was in office, Croatia had not made the advances that he, and the public, had hoped for. Progress toward EU membership stalled, and Croatia's economic growth stagnated, in part because of the global recession. Another undeniable factor contributing to Croatia's economic woes, however, was the lack of meaningful political and legal reforms, without which desirable levels of foreign investment are unlikely. None of these concerns were sufficient, at least in the eyes of the Croatian media and public, to justify Sanader's resignation. Speculation about corruption abounded both in the domestic and foreign press. Although the true reasons behind his resignation remain unknown, Sanader's appointed successor, Jadranka Kosor, is maintaining close ties to well-known members of the HDZ, reviving EU accession talks, and attempting to improve Croatia's economic prospects.[7] She has also undertaken an unprecedented campaign to combat corruption and has vowed to prosecute those involved in organized crime regardless of their political connections or wealth.

ISSUES AND ATTITUDES TOWARD REFORM: THE QUESTION OF CORRUPTION

Since the establishment of an independent state, the Croatian people have witnessed the deterioration of domestic industries and government institutions, largely because of corrupt practices that were initiated in the early postwar years. For example, the privatization of large corporations was fraught with insider dealing and political favoritism. With the goal of fostering a free-market economy, large companies that once were owned by the Yugoslav government were sold, often at well below value, to private entrepreneurs during the 1990s. Unfortunately, many of these entrepreneurs were well-connected political players with little business experience. Valuable properties were distributed according to backroom negotiations instead of an open and fair bidding process. In many cases, viable businesses were poorly managed and destroyed by these new owners who eventually sold the remaining assets for a profit, usually to larger European conglomerates. Important government positions also were distributed by virtue of political connections, producing corrupt and incompetent agencies on the federal and local level. Efforts have been made to rectify the errors of the immediate postwar years, but 21st-century debates over such issues as human rights, civil liberties, and economic reform take place against a backdrop of mistrust.

Although committed to democracy, Croatians' faith in newly established institutions is generally low, according to a series of surveys conducted as part of the European Values Survey, a social science research project covering 33 countries. As of 2003, 67.5 percent of Croatian survey participants had "low or no trust" in the government, as opposed to only 40 percent expressing such negative feelings in 1995.[8] In her article on the subject, Davorka Matic asserts that this response does not mean Croatians are rejecting democracy. Given the "difficulties associated with costs, the prolonged economic crisis, widespread corruption, high unemployment, weak institutional performance, increased social inequality and international isolation, it seems only rational that people would lose trust in institutions that they view as incompetent and responsible for many of their problems."[9] In the same analysis, Matic asserts that Croatians still favor a democratic system, although their patience may be exhausted if the government fails to transform itself from a low-quality to a high-quality democracy meeting its citizens' needs.

Matic cites a 2005 survey by Transparency International in which 80.7 percent of Croatians reported that the judiciary is the most corrupt government institution. The courts suffer from inexperienced staff and a prolonged decision-making process,[10] making speedy resolution of most cases impossible. The Ministry of Justice reported that as of September 30, 2008, a total of 941,827 cases remained unresolved. That is almost one case for every fourth person living in the country. According to a report issued by Freedom House in 2009,[11] the HDZ has "met its own limitations in terms of fighting corruption and reforming the judiciary."[12] More recent surveys confirm the public perception of the judiciary has not improved. The 2009 Global Corruption Barometer,[13] a public opinion survey conducted by Transparency International, reports that the 1,000 Croats surveyed gave the Croatian judiciary a score of 4.4 on a scale of 1 (the best) to 5 (the worst).

On a hopeful note, some progress is being made in terms of judicial reform according to the European Union Croatia Progress Report for 2008. Both a new code of ethics for attorneys and a system for assessing judges' performance have been adopted. The EU report acknowledges, however, that enforcement of judicial decisions is still a major problem. Approximately 50 percent of decisions are not enforced because the parties involved are not properly notified. Reform of the enforcement system has been undertaken, but according to the EU report, plenty of work remains to be done, with the report citing "a lack of leadership and ownership in reform implementation."[14]

Transparency International's 2009 survey also reported that corruption in government remains one of the greatest concerns for the Croatian public, with approximately 71 percent of those polled believing that the government has not stopped corruption. Croatia was ranked 62 out of 180 countries surveyed in Transparency International's 2008 Corruption Perceptions Index,[15] with a score of 4.4 out of a best possible score of 10,[16] which is a substantial improvement from 1999, when Croatia scored only 2.7. Some instances of successful law enforcement appeared in the media; however, on the surface at least, these cases seem to have little to do with larger systemic problems. For example, one prominent 2008 case involved a surgeon who was sentenced to nine years in prison for taking bribes from patients who wanted heart surgery. The same year, several professors at the University of Zagreb were arrested for taking bribes in exchange for handing out diplomas. Although one may speculate that this sort of bribery has become the norm in certain circles, current evidence to support this theory is anecdotal at best.

More significantly, organized crime in the form of mafia-like groups with ties to political and business interests is often blamed for recent violence. In 2008, the murders of several prominent figures drew public attention to the government's weakness in confronting organized crime. One of the worst, and most publicized, attacks occurred in October 2008 when Ivo Pukanic, the owner and editor in chief of the *Nacional* newspaper group, was killed along with one of his employees by a car bomb in Zagreb.[17] Pukanic often wrote about corruption in Croatia as well as other Balkan countries and was known to have sources in the mafia. In 2001, his paper made allegations linking leaders of other Balkan nations to organized crime, which eventually led to the 2004 murder of a newspaper editor in Montenegro. The bombing came within weeks of the murder of the daughter of a prominent Zagreb attorney. In response to these killings, Prime Minister Sanader replaced his ministers of justice and the interior and the chief of Croatia's police. Special courts were established to deal with organized crime and improvements were made to witness-protection programs. Finally, the police arrested 10 individuals in connection to Pukanic's murder, all of whom were described by authorities as "dangerous members of the underworld." These actions, however, have not yielded a perceptible shift in public opinion, and according to the Freedom House Nations in Transit 2009 report on Croatia, the lack of progress against corruption points out a more systemic problem, specifically, a lack of political will to aggressively deal with this issue.[18] Whether Jadranka Kosor's promise to attack these issues head-on is effective or not remains to be seen.

MINORITY RIGHTS

The rights of ethnic minorities have been a priority, at least on paper, for the Croatian government since the early days of independence. The constitution guarantees equality to all members of minorities and prescribes that citizens of the Republic of Croatia "shall enjoy rights and freedoms regardless of race, color, gender, language, religion, political or other opinions, national or social origin, property, birth, education, social status, or other characteristics. All shall be equal before the law."[19] As part of the EU membership process, the Croatian government enhanced its commitment to protect minority rights. In recent years, the general population has become more sensitive to minority issues, and negative stereotyping in the media has decreased. Substantial work remains to be done, however, and implementation of antidiscrimination policies is difficult. For example, an official program dedicated to the creation of long-term strategies for minority employment in state and local government exists, but actual policies have not been enacted. Skilled administrative staff and funding are in short supply and the lack of an adequate monitoring system to produce statistics is a major obstacle.[20] The government has also established the Councils for National Minorities (CNMs) to act as advisory bodies but their independence is questionable,[21] as they depend on local authorities for funding.

The case of Serbs living in Croatia is especially challenging. The Homeland War pitted Serbs and Croats against one another and exacerbated the prejudice and mistrust that existed for generations. Going back to the days of the Socialist Federal Republic of Yugoslavia (1943–1991), Croatians resented that the Yugoslav government, based in Belgrade, often assigned Serbians to important positions within Croatia. As Branka Magas states in her book *Croatia, Through History*, in the 1950s, Serbian hegemony "grew under cover of the ruling party's organizational principle of 'democratic centralism' and policy of 'brotherhood and unity.'"[22] This resentment never entirely disappeared in Yugoslavia and was reborn with a new ferocity during the Homeland War.

In 1991, before the Homeland War, Croatia's population was 78 percent ethnic Croatian and 12 percent Serbian. By 2001, the Serbian population shrank to only 4.5 percent,[23] primarily because so many Serbs were displaced during the war years (see Chapter 1, Geography and History, for a detailed discussion). According to a 2009 report by Freedom House, Serbs are underrepresented in local and regional government. Many Serbs who returned to their homes in Croatia still face discrimination and harassment, although less so than during the years immediately following the war.[24] The EU 2009 Progress Report for Croatia[25] also reported a decline in discrimination against the Serb minority; however, the report points out that some incidents may go unreported because of a lack of faith in authorities and law enforcement. The report also states that even Serbs who remained in Croatia during the Homeland War have trouble finding jobs, particularly in the regions most heavily affected by the war. (For details regarding housing issues for Serb refugees see Chapter 11, Architecture and Housing.)

Croatia's Roma population (also known as Gypsies, Rom, or Romany) is an officially recognized minority. According to 2001 census data, Roma account for approximately 0.20 percent (9,463 people) of the population.[26] They traditionally have existed on the fringes of society, often living in their own clan-based communities. The size of the Roma population is probably much larger than census data imply. According to a 2002 survey by the United Nations Development Programme, the population could be as large as 30,000 or 40,000[27] because many Roma identify with other nationalities for census purposes. Even during the days of the former Yugoslavia, the Roma faced discrimination and endured social and economic hardships, including consistently higher rates of poverty and unemployment than the Croatian population at large. As recently as 2006, only 18 percent of the Roma population older than 15 years of age was employed.[28]

In 2005, the Croatian government developed a plan to improve access to employment, health, housing, and education and undertook infrastructure programs for Roma settlements with the help of EU funding. The goal of integrating the Roma into Croatia's mainstream begins with education. Although countrywide statistics are not available, there are indications of increased rates of school enrollment for Romany children in Medimurje County and other areas with large Roma populations. Because a majority of Roma families speak the Romany language, their children often require special language classes. Initially such classes led to the segregation of Roma children; however, efforts are being made to include these courses in the mainstream curriculum.

According to EU reports, improvements in education for Roma still are not part of a systematic or established policy, and while rates of primary and secondary school completion are increasing, progress is slow. Problems of access to basic services are further exacerbated by the Roma's lack of personal documents and a general intolerance toward this group by many Croatians.

Croatia is in a transitional state with respect to women's rights. Traditional attitudes regarding a women's place as homemaker and mother are prevalent, but at the same time, younger women expect to complete a college education and join the workforce. As in other industrial nations, women's participation in the workforce has not freed them from domestic obligations, such as housecleaning, cooking, and taking care of the young, the old, and the sick. Not surprisingly, many Croatian women are overburdened with everyday obligations. When these women do enter the labor market, they face discrimination in terms of job opportunities and pay. In response, the government recently established the 2003 Gender Equality Act, designed to promote women's rights and gender equality, including employment rights and protection against discrimination.

According to a 2007 report published as part of the Central Intelligence Agency's Country Report on Croatia, the position of women in the labor force has not significantly improved.[29] Upon entering the workforce, women report that potential employers often ask younger women about their marital status, how many children they have, and whether they are planning on having more children. Job discrimination occurs most often against women between the ages of 40 and 50 who are denied promotions and raises or simply are passed over for jobs in favor of a male applicant or a younger person. Women typically work in the four lowest-paying areas: the textile industry, the education system, social care, and health care services. Those working in education, health care, and public administration received 20 percent less total income than their male counterparts. According to the same report, a senior official publicly stated that the effect of labor discrimination extends into retirement. For example, when women are paid less than men for doing the same job, upon retirement, women's pensions will be smaller than their male colleagues. One can extend this to mean that older women will face more economic hardship than their male counterparts. In a May 2007 conference on gender equality organized by the Croatian government, it was estimated that the average monthly gross salary for women was $1,161 (5,806 kunas) and for men was $1,298 (6,492 kunas).[30]

Although the government has taken some initial steps to improve women's status in the workplace, it has a long way to go. On the positive side, female participation in government is increasing, with women currently holding 32 (21 percent) of 153 seats in the Parliament. In July 2008, the government ratified a new act on gender equity, stipulating that women must make up at least 40 percent of the candidate list for each political party on the local and national levels. According to the aforementioned EU report, however, it is doubtful that the prescribed fines are large enough to deter violations.

NOTES

1. U.S. Department of State, *Croatia Profile, Background Notes*, September 2009, http://www.state.gov/p/eur/ci/hr/ (retrieved September 15, 2009).

2. "Vjesnik: HDZ najpopularnija stranka, Mesic najpozitivniji politicar" (in Croatian), Utorak, 10. veljace 2004 (February 10, 2004), http://ns1.vjesnik.com/Html/2004/02/10/Clanak.asp?r=tem&c=1 (retrieved October 2, 2009).

3. A. M. Rosenthal, "Back from the Grave," *New York Times*, April 15, 1997.

4. For more details, see Marius Soberg, "Croatia Since 1989: The HDZ and the Politics of Transition," in *Democratic Transition in Croatia: Value Transformation, Education & Media*, ed. Sabrina P. Ramet and Davorka Matic (College Station: Texas A&M University Press, 2007), 31–62.

5. Marlis Simons, "War Crimes Case Revives Passions in a Divided Croatia," *New York Times*, December 12, 2005.

6. *Encyclopaedia Britannica Online*, s.v. "Croatia," http://search.eb.com/eb/article-9398317 (retrieved October 1, 2009).

7. Robert Bajrusi, *People of Trust to Jadranka Kosor, Nacional* no. 720, September 1, 2009, http://www.nacional.hr/en/clanak/50380/people-of-trust-to-jadranka-kosor (retrieved October 20, 2009).

8. Davorka Matic, "Political Culture, Socio-Cultural Values and Democratic Consolidation in Croatia," in *Croatia since Independence: War, Politics, Society, Foreign Relations*, ed. Sabrina P. Ramet, Konrad Clewing, and Reneo Lukic (Munich: R. Oldenbourg Verlang, 2008), 179.

9. Ibid.

10. U.S. Department of State, *2008 Country Reports on Human Rights Practices— Croatia*, February 25, 2009, http://www.unhcr.org/refworld/docid/49a8f198c.html (retrieved September 15, 2009).

11. Freedom House is a nongovernmental agency dedicated to the study and expansion of freedom throughout the world.

12. Freedom House, "Nations in Transit 2009—Croatia," June 30, 2009, http://www.unhcr.org/refworld/docid/4a55bb3b20.html (retrieved September 15, 2009).

13. "Croatia: Judiciary Most Corrupt, Media Least," Zagreb, June 5, 2009, http://www.balkaninsight.com (retrieved October 20, 2009).

14. European Union, European Commission, *Common Staff Working Document: Croatia 2008 Progress Report*, SEC (2008) 2694, Brussels, November 5, 2008.

15. Transparency International's Corruption Perceptions Index (CPI) measures the degree of corruption as perceived by businesspeople and analysts. Scores range between 10 (clean) and 0 (very corrupt).

16. See "Corruption in Croatia Same as in Namibia," Dalje.com, September 23, 2008, http://www.javno.com/en-croatia/corruption-in-croatia-same-as-in-namibia_185243 (retrieved October 20, 2009).

17. "Still a Balkan Country, A Spate of Murders Damages Croatia's European Ambition," *The Economist*, October 30, 2008.

18. Freedom House, "Nations in Transit 2009—Croatia."

19. Articles 3 and 14 of the Constitution of the Republic of Croatia.

20. European Union, European Commission, *Commission Staff Working Document: Croatia 2009 Progress Report*, October 14, 2009, SEC (2009) 1333. http://www.unhcr.org/refworld/docid/4adc274a2.html (retrieved October 20, 2009).

21. European Union, European Commission, "Croatia 2009 Progress Report."

22. Branka Magas, *Croatia Through History: The Making of a European State* (London: Saqi Books, 2007), 615.

23. Central Intelligence Agency, "The World Factbook, Croatia," https://www.cia.gov/library/publications/the-world-factbook/geos/hr.html (retrieved September 15, 2010).

24. Freedom House, *Freedom in the World 2009—Croatia*, July 16, 2009, http://www.unhcr.org/refworld/docid/4a6452c1c.html (retrieved September 15, 2009).

25. European Union, European Commission, *Croatia 2009 Progress Report*.

26. Republic of Croatia, Central Bureau of Statistics, "2001 Census, Population by Ethnicity," Crostat Databases, http://www.dzs.hr/default_e.htm (retrieved October 22, 2009).

27. United Nations Development Programme, Bratislava Regional Center, "Avoiding the Dependency Trap: The Roma in Central and Eastern Europe," 2002, http://vulnerability.undp.sk/ (retrieved September 20, 2010).

28. European Union, European Commission, *Croatia 2009 Progress Report*.

29. U.S. Department of State, *2008 Country Reports on Human Rights Practices–Croatia*, Bureau of Democracy, Human Rights, and Labor, 2007, http://www.state.gov/g/drl/rls/hrrpt/2007/100553.htm (retrieved March 11, 2008).

30. U.S. Department of State, *2008 Country Reports on Human Rights Practices—Croatia*.

4

Marriage and Family, Gender Issues, and Education

MARRIAGE AND FAMILY

Family is the heart of Croatian life. Holidays typically spent with relatives establish traditions and solidify the bond between generations. Perhaps even more important, family members are expected to turn to one another for help with everything ranging from financial problems to child rearing. When one isn't with family, the relatives become a frequent topic of conversation. Friends often know all about each other's relationships with siblings, cousins, and elderly relatives.

Croatians not only identify with their immediate family and extended relatives, but also with the town, village, or island where the clan originated. In spite of the fact that many people have migrated from rural ancestral homes to larger cities over the last century, the notion of "hometown" is still important. This affinity for one's place of origin may be explained by Croatia's history and familial connections to the land. For centuries, Croatian territory was divided and governed by various European powers. As a result, people who identified themselves as Croatian often were culturally diverse. For example, coastal Dalmatia was historically linked to Venice and Italy, and hence the Italian language was used in schools and in an official capacity until the 20th century. In northern Croatia, the Hungarian influence was much stronger, and therefore the patterns of daily life ranging from cuisine to traditional dress resembled that of Hungary more than Dalmatia. Not surprisingly, even after migrating to the larger cities, many Croatians continued to identify with other migrants from their place of origin. These ties were strengthened by the fact that most families retain a physical link to their ancestral home, in the form of an old house or piece of property that the extended family owns and quite possibly uses as a vacation house. Selling one's familial home is seriously frowned upon; it is akin to disassociating oneself from one's roots in exchange for money. This outlook is especially prevalent along the coast where foreigners are often willing to make generous offers for properties that can be used for vacation homes.

As in most Western countries, family membership, or descent, is traced according to the paternal (father's) lineage. Traditionally, one's father's family was more relevant than one's mother's (or the maternal) side in terms of social life and family identity. For example, until well into the 20th century, a woman would expect to marry and live with her husband's relatives, either in the same home or, at the very least, in the same village and function as part of his extended familial unit. She literally would "marry into" the family and her children would identify with their paternal lineage. The maternal side of the family was secondary and would not assume as large a role in the children's lives or figure as prominently on other social levels. As people migrated away from agrarian villages and into urban areas, this pattern was no longer relevant, and the importance of maternal and paternal relatives was determined in a more spontaneous manner.

The emphasis on paternal lineage, however, lingers with respect to inheritance. Until recently, the family patrimony, which often consisted of farmland or a house, was left exclusively to the sons as a means of keeping the family farm or estate intact. Daughters were given a dowry, which usually included valuable items but rarely the land that has remained in the family for generations. In some conservative families, inheritance still is handled this way, although more often, estates are divided equally. As in other European countries, parents will give children substantial gifts of property when needed, perhaps as a wedding gift or when a child is born. These gifts are often essential to help younger generations begin their own families with a greater degree of comfort.

The nature and size of the household unit, or a group of people living "under one roof," has changed over the past century. The most obvious difference is the shift away from the large multigenerational family that lived and worked together on the family farm toward a model more suited to urban living. The extended family household was replaced by the three-generational family (grandparents, children, and grandchildren) and then by the nuclear family, and finally by an increasing number of other types of households, including single people and childless couples. By 1961, the average number of people per household was 3.6,[1] and by 2001, this average dropped to 3.0. At the same time, the number of single-parent households is rising. According to the 2001 census, one parent, usually the mother, heads 15 percent of all households with children.

Aside from migratory patterns, declining fertility is one of the most important factors contributing to smaller households. In this sense, Croatia is similar to the European Union countries where the average fertility rate declined from just under 1.6 to less than 1.5 between 1990 and 2005.[2] Croatia's rate for the 2005–2010 period is only 1.42,[3] making it a low-fertility country by United Nations standards and placing it well below the rate of 2.1, which is required to maintain the population. As a result, Croatia's population probably will decline over the next several decades. According to United Nations' statistics, the country's population will go from a high of approximately 4.5 million in 1990 to projections of 4.4 million in 2010 and 3.8 million by 2050.[4] At the same time, the number of single-parent households continues to rise.

A factor that counteracts the trends in declining household size is that children tend to live with their parents until well into adulthood. The median age for male children to move out of their parents' home is 32; for females, it is approximately four years younger.[5] Economic circumstances make it difficult for young people to establish a separate household earlier in life. For this reason, living with one's parents until marriage, and even longer, is more common in Croatia than in the United States or in many other Western European countries. When young people do leave the family home, it often is to live with others, not alone, and it is increasingly common for couples to live together before marriage.

Croatians generally believe it is important to get married before starting a family, and it is relatively rare for children to be born out of wedlock. Legally, marriage is allowed between two consenting individuals of opposite sex, who are over 18 and are not blood relatives or in an adoptive relationship. The courts can allow minors ages 16 or 17 to marry if it appears to be in the best interests of the parties involved, but this is unusual. Marriage can take place via civil ceremony or within the auspices of a religious organization that has established the proper legal relationship with the state. Thus far, only the Catholic Church enjoys this status. The number of marriages has fluctuated over the years. In 1971, there were 8.5 marriages per 1,000 citizens, going down to 4.5 per 1,000 in 1991.[6] Recent data show an increase to 5.2 marriages per 1,000 in 2007. Upon getting married, most women adopt their husband's surname. Interestingly, during the decades when Croatia was part of Communist Yugoslavia, women were given the option of keeping their maiden name or hyphenating it after marriage. Given the traditional importance of patriarchal lineage, however, few women took advantage of this option then or now.

The high value placed on family and child bearing is reflected in Croatia's maternity laws. Employed women are entitled to paid maternity leave beginning 28 days before giving birth until the child is six months old. The compensation is set on the basis of the average wage earned during the six months before the leave. Unfortunately, this generous policy is not always implemented. Employers often ask female workers to sign a contract under which they promise not to get married or have children for a prescribed number of years. Women are also hired as part-time or temporary employees, thereby exempting their employers from providing maternity benefits. Such practices are more common among smaller firms, but many companies simply prefer to hire men because they feel women are overprotected by maternity laws and therefore are too expensive.

When both parents work, relatives usually help with childcare. Whereas grandmothers are traditionally very involved in childrearing, grandfathers, aunts, and other family members may also babysit, on a daily basis if necessary. Because of an early retirement policy in the 1990s, female workers could leave their jobs at the age of 55 and begin collecting pensions (men had to wait until age 60). This system allowed grandmothers to actively participate in raising their grandchildren, thereby reducing the need for daycare services. Out of economic necessity, Croatia has raised its retirement age to 60 for women and 65 for men, penalizing those who retire early with a 0.15 percent cut in pension for every month up to 9 percent for leaving their jobs five years early. In 2010 the government proposed raising the retirement age for women to 65, citing compliance with a 2007 court ruling on gender equality. The backlash to this proposed law has been furious, with critics claiming that women need more time with their families, specifically to take care of their grandchildren.[7] Whether women will be forced to remain in the workplace an extra five years remains to be seen, but the controversy this policy has generated reflects the value that Croatians place on the role of extended family in childrearing.

In spite of the strong influence of the Catholic Church and the prevalence of traditional family values, divorce rates hover around 20 percent.[8] As in many countries, these rates tend to be higher in cities than in rural areas. Generally, divorce laws are designed to protect the rights of the children. For example, normally one or both parties can file for divorce; however, if a woman is pregnant or the couple has a child under the age of one year, the husband cannot file. If a couple has children under the age of 18, then a mediating procedure is required to arrange child custody and support.

It is expected that an agreement be reached between the parents to guarantee that the children are provided for financially and have the legal right to visit both parents. Typically, mothers are given custody and fathers are legally obliged to pay alimony, but women often face problems actually getting the financial support to which they are entitled. First, men often do not report their entire income. Many Croatians are self-employed, making it easy to hide assets. Second, unemployment is high, so even well-intentioned fathers cannot always meet their financial obligations. Although the social stigma of divorce is decreasing, women and children often face financial hardships upon the break-up of a marriage.

GENDER ISSUES

During the years that Croatia was part of Yugoslavia, the Communist government made an effort to impose gender equality. While true equality was never achieved, in some ways women living in the former Yugoslavia were given more rights than their sisters in Western Europe. They enjoyed greater participation in politics as well as in the labor force, although economic conditions probably forced women to find employment outside of the home whether they wanted to or not. In spite of the philosophical argument for gender equality, in reality Croatia and the former Yugoslavia were patriarchal societies in which a traditional division of labor remained within the home. Women were primarily responsible for childcare and housework, whether or not they had jobs outside of the house.

In the 1990s, as Yugoslavia disintegrated and Croatia emerged from the collapsed Communist state, attitudes toward women's rights became more traditional. Scholars have debated the reasons for this shift, which occurred throughout Eastern Europe.[9] Possibly, the rise of traditional values was part of a backlash against Communism, which had regularly promoted women's equality. In addition, by the 1990s, many women throughout Europe and the United States had become disillusioned with the feminist movement as they found themselves faced with the dual responsibilities of home and work, leaving most of them more exhausted than liberated. Especially for women in low-paying jobs, the prospect of returning to old-fashioned values, which meant leaving the labor force to take care of home and family, must have sounded attractive, even if it was not economically feasible. This sentiment was encouraged by the Catholic Church which used its influence to promote traditional social roles, especially with respect to the family. Finally, as Croatia faced immediate and critical issues of postwar reconstruction, policies dealing with the question of gender equality were not a high priority.

In the years since the Homeland War, Croatia has experienced a political shift away from the right-wing nationalism of the Tudjman years toward a more centrist philosophy. It is quite possible that attitudes toward women's social roles have changed as well. Few studies have been conducted on this subject especially with respect to urban populations. In Lynette Sikiæ's survey of gender attitudes among rural women in Croatia, however, she found traditional values remain deeply established.[10] Despite of the years of Communist rhetoric under the former Yugoslavia and exposure to progressive gender roles through foreign media, many women in rural Croatia consistently have placed their role as wife and mother before personal desires for education or financial freedom through employment. Sikiæ also found that, among her subjects in the rural county of Vukovar-Sirmium, some women embraced a traditional lifestyle more firmly than others. Women with more education and broader life experience tended to question prevailing values, although they felt unable to change their lives because of the social expectations and economic constraints that limited any control over their personal development.

It is possible that rural women interested in defying traditional norms eventually left their birthplace to attend college or find jobs in an urban area, but they still faced the effects of postwar "retraditionalisation," as well as the long-standing prejudices against women that continue in many patriarchal societies. The Croatian Constitution guarantees nondiscrimination in the workplace as well as gender equality, but in practice many problems still exist. For example, the U.S. State Department's 2008 country report on Croatia states that unemployment is disproportionately high among females, and salaries are significantly lower than those of men with similar qualifications. According to the report, women received approximately 20 percent less than men in the fields of education, health care, and public administration. This inequality will affect women into retirement as pensions are linked to income earned during one's career.

Croatian law also prohibits sexual harassment in the workplace; however, according to a 2006 survey by the International Unions' Confederation, approximately 18 percent of women experience harassment at work.[11] Croatia lacks a systematic approach for dealing with this situation and awareness of the problem is limited. Many people, male and female, do not recognize sexual harassment as a serious concern. Rather, it is viewed as an uncomfortable aspect of the workplace that "comes with the territory," especially if a woman is young and attractive. Given this mentality, women often are afraid of complaining. They may be labeled as overly sensitive or become the object of more serious reprisals, including character attacks and job loss. Given Croatia's chronically high unemployment rate, many women would rather tolerate harassment than jeopardize their livelihood.

Although women still face discrimination on many levels, the government has taken positive steps. With the help of influential women's NGOs (nongovernmental organizations), Croatia has adopted a national gender equality policy for 2006–2010 to address women's status in the labor market while also introducing gender-sensitive education and raising awareness with respect to domestic violence. Additionally, the government has made an effort to increase women's participation in the political process, which has been enhanced by the introduction of Jadranka Kosor as prime minister in 2009.

Reproductive rights are a source of controversy in many countries and remain so in Croatia, with abortion at the center of the debate. Croatia inherited a policy of abortion on demand from the Yugoslav era, but since independence, both pro-life and pro-choice movements have been organized. Abortions are available to women 16 years of age and older up to 10 weeks after conception. After that, a special commission must approve termination of pregnancy. For women less than 16 years of age, parental consent is required. Croatian law demands mandatory counseling for any woman who requests an abortion. In the meantime, the Catholic Church has taken an active role by establishing its own network of pro-life counseling centers.

The number of abortions performed in Croatia has declined sharply over the last 20 years. The abortion ratio (defined as the number of abortions per every 1,000 live births) dropped from 921.1 in 1989 to only 204 in 2008.[12] The most obvious reason for this decline is the increasing influence of the Catholic Church and the shift in cultural values in favor of the Church's pro-life position. Along with this sentiment, many policy makers proclaimed their opposition to abortion and doctors refused to perform the procedure on moral grounds, thereby making it less accessible.[13] Because few studies have been published on the use of contraceptives in Croatia, it is difficult to assess the role of family planning in the declining abortion figures. Legislative attempts to formally limit the availability of abortion have met with swift opposition by well-organized women's groups who have successfully forced lawmakers to back away from the most restrictive policy changes.[14]

In Croatia, the notion of gender equality usually is limited to the status of women in society. Gay rights lag far behind and are rarely even a point of discussion. During the Yugoslav era, homosexuality was not mentioned until the AIDS epidemic of the 1980s, and then it was represented in an extremely negative context, along with prostitution and drug abuse. Even within the context of human rights discussions after the establishment of an independent Croatian state, homosexuality was effectively marginalized.

Given the predominance of conservative traditional values in Croatia, the stigmatization of gays and the predominance of gay stereotypes is hardly surprising. Although homosexual relations between consenting adults are not illegal, many Croatians are uncomfortable with the issue. According to surveys quoted in the *International Encyclopedia of Sexuality*,[15] about half of the respondents are extremely homophobic and slightly more stated that they would not like to have a homosexual person as a neighbor. Women and younger people living in urban areas displayed more tolerance. At the same time, homosexuals are slowly coming out of the closet and organizing to advance gay rights but the process has not been easy.

Croatia's first gay pride parade took place in Zagreb in 2002 with the theme *Iskorak Kontra Predrasuda* (Coming Out Against Prejudice). Approximately 300 people participated, but the day ended in violence. The parade's master of ceremonies was physically attacked, opponents yelled homophobic slogans, and the event ended with tear gas thrown at the crowd. Most observers left the scene safely while the police escorted more prominent (and recognizable) gay activists to their homes. At this point, a group of self-styled skinheads harassed and beat up at least 20 people, some of whom attended the parade and others who were simply bystanders. The following year, the gay pride parade was accompanied by a larger police presence and violence was avoided. The parade has become an annual event in Zagreb, but as recently as 2008, massive police protection was still deemed necessary. Normally the police presence in Zagreb is far less noticeable than in the average U.S. city. On the day of the parade, however, groups of officers in full riot gear were stationed on every street corner. Violence was avoided, but the police presence stands as a reminder of the perilous situation faced by gays and lesbians who dare to publicly come out and celebrate their community. In 2003, the Croatian government passed legislation on same-sex unions granting gays and lesbians property rights, while also forbidding discrimination on the basis of sexual orientation. Although same-sex couples still do not have all the protections afforded heterosexual couples, this legislation puts Croatia among the most progressive countries in Central and Eastern Europe with respect to gay rights. In 2004, the policy was expanded to specifically address education, the media, and the workplace.[16] In addition, gays and lesbians have assumed a higher profile on the cultural scene. Cafés and bars catering to a gay clientele have opened and Queer Zagreb, a cultural festival, is an established annual event.

EDUCATION

Croatia's educational institutions are among the best in Southeastern Europe.[17] This is not surprising because Croatians place a high priority on schooling their children. For many families, education is the ticket to social mobility and financial security. Even in the former Yugoslavia, the government understood that a good educational system advanced both the individual as well as the country at large. Croatian schools are not perfect, but literacy rates are high, and children are guaranteed the right to an education almost entirely free of charge.

Most students first attend preschool, whether public or private. These schools serve children from the ages of one to five years and are not compulsory. After that, children attend primary school for eight years and their education is divided into two phases. Between first and fourth grade, students have a single teacher who covers the full range of subjects, including mathematics, reading, science, physical education, religion, and English language. From the fifth through eighth grade, teachers are more specialized and students receive instruction from several different faculty members.

Primary school education is compulsory, meaning all Croatian children should complete at least eight years of schooling. During this phase, students are exposed to the various sciences, including biology, chemistry, and physics. They also begin to study a second foreign language, usually German or Italian. Ninety-one percent of children complete their primary education, contributing to the country's 98.5 percent literacy rate.[18] As of 2010, Croatia had more than 900 primary schools that fell under the jurisdiction of local government. The pupil-to-teacher ratio is relatively low at 14.7 students for every teacher.[19]

Secondary education was optional until 2006 when it became compulsory. This is not a radical reform, as nearly all students would have enrolled anyway. At this point, students must decide to either attend a gymnasium or a vocational school. A small percentage of students select specialized art or music academies.

Gymnasiums are academically oriented, and students must pass a standardized entrance exam to enroll. Once a student is accepted, he or she must select one of four curriculums: (1) a mathematics and computer science curriculum, (2) a curriculum emphasizing the classics, including Latin and Ancient Greek, (3) a curriculum emphasizing foreign languages, or (4) a general education curriculum. Typically, it takes four years to graduate from the gymnasium, although many vocational schools only require three years. Upon completion of course work, gymnasium students must take a final exam called a *matura*, which the student must pass to attend a university. A new standardized test will be introduced at the end of the 2009–2010 academic year, featuring three mandatory subjects: Croatian language, mathematics, and one modern foreign language (English, German, Italian, or French). Students completing the classical track also will have the option of Latin or Ancient Greek. Optional subjects for testing include specific scientific fields, such as biology, chemistry, and physics as well as history, visual arts, music, and computer science, to name a few.

After secondary school, students may attend one of seven public universities located in Zagreb, Split, Rijeka, Zadar, Pula, Osijek, and Dubrovnik.

In addition, Dubrovnik is home to Croatia's first private university. Established in 2008, Dubrovnik International University is known primarily for its emphasis on diplomatic studies and international affairs. At the public universities, education is almost entirely free of charge, but students must pay for dormitories if they cannot live at home. Approximately 40 percent of individuals of college age are enrolled in a university.[20]

According to a recent United Nations Children's Fund report on education in Croatia,[21] inequities still exist with respect to access. Problems are most evident upon comparisons between ethnic groups. Roma and Serb children do not have the same access to quality education that the majority of Croatian children enjoy. The report cites deep-seated problems of discrimination against minorities as the major factor contributing to educational inequities. Other problems cited in the report include relatively low primary school enrollment by minorities of 85 percent compared with 92 percent for the population at large and low preschool attendance of 46 percent. Secondary school enrollment compares favorably to the regional average at 85 percent. On the positive side, Croatian students performed on par with their Central European neighbors on the 2006 Programme for International Student Assessment (PISA) assessment, which measures 15-year-old students' capabilities in reading, mathematics, and science. On a global level, however, Croatia has plenty of room for improvement. Out of 57 participating countries, Croatia ranked 26th in science, 36th in mathematics, and 30th in reading.

In 2005 the Croatian government began to adopt reforms aimed at improving all levels of education. For example, the Ministry of Education, with support from the World Bank, opened 29 new preschools in underserved areas. Foreign language programs were either introduced or enhanced at the preschool level and efforts were made to standardize elementary school education. Finally, the government decreed that all children should have access to free textbooks. Along with many other European countries, Croatia has instituted the reforms recommended by the Bologna Process, established by the European Union to, among other things, standardize university degree programs across European countries and promote lifelong learning.

Notes

1. Francis H. Eterovich and Christopher Spalatin, eds., *Croatia: Land, People and, Culture,* Vol. 1 (Toronto: University of Toronto Press, 1964).

2. European Commission, Eurostat, "EU Labour Force Survey," in *The Life of Men and Women in Europe, a Statistical Portrait* (Eurostat Statistical Books, 2008).

3. Population Division of the Department of Economic and Social Affairs of the United Nations Secretariat, "World Population Prospects: The 2008 Revision," http://esa.un.org/unpp (retrieved June 2, 2010).

4. Ibid.

5. European Commission, Eurostat, "EU Labour Force Survey."

6. European and North American Women Action (Enawa), "The Status of Women's Rights in Croatia," Fall/Winter 2000, www.enawa.org/NGO/Croatia1 .htm *(retrieved May 30, 2010).*

7. Radic, N. "Croatia to Postpone Retirement for Women," SETimes.com, June 8, 2010. http://www.setimes.com/cocoon/setimes/xhtml/en_GB/features/setimes/ blogreview/2010/08/06/blog-04 (retrieved September 16, 2010).

8. Republic of Croatia, Central Bureau of Statistics.

9. See Robert M. Kunovich and Catherine Deitelbaum, "Ethnic Conflict, Group Polarization, and Gender Attitudes in Croatia," *Journal of Marriage and Family* 66, no. 5 (December 2004): 1089.

10. Lynette Sikiae, "Gendered Values and Attitudes among Rural Women in Croatia," *Journal of Comparative Family Studies* 38, no. 3 (2007): 459–479.

11. U.S. Department of State, *2007 Country Reports on Human Rights Practices– Croatia*, Bureau of Democracy, Human Rights, and Labor, March 11, 2008. http:// www.state.gov/g/drl/rls/hrrpt/2007/100553.htm (retrieved June 2, 2010).

12. "Historical Abortion Statistics, Croatia," comp. Wm. Robert Johnston, April 25, 2010, http://www.johnstonsarchive.net/policy/abortion/ab-croatia.html (retrieved April 25, 2010).

13. Sanja Cesar, "Reproductive Health Services in Croatia," Center for Education and Counseling of Women, http://www.astra.org.pl/CROATIA.pdf (retrieved April 22, 2010).

14. Jeremy Shiffman, Marina Skrabalo, and Jelena Subotic, "Reproductive Rights and the State in Serbia and Croatia," *Social Science & Medicine* 54, no. 4 (2002): 625–642.

15. The studies quoted are A. Stulhofer, "*Seksualno stanje nacije 1999*" (Sexual state of the nation 1999) *Globus* 452 (August 6, 1999): 58–63; G. Crpic and I. Rimac, "*Pregled postotaka i aritmetickih sredina: Europsko istrazivanje*," 2000, *Ency-clopedia of Sexuality Online*, http://www2.hu-berlin.de/sexology/IES/croatia.html#1 (retrieved April 22, 2010).

16. For good synopsis of gay and lesbian rights in Croatia, see Dean Vuletic, "Gay Men and Lesbians," in *Croatia since Independence: War, Politics, Society, Foreign Relations*, ed. Sabrina P. Ramet, Konrad Clewing, and Reneo Lukic (Munich: R. Oldenbourg Verlang, 2008).

17. UNICEF Country Profile, "Croatia: Education in Croatia." http://www .unicef.org/ceecis/Croatia.pdf (retrieved April 23, 2010).

18. Statistic from UNESCO UIS Data, UNESCO Institute for Statistics, http:// www.nationmaster.com/country/hr-croatia/edu-education (retrieved April 23, 2010).

19. Statistic from the World Bank, *World Development Indicators* database, http://www.nationmaster.com/rcd/country/hr-croatia/edu-education&all=1 (retrieved April 23, 2010).

20. World Bank, *World Development Indicators* database, http://www.nationmaster .com/time.php?stat=edu_sch_enr_ter_gro&country=hr (retrieved April 23, 2010).

21. UNICEF Country Profile, "Croatia: Education in Croatia."

5

Holidays and Leisure Activities

The 11 official holidays on the Croatian calendar are both secular and religious, each having a particular tradition and history. But as in the United States, many people look forward to these holidays primarily because they represent at least one day off from work. Government offices are closed, as are many private businesses and shops, while ferries, buses, and trains usually run on a modified schedule. If the holiday is planned to create a three-day weekend, crowded travel conditions are the norm, especially in the summer months. If groceries are needed on a holiday, it is best to go shopping in the morning, because at least one local store will be open but for only half a day. Outdoor markets usually are empty as are most streets, even in larger cities. As noted in several travel guides for Croatia, visitors generally have a hard time figuring out exactly what is being celebrated during most holidays.

Listed below are Croatia's official holidays, including explanations for the less familiar ones and a brief discussion of how each is celebrated. Christmas and Easter are covered in more detail at the end of this section.

- January 1, New Year's Day: Croatians hit the streets on New Year's Eve with large outdoor celebrations. Ban Jelacic Square in Zagreb gets particularly raucous with vendors selling *rakija*, an alcoholic beverage made of distilled fruit (often grapes), and wine alongside fireworks and musical performances. The party goes on well past midnight and the event is free. In addition,

New Year's Day is also the Feast of Mary, Mother of God, and a holy day of obligation in the Catholic Church, so many Croatians celebrate the day by going to Mass and then feasting on a traditional meal of *sarma* (stuffed cabbage) and pork.

- January 6, the Feast of the Epiphany: This marks the end of the Christmas season and celebrates the appearance of Christ in human form. It also honors the Three Kings (or the Three Wise Men) who saw a star above Bethlehem and followed it to visit the Christ Child on January 6. Although this is not a holy day of obligation, many Croatians attend Mass anyway.

- March/April, Easter Monday: Croatians take the day after Easter off from work and school to visit friends and relatives. The holiday is observed in many other Christian countries, but it also dates back to a tradition of secular celebrations following Easter.

- May 1, Labor Day: This day signals the beginning of the vacation season. Everyone does their best to take a trip to the coast or mountains. Traditionally Labor Day honors the achievements of workers and was an important holiday during the Communist era. Companies would organize picnics and parties for their employees and every woman would wear a red carnation.

- June, Corpus Christi: Catholics celebrate the Eucharist on this holiday, which falls on the Thursday after Trinity Sunday. This is not a holy day of obligation, but many Croatians still attend Mass.

- June 22, Anti-Fascist Resistance Day: This holiday was established in honor of the uprising led by Josip Broz (Tito) against the Germans who had conquered Yugoslavia during World War II. The Germans eventually were defeated and Tito established the Socialist Federal Republic of Yugoslavia.

- June 25, Croatian National Day: On June 25, 1991, the parliament voted for independence from Yugoslavia.

- August 5, Victory Day and National Thanksgiving Day: On this day in 1995 the Croatian Army took the city of Knin during Operation Storm, which effectively put an end to the Republic of Serbia Krajina and the Homeland War. The biggest celebration takes place in Knin, where Croatian dignitaries join the public in a Mass followed by a ceremony commemorating those who lost their lives in the war. The high point of the day comes when the Croatian flag is hoisted above the 10th-century Knin fortress that overlooks the city. Thousands of people from all over the country attend this celebration.

- October 8, Independence Day: Although the Croatian Parliament proclaimed independence on June 25, 1991, Croatia did not formally cut ties with Yugoslavia until October 8. A three-month moratorium was placed on independence activities, while an agreement was negotiated to resolve the situation peacefully.

- November 1, All Saints Day: This is a traditional Catholic holiday honoring martyrs. Croatians also pay respects to their deceased friends and relatives by bringing flowers to cemeteries and attending Mass. This is a holy day of obligation for Catholics.

- December 25, Christmas Day: This is a traditional Catholic holiday honoring the birth of Christ, and is a holy day of obligation for Catholics.

Christmas Traditions

Traditionally a religious holiday, in recent years Christmas has acquired a familiar secular tone. American and Western European traditions—including Santa Claus, elves, and reindeer along with an emphasis on gift giving—have begun to characterize the season. This just adds another layer to a Christmas which is laden with diverse traditions rooted in the varied histories and physical landscapes that have molded Croatian culture. The secularization of Christmas is ironic as the holiday could not be publicly celebrated during the Yugoslav era because of its religious nature. But in spite of the recent commercialization of the day, Croatians maintain their traditions, religious and otherwise.

From a religious standpoint, preparations begin with the season of Advent,[2] which includes the four Sundays before Christmas and represents a period of preparation for the birth of Christ characterized by prayer, fasting, and attending Mass. Croatia is rich in folk traditions for the Advent period, the most common taking place on December 13, Saint Lucy's Day, when wheat seeds are planted in a shallow dish. By Christmas Eve, the wheat has sprouted and candles are placed in the dish as a decoration that also symbolizes the spiritual light of Christmas. In agricultural regions, the height of the wheat is thought to predict next year's harvest. The feast of Saint Thomas on December 21 marks the beginning of preparations for the Christmas feast. Pork is the most common main dish, but roast duck, goose, or turkey also is served. Women begin making pastries, including a Christmas cake called *cesnica*[3] or *krstnica*, which is round and inscribed with a cross. Each of the four corners of the cross is decorated with a figure of a bird made of pastry dough. A candle is placed in the middle of the cake and remains on display until New Year's Day when it is eaten. The *cesnica* is loaded with symbolism: the birds represent the four evangelists, the candle represents Christ as the light of the world, and the cross symbolizes spiritual salvation.

For many families, Christmas celebrations commence on Christmas Eve when a modest dinner featuring a meatless main course is served after a short prayer. In Dalmatia, *bakalar* (dried cod) is the traditional dish followed by a dessert of *fritule*, a small round pastry made of fried dough. Many Croatians attend Christmas Eve Mass that features lots of music and usually is less than two hours long. In Bosnia and Herzegovina, however, Christmas Eve Masses have been known to last until dawn.

Homes are decorated during the holiday season with lots of greenery and wreaths. Croatians also have adopted the tradition of placing Christmas trees in their living rooms, and although the trees originally were decorated with nuts and dried fruit, glass figurines and shiny ornaments have become popular in recent years. Brightly painted red Licitar hearts made of dried dough also are placed on the tree. These hearts are the traditional symbol of Zagreb and appear throughout the city during the holiday season with thousands of them decorating the giant tree in Ban Jelacic Square. Gifts are customarily given to children on Saint Lucy's Day and Saint Nicholas Day (December 6). The practice of gift-giving on Christmas day is relatively new, and the children are told that their presents, usually small items, came from the Baby Jesus, although Santa Claus is increasingly referenced.

Easter Traditions

Preparation for Easter begins with the Lenten season, which takes place during the 40 days before Easter and is marked by a period of fasting and prayer leading up to Holy Week, when Croatians, like Catholics throughout the world, are especially intent upon abstaining from things they like (alcohol, cigarettes, sweets) as a means of purification. Holy Week begins with Palm Sunday, when palm branches are blessed in honor of Jesus' entry into Jerusalem during which bystanders threw cloaks as well as palms before the donkey he rode. Jesus' reception worried the Roman authorities who began to view him as a threat, and thus began the sequence of events leading to his crucifixion. Today Croatians are offered palm branches in church; however, until recently, few palm trees grew in Croatia so other types of plants were used, including willow, olive, and rosemary branches. Holy Thursday commemorates the Last Supper and begins a period of intense contemplation and prayer. Church bells remain silent for the next three days and according to tradition, farmers do not work in their fields. The next day is Good Friday, which honors Christ's crucifixion and death at Calvary. Masses are not held, and Croatians tend to spend this time with their families. Holy Thursday and Good Friday are not official holidays, but many people take these days off from work. Businesses are closed and city streets are quieter than usual. Holy Week ends with Easter, the celebration of Christ's resurrection from the dead after his crucifixion.

Easter Sunday begins with a morning Mass to which people bring baskets of food to be blessed for the feast that follows. In addition to a large meal, a number of traditional desserts are prepared, such as *uskrsna pogaca* or *sirnica* (Easter bread made with lots of eggs and sugar), *orehnjaca* (walnut cake), and *krafne* (jelly-filled donuts). Croatians practice other traditions including the common European custom of decorating Easter eggs. The old-fashioned method involves first drawing on an egg with a wax crayon. Designs can range from written text to floral or geometric patterns. To dye the eggs, they are placed in a pot full of boiling water along with a combination of roots and herbs that release natural colors. The wax is then removed to reveal a decorative pattern. Polishing the eggs with a little bit of oil finishes the process. The eggs are called *pisanice* which is derived from the phrase "to write" in reference to the process of drawing (or writing) on the egg with wax. Although this method was practiced for generations, it is rarely used today because most people buy prepackaged egg-dying kits at the supermarket. The eggs are a fun tradition, but for most Croatians the best aspect of Easter is the opportunity to spend a relaxing day at home with their families. The city streets tend to be quiet on Easter Sunday and few businesses or restaurants are open.

FAMILY EVENTS

Weddings

Many young Croatians expect to have a large wedding, and parents do their best to oblige. First the couple has to decide whether they want a civil or a church ceremony. Both are legally recognized as long as the religious ceremony is officiated by a Catholic priest in a Catholic Church. The law does not honor marriage ceremonies performed by representatives from other faiths, so if the couple is not Catholic, they must have a civil ceremony prior to a religious one. In small towns, weddings usually involve the entire population. If the marriage takes place in a city, then the bride and groom's extended families are expected to come, along with friends and neighbors. In either case, celebrations can easily involve more than 200 guests, and the couple's parents usually find a way to provide plenty of food, drink, and music no matter what their financial situation is.

Weddings usually take place on Saturdays, and in larger cities one can see ceremonies taking place in churches and hear lots of cars honking in honor of newly married couples. On the day of a wedding, the bride and groom arrive at the church separately, the groom usually gets there first and then the bride arrives in the nicest vehicle available. It can be a Mercedes, a BMW, or even a horse-drawn carriage. As in the United States, the bride wears white and her bridesmaids are arrayed in matching gowns of a specified color, while the groom and best man usually are dressed in dark suits. Unlike in the United States, after the wedding vows are taken, the priest does not tell the groom that he may kiss the bride. The kiss must wait until the couple leaves the church.

Croatian wedding receptions are similar to those in the United States, except that the party often lasts even longer and food and drink are even more plentiful. Traditionally, receptions were held at the groom's home or in a church or city hall, however restaurants are becoming increasingly popular. The wedding cake is usually multilayered and may or may not have figures of the bride and groom on top. At least as important are the *koaci,* small bite-size pastries that are served and available in a seemingly infinite supply throughout the reception.

As for gifts, money is always appreciated and 100 euros is the standard amount. In some cases, a couple may specify items they would like to receive and guests coordinate their gift giving to meet the couple's needs.

Birthdays and Name Days

Traditionally, name days were celebrated far more often than birthdays. In the Catholic calendar, each saint has a day of the year dedicated to his or her memory, and because Croatians tend to give their children Christian names, one simply needs to find which day of the year corresponds to one's name. Usually, name days are celebrated with a small dinner and modest gifts. Interestingly, one may receive more congratulations on a name day than a birthday because more acquaintances know an individual's name than his or her birthday. Name day celebrations are not a uniquely Croatian tradition but have been practiced throughout Europe as well as some Latin American countries.

Younger generations celebrate birthdays rather than name days. Birthday parties tend to be on the small side, with a group of close friends getting together for dinner either at the home of the person who is having the birthday or at a restaurant. While the celebrations may look similar to those in the United States, there is one big difference. The person who is turning a year older has to foot the bill for the party. The honoree will receive gifts, but in exchange he or she will have to finance the celebration.

LEISURE TIME

In her book on Croatian culture, Irena Ban echoes a common complaint heard in Croatia: people have less and less leisure time, especially in comparison to the days before independence. When the country was part of Yugoslavia, businesses were state-owned and the workday was limited to eight hours. One had little incentive to work more because salaries were steady and job security was guaranteed. Today, with the advent of private enterprise and decreasing governmental support, career-minded people find themselves working longer hours and having to occasionally work on weekends. When one has free time, it usually is spent socializing with family and friends or engaging in sports. Families often will have at least one large meal together over the weekend.

This usually takes place at home because better restaurants are often too expensive for the average family. Besides, both men and women tend to be good cooks.

Croatians generally spend as much time as possible outdoors, although not necessarily engaging in strenuous exercise. Fitness is approached with moderation. On a nice day walkers, joggers, and bicyclists descend on public parks in droves although most of them seem more intent on socializing than getting an aerobic workout. During the summer months, nearly everyone wants to go to the coast, at least for a week or two. Ideally, one has access to a vacation home in Dalmatia or Istria so that an expensive hotel bill can be avoided. Many Croatians have vacation property, although most of these homes were not purchased recently, rather they have been passed down from generation to generation. Decades ago, when families migrated away from idyllic coastal villages for economic reasons they usually opted not to sell their homes. They simply locked them up and returned in the summer to relax, visit with loved ones, and perhaps plant a vegetable garden. Although coastal real estate has become very valuable, few families sell their ancestral homes. Aside from the sentimental connection, sales can become complex as a single property may have several owners and it is difficult to get everyone to agree on the terms of a sale. Often it is easiest to keep the house in the family and enjoy it.

Ban points out that many Croatians have become recreational shoppers, a pastime that came with the recent shift toward a capitalist economy. During the Yugoslav era, shoppers did not have a wide range of stores or merchandise from which to select. Imports were limited and domestic fashions simply were not that interesting. In those days, people from all over Yugoslavia would organize excursions to border towns like Trieste, Italy, to do their shopping. With independence came an influx of investment that included international clothing chains offering everything from designer suits to cheap trendy imports. Shopping centers and malls were built to accommodate these businesses, and families soon began spending time there even if they did not plan to spend any money. Window-shopping and a cup of coffee at the mall has become a popular way to enjoy an afternoon. For those with extra kuna to spare, these new retail centers are even more exciting with so many new international brand-name stores in one place. For some shoppers, however, the smaller neighborhood boutiques offer one important advantage—they allow a familiar customer to purchase an expensive item on a payment plan. Few Croatians can afford high-end clothing or shoes, but they can make smaller payments over time and eventually purchase the item. This is a valuable option for the shopper with a taste for fine designer clothes and limited funds.

As for nightlife, most discos and nightclubs cater to a young crowd, mostly under the age of 30. All generations patronize cafés, day and night. Croatians

Sailboats docked in the marina of Milna, a town on the island of Brac. (Courtesy of the author.)

love to sit and talk, often with a cigarette, while sipping an espresso, although alcoholic beverages are also popular. During warmer months, these cafés provide outdoor seating and the socializing usually continues until the wee hours.

Along the coast, sailing is a popular way to spend one's leisure time, especially in Dalmatia. According to legend, the first description of a Croatian sporting event dates back to a regatta held back in the late 16th century.[4] More than 70 wooden sailing boats raced from Komiza harbor on the island of Vis to the islet of Palagruza, a distance of more than 40 miles (64 kilometers). The type of boats that raced were known as *falkusa,* a particularly graceful, narrow-hulled fishing boat used until the mid-20th century when motorized engines rendered them obsolete. Because of its elegance, the *falkusa* often appears in paintings by local Dalmatian artists who use it as a romantic symbol of the region's seafaring heritage. Many locals still own small boats and are taught to sail and fish at an early age. Although motorboats are increasingly popular, it is not difficult to find someone familiar with the rudimentary aspects of sailing. Entrepreneurial Croats have capitalized on the fine sailing conditions on the Adriatic by sponsoring sailing tours and boat rentals to attract tourists who want to spend their summer on the water.

Sports are popular in Croatia, and although the population never has been as fitness obsessed as Americans, they enthusiastically watch, if not participate in, a variety of team and individual sports. The most popular team sports include soccer (known as football in Europe), handball, water polo, and basketball. Individual sports include tennis, skiing, swimming, and chess. Of all of these, soccer (*nogomet*) attracts the most media attention and is the object of the most intense emotions.

Fans' passionate devotion to their favorite teams is based on a combination of civic pride and history of (for the most part) good-natured rivalries. The long-running competition between Split and Zagreb exemplifies the excitement and hard-core devotion that Croatian soccer inspires. Matches between the two teams are called the Eternal Derby (*Vjecni derbi*), a term used for games between the best and most popular European clubs. In this case, the Eternal Derby dates back to the 1920s when Zagreb's team, then called Gradanski, regularly competed with Split's Hajduk for the Kingdom of Yugoslavia championships. Zagreb's club, now called Dinamo, has an impressive record, having won 12 Prva Hrvatske Nogometne Lige (HNL, Croatian Soccer League) titles. Hajduk, on the other hand, is one of Croatia's oldest and most respected soccer organizations with an extraordinary legacy. When the Croatian national team came in third place for the World Cup in 1998, 5 of the 11 players on the starting team had played for Hajduk. While extremely popular in Dalmatia, the club also has an international following with a significant fan base in the United States, Brazil, Chile, and New Zealand. Dinamo–Hajduk matches generate plenty of fan and media attention, and the games rarely end without incident, becoming among the most violent in Europe. A March 2010 match in Zagreb required 500 police officers and 200 security guards to maintain order among 15,000 fans.[5]

Croatian soccer fans put aside their regional rivalries to support their national team, which has won all but one home game since its admission to the International Federation of Association Football (FIFA) in 1993 (they lost to England in 2008).[6] When the Croatians entered the FIFA, they were ranked 125th, but by 1998, the team advanced to third place, an especially uplifting development for their fellow citizens who were suffering from the aftermath of the Homeland War. The players are considered national heroes and the team's legendary status has led to several musical tributes. The most famous is by Slaven Bilic, a famous player turned coach, who celebrated his team by recording a hit song called "*Vatreno Ludilo*" ("Fiery Madness") with his band Rawbau. Other artists, including *Prljavo Kazaliste* and Dino Dvornik, have also recorded songs in honor of the national team.

Home games usually are played at either Zagreb's Maksimir Stadium or Split's Poljud Stadium. Although Croatian fans rarely fight with one another at international matches, fan behavior has repeatedly led to Union of European Football Associations (UFEA) sanctions. One of the most common points of contention is the use of flares to inspire the home team by creating what appears to be smoky bonfires in the stands (the inspiration for Bilic's *Vatreno Ludilo*). These devices are prohibited at international matches and are regularly confiscated. More seriously, in the Bosnian town of Mostar, Croatian fans went on a rampage after their team lost a qualifying match for the 2006 World Cup to Brazil. They smashed cars, broke windows, and before it was over six police officers were hurt and one person was seriously injured by gunfire.[7] Such incidents occur every year, and while the majority of Croatian fans are law abiding, a small minority engage in hooliganism that results in fines for the Croatian Football Association and damages the country's reputation.

Basketball enjoys a huge domestic audience and, like soccer, has a long history dating back to the 1920s. In recent years, Croatia has been viewed as an "inexhaustible source of basketball talent"[8] with many players going to European clubs as well as the U.S. National Basketball Association. The national team enjoyed tremendous success in the 1990s with a silver medal at the 1992 Olympics (losing to the American "Dream Team") and a third place finish in the 1994 World Championships. These victories raised the international profile of Croatian basketball and made the sport even more popular at home. Several Croatian players went on to careers in the NBA, most notably Toni Kukoc who joined the Chicago Bulls and Drazen "Dragon" Petrovic whose promising career with the New Jersey Nets was cut short in 1993 when he died in a car accident. In addition to the national team, Croatia has local clubs that play in the NLB League (also known as the Adriatic League), which covers the region of the former Yugoslavia (now Slovenia, Serbia, Montenegro, and Bosnia and Herzegovina) as well as in the domestic Croatian A1 League.

Basketball fans are passionate about their favorite teams and, as with soccer, sometimes small groups resort to violence when the home team loses. One of the most highly publicized incidents occurred in 2009 as the Belgrade team prepared to head home after narrowly defeating Split, 67 to 62. Approximately 20 disgruntled fans arrived at the Split airport and threw rocks and bottles at the team while they waited for their flight. Several players were hurt, as were bystanders.[9]

Disgraceful incidents like this draw a great deal of media attention and distract from the fans' true passion for sports, which is particularly true in Split. Few cities are as obsessed with sports and have produced as many talented athletes. The aforementioned Toni Kukoc and Dino Radja (of the Boston Celtics) are both Split natives who began their careers with KKSplit, the local professional team, before being drafted by the NBA. Tennis great Goran Ivanisevic was also born in Split and upon winning the men's singles title at Wimbledon in 2001 was treated to a homecoming party with 150,00 of his fellow Splicani,

Croatian basketball star Toni Kukoc.
(Courtesy of Risha Cupit, Risha Cupit Photography, Milwaukee, WI.)

as citizens of Split are called, a remarkable turnout considering the city has a
population of only 200,000. That same year, Ivanisevic was given the opportunity to play for Hajduk, which he described as the fulfillment of a lifelong
dream.[10] Croatians also love handball (*rukomet*) and Split has produced one
of the world's best players—Ivano Balic, who helped lead the Croatian team
to an Olympic gold medal in 2004 (the team also won a gold medal in 1996).
One of the 21st-century's top female athletes, world champion indoor high
jumper Blanka Vlasic, is also a Split native. She brought home an Olympic
silver medal from the 2008 Beijing games.

   In addition to high-profile athletes and a famous soccer team, Splicani are
also known for a local game called *picigin*, which is played on a local sandy,
shallow beach called Bacvice. *Picigin* is a strictly amateur sport that resembles
aquatic volleyball, sans the net. Ideally, the game is played with a tennis ball
stripped of its exterior layer so that only the rubber remains. Players pass the
ball to one another by hitting it with their palms. When the game is in full
swing, the players often make acrobatic maneuvers to keep the ball from

landing on the water. Both men and women enjoy the sport and play continues year-round, including a traditional game on New Year's Day that takes place regardless of the weather or water temperature.

For those interested in more conventional aquatic sports, water polo is a popular option. The first game was played in 1908 at Bacvice Beach and has remained part of the Croatian athletic scene ever since. The fact that the waterpolo team carried the Croatian flag during the opening ceremony of the Beijing Olympics reflects the importance of the sport. Most towns have pools that are appropriate for training, and many boys and young men play, especially in coastal Dalmatia where the sea is calm enough for practice or a casual game. Larger cities have their own teams, which compete domestically but also play on an international circuit. The national team has a stellar record, having won the 2007 World Championship and taking third place in 2009. The future for this sport looks bright as the country has a strong youth training program.

Although Croatia is famous for its beaches, it also boasts plenty of wonderful hiking and skiing. At higher elevations, the mountain ranges provide a respite from the oppressive summer heat as well as perfect locations for winter sports and a number of small and unpretentious ski resorts. The accomplishments of Croatian skier Janica Kostelic and her brother Ivica have drawn the attention of skiers from around the world. Janica won three gold medals and one silver at the 2002 Winter Olympic Games at Salt Lake City, and a gold and silver at the 2006 Games in Turin; Ivica won a silver medal at the 2006 games, and two silver medals in the 2010 Winter Olympics in Vancouver. Thanks to the popularity of the Kostelic siblings, the International Ski Federation granted Croatia the privilege of hosting a women's World Cup slalom competition in 2004 at Mount Sljeme near Zagreb. The event, dubbed the "Snow Queen Trophy," inspired citywide festivities, but the treacherous course led the media to compare the event to Roman gladiator battles[11] which probably explains why interest exceeded Mount Sljeme's 25,000-person capacity.

With Croatians' great love of sports and so many successful athletes, it may come as a surprise that people spend an enormous amount of time indoors on their computers. As of June 2009, approximately half of the population used the Internet, up from only about 33 percent in 2006.[12] While some of this increase represents work-related computer use, such a spike also indicates more recreational computing, including social networking, gaming, or Web surfing. Although computer literacy is admirable, sitting in front of a laptop for hours at a time goes against Croatians' traditional ideals of leisure time. It is too solitary and sedentary, at least up until now. But given current trends in Internet use, technology is clearly changing how leisure time is spent. One only has to hope that 10 to 20 years from now at least a few people will have the interest and the stamina for an old-fashioned game of *picigin* on a cold New Year's Day.

NOTES

1. For more information, see Irena Ban, *Culture Smart! Croatia* (London: Kuperard, 2008).

2. Marko Dragic, "Advent in Liturgy and National Culture of the Croats," *Church in the World* 43, no. 3 (September 2008). This is a Croatian language paper, but the abstract is available in English at http://hrcak.srce.hr/index.php?show=clanak&id_clanak_jezik=46556&lang=en (retrieved February 17, 2010).

3. James Monti, "Croatian Christmas Traditions," *The Magnificat* (Advent 2006): 2–5, http://www.croatia.org/crown/articles/8874/1/Croatian-Christmas-Traditions-by-James-Monti-published-in-The-Magnificat-Advent-2006/Advent-2006.html (retrieved February 17, 2010).

4. "Rota Palagruzona" (in Croatian), http://www.santamaria-cruising.hr/prospekt%20-%20ROTA%20PALAGRUZONA.PDF (retrieved February 20, 2010).

5. "Security Will Be Heavy at Dinamo-Hajduk Game," *Croatian Times,* March 23, 2010.

6. Jonathan Stevenson, "Croatia 1-4 England," BBC Sport, September 11, 2008, http://news.bbc.co.uk/sport2/hi/football/internationals/7602774.stm (retrieved February 17, 2010).

7. "New Clash in Scarred Bosnia City," BBC News, June 24, 2006, http://news.bbc.co.uk/2/hi/europe/5079328.stm (retrieved February 18, 2010).

8. Boris Jakimenko, "Croatian Basketball and Its Young Players," *FIBA ASSIST MAGAZINE*, December 2005, 9–11.

9. "Crvena Zvezda Basketball Players Attacked In Split," Dalje.com, January, 21 2009, http://dalje.com/en-croatia/crvena-zvezda-basketball-players-attacked-in-split/226468 (retrieved February 17, 2010).

10. "Goran's Split Loyalties," BBC Sport, July 24, 2001, http://news.bbc.co.uk/sport2/hi/football/europe/1438564.stm (retrieved February 17, 2010).

11. Nathaniel Vinton, "Zagreb Is Set to Crown a New Queen of the Hill," *New York Times*, December 3, 2006.

12. Central Intelligence Agency, "The World Factbook: Croatia" https://www.cia.gov/library/publications/the-world-factbook/geos/hr.html (retrieved February 17, 2010).

6

Cuisine and Fashion

CUISINE

Croatia's cuisine is regional. Every city, valley, and island is known for its own specialties. The diversity is a product of history and geography. For centuries Germans, Hungarians and Turks governed, fought over, or immigrated to the interior regions of Croatia, making their mark on local cuisine. Meanwhile, the coastal regions have a Mediterranean tradition reflecting their strong historical ties to Italy. Croatia's diverse geography also contributes to regional specialization. The interior flatlands are more conducive to traditional farming, whereas most of the rocky coast can support only a limited harvest of olives, some vineyards for wine production, and small-scale vegetable farms. Finally, parts of the country were geographically isolated before the 20th century. Smaller remote island communities or villages in mountainous areas developed culinary traditions that were quite removed from those of cosmopolitan cities like Zagreb.

Before discussing regional specialties, some general observations can be made about common practices and traditions. For starters, most domestic produce, meats and many cheeses come from small farms that use few chemicals. Genetically modified crops are not grown. Produce can be purchased at small food shops and supermarkets, but most Croatians rely on large outdoor farmers' markets for fresh fruits and vegetables. Local cheeses can also be purchased directly from farmers at these markets, although one must taste the cheese before buying since quality varies greatly. Packaging and sale of milk and yogurt is regulated, and these products are available only in stores.

Croatians usually eat three meals a day. Breakfast is light; a typical continental breakfast comprises coffee; bread with butter, cheese, or jam; and yogurt or fresh fruit. Sometimes cold cuts are served, *pursut* (prosciutto) being the most popular. The traditional American breakfast of bacon and eggs is an imported concept and can be found in tourist areas. Lunch is the main meal of the day, with dinner typically being lighter and less formal. Lunch often starts with a light soup, usually a chicken or beef broth base, followed by an entrée, often meat or fish. Pasta or salads are also served as first courses. Finally the meal ends with dessert, usually a homemade cake or pastry, and coffee. Traditionally the working day is scheduled to accommodate a long lunch. Shops and offices open early in the morning and then close around lunchtime, to open again late in the afternoon so that everyone can enjoy a leisurely meal that is often followed by a nap. This tradition is rapidly disappearing, as more businesses remain open all day in conformity with other European countries.

As tourism flourished over the last decade, fine restaurants have opened throughout Croatia. Most Croatians agree, however, that the best meals are found at home. Croatians are good cooks and value their culinary traditions, passing them along from one generation to the next. One practical reason for

The fruit and vegetable market in Koprivnica. (Courtesy of the author.)

this is that restaurant meals are too expensive for the typical family budget and low-cost fast food is not seen as a viable option, particularly by older generations. If one does want fast food, pizza is available everywhere and the quality is usually good. McDonald's restaurants can be found in larger cities along with local eateries that serve sandwiches as well as *cevapcici* (pork or beef meatballs), *raznijci* (Croatian shish kebab), and *burek* (filo pastry dough filled with meat or cheese), which is available in pastry shops throughout Croatia. Traditionally served as a breakfast food for farmers and fishermen, *burek,* along with *cevapcici* and *raznijci* were popular throughout the former Yugoslavia. All three of these dishes originated in the Ottoman Empire and similar versions are found in several other Slavic countries as well as throughout the Arab world.

As in the United States, certain foods are associated with specific holidays in Croatia. Because Croatia is a predominately Catholic country, the most important holidays are Christmas and Easter. Although some regional variation exists in the traditional Christmas menu, most Croatians observe the Catholic tradition of abstaining from meat on Christmas Eve and instead serve fish. Dalmatians often prepare *bakalar,* a dried salted cod dish that often is made with potatoes, onions, parsley, and tomatoes. On Christmas Day, meat returns to the table in the form of a large roast of some sort, usually turkey or pig, accompanied by stuffed cabbage or peppers. Popular fried desserts include *hrostule,* which is made of a strip of dough tied into a bow and then quickly deep fried, and *fritule,* also known as Dalmatian fritters. Ideally neither of these desserts is greasy or too heavy. Dried figs and nuts are often served after the meal as well. Easter observances begin with a meatless Good Friday, while the main Easter meal qualifies as a feast, usually featuring roast lamb or pork with a variety of side dishes. Several different desserts are served, including cakes, tortes, and cookies with colorful Easter eggs to decorate the table.

The high salt content of certain dried fish and cheeses aside, Croatian cuisine is not particularly spicy. As expected, northern areas with a stronger Hungarian tradition use more paprika and have a somewhat zestier cuisine than that of Dalmatia, for example, which retains an Italian culinary tradition. Other than basic salt and pepper, the seasoning that appears in almost every Croatian kitchen is Vegeta, the popular powdery condiment produced by Podravka, a company located in the northern town of Koprivnica. Although Vegeta's precise contents are a trade secret, the packaging lists salt as the primary ingredient with dehydrated vegetables and monosodium glutamate coming in second and third. The label is not precise about the other spices included in Vegeta, but the end result is a condiment that is popular throughout the land. Originally introduced to the Yugoslav marketplace in 1959, Vegeta is available in all Croatian supermarkets by the kilo. It has also been exported since the early 1970s when it was introduced to Hungary and Russia and soon afterward to Austria, Sweden, West Germany, and Czechoslovakia. Today, it also can be found in specialty stores in the United States.

The regional differences that characterize Croatian cuisine can be divided between the inland area of Croatia and the coast, where the culture and economy traditionally have revolved around the sea and fishing. Roman Emperors were the first to farm oysters on the coast of Mali Ston, a small town on the Peljesac Peninsula on the Dalmatian coast, where to this day oyster farming continues. Even one of Croatia's most famous literary figures, Renaissance poet Petar Hektorovic, provided a fascinating detailed account of a three-day fishing trip taken near his home on the island of Hvar. Written in 1556 in the form of a letter to his cousin, Hektorovic describes, among other things, what the fishermen ate, the various tools they used, and how they prepared their catch. The piece is a fascinating reminder of the extent to which fishing has always been an integral part of life in Dalmatia.

The Adriatic Sea teems with a large variety of fish, approximately 400 species, although no single type is particularly plentiful. The most common species include mackerel, sardines, sea bass, squid, octopus, and mullet. In smaller towns, one usually can buy fish directly from the fishermen early in the morning when they return from a night at sea. The availability of any particular type of fish is unpredictable, so good cooks have learned how to improvise their menus accordingly. For example, *brodet* is a generic term for fish stew with polenta that can be made with a variety of fish and shellfish. Although every cook has his or her own recipe for the dish, flexibility is essential because even in larger coastal cities like Split, the catch varies from day to day. The general consensus is that the most authentic seafood meals are found in smaller fishing villages, usually on the islands. Because of the rise in tourism, one often must pay top dollar for high-quality fish, even in these locations. Over the last several years, fish farms have been established along the coast of the island of Brac as well as along the Peljesac Peninsula, where in addition to the aforementioned oysters, one can find a reliable supply of farm-raised sea bass, orada, and tuna.[1]

In addition to *brodet,* Dalmatians also serve *bakalar,* a specific type of fish stew made of salted cod. Although it is a Christmas Eve tradition, it is served throughout the year as well. Cod is not found in the Adriatic, but generations of Dalmatian sailors returning from the North Atlantic brought this dried and salted variety home. Because the fish is preserved, it is easy to transport and is found in cuisines throughout the Mediterranean as well as inland regions, including Serbia. Before it is cooked, dried cod is hard, almost like a piece of wood. Most Croatian cooks have their own recipes for *bakalar,* but generally the fish must be soaked in water, sometimes for up to 48 hours before cooking, to soften it and remove the extra salt.

Summers are quite hot along Croatia's coastline, so rather than heat up the kitchen for a stew or risotto, fish is grilled outdoors. Before World War II, when large olive orchards were common, olive wood was used for grilling to give fish extra flavor. Unfortunately, many of these orchards have been abandoned and most Dalmatians now rely on charcoal. Because the majority of fish caught in the Adriatic are small, they are not cut into fillets, but rather grilled whole and served with the head still attached. While a visitor may try to navigate the maze of bones in these small fish with a knife and fork, Dalmatians are not shy about using their fingers, which is certainly the most practical way to approach a grilled mackerel. Thanks to years of practice, most Dalmatians can eat a whole fish with minimal use of silverware while maintaining a sense of propriety at the dinner table.

Shellfish, particularly mussels, are also popular in Dalmatia and are prepared in variety of ways, but most commonly as a risotto or steamed and served with a sauce or topping. Both of these dishes are considered appetizers. Traditionally *prstaci*, also known as date mussels, are the most prized shellfish. They often are compared to standard mussels but have a narrower brown shell and a subtler flavor, making them a delicacy. Unfortunately, the process of collecting *prstaci*, which live deep within rocky crevices, is destructive to the environment.[2] In 2001, the Croatian government launched a campaign to protect the biological diversity of the Adriatic and banned the hunting of this species. Restaurants are closely monitored and violators are heavily fined, yet *prstaci* occasionally manage to make it to the dinner table.

The cuisine along the coast is so diverse that each island has its own unique specialties. For example, Hvar and Korcula are known for their octopus (*hobotnica*) dishes, and Lastavo is known for its fish stew. Older cookbooks, in particular, are filled with recipes for regional island desserts. However, the most famous island specialty is *Paski sir,* cheese from the island of Pag (*sir* is the word for cheese). Made from sheep's milk, this cheese has won awards throughout Europe and achieved remarkable fame, especially considering so little of it is exported. Pag's arid climate and rocky terrain make mass production of *Paski sir* impossible. Small herds of sheep graze on the herbs and grasses that are indigenous to the island. The soil has a high salt content because of the constant winds that blow a sea mist onto the shore. The result is a firm, yellow cheese with a piquant, salty flavor that blends well with meat and fish but is best served alone as an appetizer.

The aforementioned risotto, a rice dish that originated in northwestern Italy where rice paddies are common, also is a Dalmatian staple that usually appears as an appetizer on most restaurant menus but is hearty enough for a main dish. Risotto does not demand much meat and is a versatile dish that for centuries suited Dalmatia's limited farming capacity. Risotto can include vegetables, chicken, or fish, but black risotto made using the ink from cuttlefish is one of the most famous coastal specialties.

Although Dalmatia's terrain is too rocky for extensive cattle farming, beef does appear on the menu, most traditionally in the form of *pasticada,* consisting of a round of beef that is heavily seasoned with bacon and a sauce made of vegetables and herbs. Large cuts of meat usually appear in the form of lamb or pork, which do not require significant territory for grazing and, as a result, are a bigger part of a traditional menu than beef.

The most popular form of ham is a cured and dried version served uncooked in thin cold-cut slices known as *prsut,* or prosciutto. The term "prosciutto" is Italian for ham and, although this delicacy is found throughout the country, it is traditionally associated with the Istrian Peninsula and Dalmatia. The procedure for making prosciutto is time-consuming, ranging from 9 to 18 months, depending on the size of the ham. Basically the meat is cleaned and salted and then left to hang in a dry, cool place for a number of months. In Dalmatia, the meat also is smoked using various types of wood to achieve specific flavors. The Istrian version usually is dried in fresh air and seasoned with a combination of spices, including but not limited to salt, pepper, and rosemary. Because the climate near the coast is too humid for drying meat, prosciutto is produced at least a few miles inland.

To preserve the quality of Croatia's traditional prosciutto, it is now covered by an EU Protected Designation of Origin (PDO), which sets criteria for traditional products produced in specific geographic locations. This designation ensures that products labeled as originating from a certain region really were produced there and are made of traditional ingredients. The PDO designation is relevant because cured ham is made throughout southern Europe. For a cured ham to qualify as Dalmatian prosciutto (*dalmatinski prsut*), it must not only be produced in Dalmatia, but also should have a certain salt content and the color should be relatively dark and dry. The Istrian variety usually is less salty and dry, with a milder flavor.

Many of the Istrian Peninsula's culinary specialties are influenced by nearby Italy. Pastas and gnocchi are popular along with *menestra,* a vegetable and bean soup similar to minestrone. Istria's greatest culinary distinction, however, lies in the wild truffles that grow in the peninsula's interior and that are used in risotto and pasta dishes. Istrian truffles have gained popularity throughout Europe in recent years, in part because they are fairly inexpensive and have a comparable flavor to more costly French and Italian varieties. The truffle business is fairly new to Istria. According to local lore, the Italians who occupied the region before World War II noticed the truffles and began hunting them, using highly trained dogs that are essential to identifying the prized fungus. Over the last few decades, the industry has grown and an established truffle-hunting season now begins in October and runs through January, during which 3,000 people and approximately 10,000 dogs wander through the Istrian forests searching for the valuable delicacy.[3]

The cuisine found in Zagreb and northwestern Croatia is heavier than along the coast, and bears a strong Viennese influence, dating back to the days of the Austro-Hungarian Empire. Meats, including lamb and pork, are commonly roasted on a spit, often outdoors. Roadside restaurants usually entice customers by setting up large outdoor barbecues featuring large chunks of meat or entire roasted pig and lamb carcasses within sight of passing motorists. An example of a more elaborate entrée typically found in Zagreb restaurants is veal stuffed with ham and cheese and then fried in breadcrumbs. Side dishes include roasted potatoes or *mlinci* (baked noodles). *Strukli*, a pastry made with flaky filo dough filled with cheese can be salty or sweet and offers an alternative to the meat dishes commonly found in this area.

Traveling eastward into Slavonia, the menu becomes spicier, reflecting a Hungarian influence. Goulash is a popular meat-based main dish, typically flavored heavily with garlic and paprika. The Drava River is a good source of freshwater fish, including carp and pike, which often are cooked in a traditional paprika sauce to make a fish paprikash. Slavonia also produces Kulen, a paprika-flavored sausage that can be served in a variety of ways, including in a pickled vegetable dish called *tursije*. Finally, *palacinka,* thin, crepe-like pancakes filled with cheese, jam, or chocolate, are a popular dessert that originated in this region and have become ubiquitous throughout Croatia.

Lunch and dinner usually include domestically produced wine. Winemaking is a centuries-old Croatian tradition, and today the country produces hundreds of varieties. Red wine has been a traditional part of the coastal economy for centuries because of the combination of mountainous terrain and climate allowing for small vineyards and olive groves, but little else. White wine is more commonly produced in the interior. Many varieties of grapes are available, but for red wine, a grape called *plavac mali* is considered the best. For white wine, *Posip,* grown on the Adriatic island of Korcula, and *Malvazija* from Istria are highly regarded.

In the past, few of these wines were exported to the United States, in part because of the relatively small amount that was produced as well as their inconsistent quality. In the last several years, exports have increased and Croatia's wine industry is gaining an international reputation. In 2009, Croatia won eight gold medals in the Decanter World Wine Awards. Sweet wines and Sherry gained most of the recognition but the quality of the dry wines, particularly the white wines, is attracting attention.

A man selling homemade liquor in Vrsar. (Courtesy of John Kruth.)

Croatians often mix red wine with water to make a drink known as *bevanda,* which originated centuries ago when water quality was not reliable. The addition of at least a small amount of wine made well-water more palatable, especially in arid coastal regions that had a limited supply of fresh water. White wine is also mixed with carbonated mineral water to make a drink called *gemist.* Stronger alcoholic beverages, usually made from local fruit, are frequently served before meals as an aperitif. Among the most popular of these is *sljvovica* (plum brandy), although *travarica* (herb brandy), *medovica* (honey brandy), and *orahavica* (walnut brandy) are also common. Supermarkets sell these products, but many are homemade and can be purchased at roadside stands during the tourist season.

Croatians are dedicated coffee drinkers. Every town, no matter how small, has a café where beverages are sold, often without food, and coffee is the drink of choice. The origins of this obsession are traced to the days of Ottoman invasions. The invaders eventually departed but left a country of coffee addicts behind. In the days of the former Yugoslavia, Turkish coffee, also known as Greek coffee in the United States, was the most popular both at home and in cafés. Today most cafés serve espresso with cappuccino and lattes available upon request. Turkish coffee is almost extinct outside of the home.

Coffee, the national beverage. (Courtesy of the author.)

According to an article in Javno.com, a Croatian news Web site, Croats drink approximately 22,500 tons of coffee per year and spend about 2.25 million hours consuming it.[4]

FASHION

Traditional Dress

Croatians are dedicated followers of fashion and even those unconcerned with the latest trends always make an effort to dress appropriately for every occasion. An interest in clothing is not new in Croatia, where a rich tradition of folk costume has been preserved into the 21st century. Each region has its own historical costumes that are not only integral to local musical and folk dance traditions, but also function as a symbol of national heritage and local identity in contemporary Croatia. To put the 21st-century fashion scene into context, a short discussion of the evolution of dress in Croatia is needed.

Ethnographic museums in Split and Zagreb have extensive collections of folk costume from throughout the country that represent a wide variety of textile weaving, lace making, and embroidery, all handicrafts which were part of peasant life for centuries. A sense of village identity, geography, and history

Folk costume from the interior of Dalmatia.
(Courtesy of the author.)

are evident in the specific designs associated with local costumes, which vary significantly throughout Croatia. Typically, cotton and linen textiles were woven in agricultural areas, whereas wool was used more frequently in mountain villages. The inspiration for the patterns woven or embroidered into these textiles ranged from the local flora and fauna to popular legends and ancient myths. Although delicate lace and floral imagery were common to women's costume, swords and guns accessorize men's folk dress, particularly in areas that were subject to Ottoman invasion.

Accessories for women included gold or silver jewelry and buttons, typically in the filigran style, as well as beads made from coral found in the Adriatic and coins strung on necklaces. The quality and quantity of these accessories reflected family wealth and social standing. It was common for a woman to wear her finest jewelry (which represented a good part of her dowry) for all to see during holiday celebrations. Her wealth—in the form of bracelets, rings, necklaces and other precious accoutrements—was easily carried with her should she need to leave home quickly. During Croatia's turbulent history, many families had to escape invading armies, especially during the Ottoman incursions of the 16th century. By the time this threat diminished, heavy accessorizing with coins, either in the form of a necklace or sewn to a bodice or vest, further accompanied by rows of silver or gold buttons, had become a traditional style. The regional variety of folk costume is further complicated by the influences of foreign cultures as Croatia borders both Eastern and Western Europe and was, at various times, controlled by Venetian, Austrian, and Turkish powers.

Items considered folk costume in the 21st century should not be confused with clothes that peasants wore on a daily basis. The richly embroidered women's garments seen in museum displays typically were reserved for special occasions, while simpler items, which were easier to clean and replace, were worn when working in the home or fields. Clothing styles evolved gradually because most Croatian villages were well beyond the influence of European fashion trends. Designs were determined by local women whose finest

Folk costume from the region of Omis in the interior of Dalmatia. (Courtesy of the author.)

creations would be passed down from generation to generation. Many pieces of clothing and jewelry are still in family collections and are regarded as heirlooms, which are sold only in case of financial desperation. Croatians value traditional dress to the extent that local merchants who display indigenous antique jewelry regularly refuse to sell these items to tourists.

Folk dress can regularly be seen in photos until World War I, although the adoption of standard European fashions occurred gradually and unevenly throughout the territory that constitutes present-day Croatia. By the mid-19th century most residents of larger towns had given up traditional styles, although elements of indigenous costume endured in certain rural areas until after World War II. Men's dress changed more rapidly than women's as young men tended to migrate to cities for work in greater numbers and adopted cosmopolitan attire in the process. At the same time, the young intellectuals inspired by the Illyrian movement and a desire for cultural and political independence from Austria-Hungary recognized folk dress as a symbol of Croatian national identity. Families were encouraged to preserve their costumes and wear them during holidays and for special events. Although this custom gradually faded, elements of traditional dress occasionally have appeared in some contemporary fashions.

Croatia's most significant contribution to modern dress is the men's necktie, which dates back to the Thirty-Year's War (1618–1648). Although known for their military prowess and daring, Croatian mercenaries made a significant impression on the French military leaders with their neckwear. The French wore stiff linen collars known as ruffs, but were quick to adopt the softer scarves worn by the Croatians.

This accessory became known as a "cravat" which, according to legend, is derived from a French mispronunciation of "Hrvat" (that is, a Croatian). Although men's neckwear has come a long way from the original cravat, which resembled a white scarf tied in a floppy bow around one's neck, Croatia is still credited with inventing the necktie. Today ties are sold in souvenir shops throughout the country and are marketed as a Croatian innovation.

Fashion in Contemporary Croatia

Croatians are followers of fashion trends from Europe and the United States, but they also have succeeded in establishing a vibrant domestic fashion scene. The latest styles for both men and women are visible on the streets of Zagreb and Split where one can find a dizzying range of shopping opportunities. Designer boutiques abound, as do international chains such as Benetton and Diesel. One can also buy far less expensive items at outdoor markets that carry garments typically imported from China, India, or Turkey and other countries where production is cheap.

Like many Europeans, Croatians value quality over quantity and are more likely to save to buy one expensive, high-quality item than to purchase several cheaper things in its place. As a result, Croatian's closets are not as full as those of many Americans and one may see the same outfits recycled over and over. But no matter how small one's budget, Croatians understand the importance of appearance and a well-coordinated look. Clothing is meticulously cared for and always pressed and neat, and shoes are shined. The typical Croatian does not easily embrace the notion of "sloppy chic." Whenever possible, natural textiles such as silk and wool are preferred to synthetics, and during the summer months, white cotton and linen are extremely common, especially in Dalmatia.

Larger cities organize fashion events allowing local designers to show off their creations that usually are available at nearby boutiques. The most significant of these take place in Zagreb and include prominent domestic names as well as a few invited foreign designers. One of the most established events is Zagreb's Cro a Porter Show, which receives media coverage and is the closest Croatia comes to New York's Fashion Week. Other large shows also take place in Varazdin, Split, Zadar, Dubrovnik, and Rijeka. These events are a cultural as well as economic boost for any given town as the clothing shown is almost entirely produced by local men and women.

Croatian fashion Web sites and publications do a good job of covering international events and personalities, but some have argued that insufficient attention is given to the domestic fashion industry. This frustration was expressed in an open letter published in the Croatian press in 2009, in which designer Nada Dosen, with 20 years of experience to her credit, lamented the "chaotic state" of the domestic fashion industry.[5] One only needs to walk through a shopping district in any city to sympathize with her perspective. She described the Croatian market as "suffocated with imported brands," and noted that Croatian shoppers tend toward trendy foreign brands over clothing by lesser-known local companies. These are common observations, but she also argued that many locals perceive domestic fashions, which are designed and produced in Croatia, as too expensive. She presents the case that economic survival is nearly impossible given the financial challenges faced by designers and the lack of any concerted effort by the government, media, or industry to support this domestic industry.

To complicate matters further, many cheap copies (knockoffs) of designer accessories are readily available at outdoor markets throughout Croatia, much as they are elsewhere in the United States and Europe. The copies of Louis Vuitton and Coach handbags that sit alongside fake Ed Hardy hats are particularly prevalent at beachside stands during the summer tourist season. The quality of these reproductions is poor, but they provide a means for tourists and locals alike to purchase a designer look at a low price. The ubiquitous

Ed Hardy knockoffs for sale in an outdoor market.
(Courtesy of the author.)

nature of these items, illegitimate cheap reproductions that they are, only reinforces the fascination with big international brands in Croatia.

It is true that the homegrown fashion scene lacks the financial backing of its international competitors, but Croatian designers are making inroads domestically and slowly are gaining broader recognition, largely through younger designers who have won prizes in international competitions. One of the most prominent of these is Igor Galas, a recent graduate of the Faculty of Textile Design in Zagreb. Known for his eclectic hand-knitted collections, Galas won the 2010 iD Emerging Designer Award in New Zealand and has shown collections elsewhere in Europe and Asia. Zoran Aragovic is another young up-and-coming name in Croatian fashion. A graduate of the Profokus School of Fashion Design in Zagreb, he has shown his collections domestically and has established his prêt-à-porter (ready-to-wear) line called BiteMyStyle. Like Galas, Aragovic's designs are distinctive and feature a dizzying variety of patterns and appliqué.

Although many domestic designers work on a small scale, produce few items, and depend on custom orders, several larger prêt-à-porter companies have become lasting fixtures on the Croatian fashion scene. Designer Neda

Makjanic-Kunic founded MAK, originally a small one-woman tailor's shop in Split, in 1986. Today the company has its own design and garment manufacturing facility along with a chain of retail stores throughout Croatia plus three so-called concept stores. MAK produces sportswear, a line of business wear, and a more formal cocktail collection. The company also has an exclusive atelier line, which is the product of collaborations with various designers and celebrities. Image Haddad is another significant prêt-à-porter company, which was founded in 1988 by the husband and wife team Zrinka and Samir Haddad. Specializing in quality sportswear, they own and operate a chain of retail boutiques and have launched other brands, including H2, Haddad Vintage, and H2 Jeans. Of the newer domestic brands, designer Durdica Vorkapi's label, Hippy Garden, founded in 2000, appears to be making the most significant inroads internationally as well as domestically. The company is known for its combination of urban chic and flower-child femininity that made news when Vorkapi's Winter 2010 collection was showcased at London's Fashion Week.

While some trend-conscious Croatians will always gravitate toward familiar international names, local designers are clearly making an impact on the domestic fashion scene. The extent to which the country's clothing industry develops is subject to a variety of economic factors, but anyone who explores Zagreb's more elegant boutiques can attest to the talent and commercial potential of Croatia's young designers and fashion professionals. As the country's economy develops and financing becomes more available, one can expect to see local talent dominate a larger portion of the domestic market.

NOTES

1. For more information on fish and fishing, see Boris Marelic, "Fish and Fish Specialties of Dalmatia," http://www.find-croatia.com/fishing-croatia/fish-and-fish-dishes-of-dalmatia.html (retrieved June 10, 2009).

2. Eugen Draganovic, "Collecting of Date Mussels in Mediterranean Countries and Protection of Rocky Bottom in Croatia (abstract)," *Sixth Congress of Croatian Biologists* with international participation, Opatija, Croatia, September 22–26, 1997, http://www.vef.hr/dolphins/radovi/pdf%202009/gomercic%201997%20HBD%20sred%20med.pdf (retrieved July 13, 2009).

3. Jeanne Oliver, *Lonely Planet, Croatia Country Guide,* 4th ed. (Footscray, Australia: Lonely Planet, 2007), 131.

4. "Croats Spend 2.25 Million Hours on Drinking Coffee," Javno.com, September 3, 2009, http://www.javno.com/en-economy/croats-spend-225-million-hours-on-drinking-coffee_274953 (retrieved June 10, 2009).

5. "What Is the Point of Croatian Fashion Design?" trans. Karmen Horvat, Dalje .com, March 13, 2009, http://dalje.com/en-lifestyle/what-is-the-point-of-croatian-fashion-design/242566 (retrieved June 10, 2009).

7

Literature

Croatia's rich literary tradition reflects the region's complex history. A variety of Croatian dialects have existed and evolved over the years, but until the 19th century other languages were used in an official capacity. Because Croatian territory often was under the control of foreign powers, such languages as Italian, German, or Hungarian were spoken in the courts, government offices, and schools. For centuries, the vernacular Croatian language was reserved for common conversations and informal occasions, and until the advent of the Illyrian movement, little written material was published in Croatian. In spite of the inferior position of this vernacular language, over time, a uniquely Croatian literature emerged. This chapter reflects the development of that tradition and the language that is still in the process of evolving in the aftermath of the Homeland War and Croatia's independence.

GLAGOLITIC SCRIPT AND EARLY LITERARY TRADITION

One cannot begin to discuss Croatian literature without mentioning Glagolitic script, the oldest Slavic script and the original alphabet of the Croatian language that has enjoyed a revival of interest in recent years. "Glagolica," as it is called in Croatian, was used during the Middle Ages throughout Eastern Europe, but it was of particular significance along the

Dalmatian coast where it played an important role in the historic 10th-century conflict between local priests and the pope. The Dalmatian clergy, led at the time by Bishop Gregory of Nin (also known as Grgur Ninski), insisted on performing the Mass in Croatian and used Glagolica, as opposed to the standard Latin language and script. While Rome objected, the Croatian priests continued thus for more than two centuries. Finally, in 1248, the bishop of Senj received special permission from Pope Innocent to use the Croatian language in the liturgy, making Croatians the only group to ever receive this privilege before the Second Vatican Council in the 1960s when parishes were given the option of using vernacular language. More than two centuries later, in 1494, Croatia's first printing press was installed in the town of Senj, and not surprisingly, the first publication was a missal (a book containing all of the prayers and readings for daily Mass) in Glagolitic type. Although most Slavic groups converted to Cyrillic script by the 12th century, regular use of Glagolica continued until the 17th century when Venetian domination of Dalmatia and Istria led to the widespread adoption of the Latin alphabet.

Glagolica survived in Croatia largely because of Dalmatian and Istrian priests, who continued to use it well into the 19th century, and even today Masses occasionally are performed using archaic Croatian language based on Glagolitic texts. Recently, however, the script has reentered popular consciousness as a symbol of Croatian culture and ethnicity. Because of the fascinating patterns created by the letters, it frequently appears on souvenir items, including jewelry and neckties.

As for literature in Croatia, the influence of Italy is inescapable. Historically, clergy members went to Italy for higher education, as did the children of wealthy families. Latin was the language of the educated classes and used for important written documents and literature. Glagolitic writings, on the other hand were limited to the aforementioned religious purposes, as well as translations of ecclesiastical documents originally written in Latin. Generally, Croatian was not considered viable, or appropriate, for poetic endeavors. By the beginning of the 15th century, this began to change; the language evolved sufficiently to support purely literary efforts, and the earliest signs of truly Croatian literature began to emerge.

The first Croatian poets who started using vernacular language were well educated and embraced the humanistic ideas emanating from Renaissance Italy. By the 15th century, Dante had already written his *Divine Comedy* in vernacular Italian, thereby making the use of spoken language in literature that much more acceptable. Still, the most memorable literature of the 15th century, including the love poems and historical works of Juraj Sizgoric of Sibenik were written primarily in Latin.

Glagolitic script in Zagreb Cathedral. (Courtesy of Risha Cupit, Risha Cupit Photography, Milwaukee, WI.)

FOLK TRADITIONS IN LITERATURE

The Croatian literary tradition started in earnest during the 16th century, as important works not limited to the conventional Latin-based literary forms began to emerge. Croatians, along with other Slavic cultures, had a remarkable oral tradition of folk songs and poems, and ultimately these became a part of Croatia's earliest significant literature. Dalmatian-born Marko Marulic's (1450–1524) vernacular poem "The History of the Holy Widow Judith Composed in Croatian Verses" (also known as "*Judita*" in Croatian) was the first major work published in Croatian. The poem tells the story of Judith, a beautiful Israelite widow, who defends her people from Assyrian invaders by using her feminine wiles to behead Holofernes, the enemy's general—an inspiration for the Croatians who were struggling against the invading Ottoman Turks. At least as important as the story was Marulic's elegant merging of established Italian literary forms with traditional Croatian folkloric verse. Marulic, one of the most widely read authors of his time, primarily because of his substantial body of work in Latin, did not claim to have created a literary masterpiece with respect to Judith. Rather, he wanted to provide an enlightening book for ordinary people who could not read Latin or Italian; in the process, however, he created one of the first uniquely Croatian pieces of literature.

By the 15th century, Dubrovnik emerged as a center for Croatian literary activity. Northern Dalmatian cities such as Split, where Marulic was born, and Zadar had come under Venetian control leading to the secondary status of Croatian, relative to the Italian language. Meanwhile, Dubrovnik remained a free and wealthy, albeit small, republic in which Croatian was not only the most commonly spoken language but also used for all official purposes. Its citizens were well educated and especially inclined to create and appreciate literature. By the early 17th century, writers from Dubrovnik brought Croatian literature to an unprecedented level of artistic accomplishment. Among the contributing authors is Petar Hektorovic (1487–1572), whose famous poem "Fishing and Fishermen's Talk" (*Ribanje i ribarsko prigovaranje*) is considered essential Croatian literature, incorporating folk songs with standard Italian literary forms.

Born into an aristocratic family, Hektorovic turned to the lives of ordinary people for inspiration. "Fishing and Fishermen's Talk" was based on a three-day trip the author took with two local fishermen to the islands of Hvar and Solta. The narrative poem describes the trip in detail, down to the types of tools the fishermen used, the fish they caught, and the sea itself, while also including two songs as sung by his companions in traditional folk meter. The realism of the work is unusual for its time. Hektorovic approached his subject with a journalistic desire to create an honest image of fishermen's lives,[1] and he spoke to the importance of treating others with respect and humanity, regardless of class or social standing. Contrary to the norms of 16th-century society, Hektorovic treated his subjects as equals, creating dialogue that gave them a dignity usually reserved for his fellow aristocrats. His message was particularly relevant in light of the peasant revolts that occurred during his lifetime.

One of the most popular literary works preceding the modern era is Andrija Kacic Miosic's (1704–1760) "A Pleasant Discourse about the Slavic People" (*Razgovor ugodni naroda slovinskoga*). It was first published in 1756 and became an instant hit leading to a second publication three years later—a rare feat for an 18th-century poem. The work was read beyond Croatian lands into Serbia, Slovakia, Macedonia, and Slovenia.

Kacic was an educated Franciscan monk, a student of Enlightenment thinking, and teacher to both monks and lay people. As Bogdan Rakic states in his insightful article on South Slavic literature from the 16th through 19th centuries,[2] Kacic's motivation was "both patriotic and pedagogical." He wanted to educate his readers about the more inspiring episodes in Croatia's history, while also implying that a great future was possible. Almost prescient in terms of his approach of presenting Slavs as a unified people, much as the proponents of the early Illyrian movement would in the 19th century, Kacic writes of Croats as well as the heroes of other South Slav peoples with equal enthusiasm.[3] He relied on vernacular language and used traditional folk song forms familiar to his native Dalmatia, where epic poems were traditionally memorized and sung by the largely illiterate peasant population. His book was perceived by many as more of a songbook than a historical text, perhaps contributing to its popularity. This was fine with Kacic who is quoted in Rakic's article as stating, "our Lord endowed our people with the natural ability to sing about the same things that other nations put into their history books." Kacic's "A Pleasant Discourse about the Slavic People" is considered a cultural milestone of Croatian literature. It lives on in the form of a traditional folk song and as well as in the written word. Kacic is also commemorated by Ivan Mestrovic in a life-size portrait made in 1957, as well as by Ivan Rendic, whose portrait is in the center of the main square, named after the writer, in the coastal town of Makarska, not far from Kacic's birthplace.

CROATIAN IDENTITY AND LANGUAGE

Ivan Gundulic (1589–1638), is Croatia's most significant historical literary figure. Like Hektorovic, Gundulic was born to an aristocratic family. Unlike some of his predecessors, however, his themes were more traditional, inspired by his Christian faith and patriotic love for his birthplace and hometown, Dubrovnik, which was still an autonomous state during his lifetime. For example, his poem "The Tears of the Prodigal Son" (*Suze sina razmetnoga*) deals with repentance for sins and rejection of earthly pleasures in favor of devotion to God. His play "Dubravka" uses romantic love as a vehicle for issues of freedom and the autonomy of Dubrovnik.

Gundulic's most famous work is an epic poem called "Osman." Modeled on Italian literary forms, "Osman" was based on contemporary events surrounding the defeat of Sultan Osman II by the Poles and his subsequent death at the hands his own army. The tale was particularly relevant as Ottoman invasions were a constant threat to the region. The struggle between Christians and "infidels" allowed for passionate expressions of faith and rhetorical flourishes that were typical of the writings from this period. Although this Baroque style of writing has fallen out of favor, Ivan Gundulic's "Osman" remains relevant as a statement of independence and autonomy for the city of Dubrovnik and for Slavs in general, in the face of foreign oppressors.

Out of concern that Dubrovnik might become a target for Turkish aggression, "Osman" was only circulated via handwritten copies and not formally published until the 19th century when the leaders of the Illyrian movement (sometimes referred to as the Croatian Revival) embraced Gundulic's work as representative of the pan-Slavic consciousness they were trying to cultivate. In his seminal book *Croatia: A Nation Forged in War*, Marcus Tanner traces the Illyrians' fascination with Dubrovnik to the fact that unlike the rest of Croatia, which was under foreign rule (Dalmatia had long been controlled by Venice and northern parts of Croatia were governed by Hungary), Dubrovnik remained independent, thereby making it especially representative of Croatian culture.

The relevance extends beyond mere inspiration as the Illyrians recognized that a standardized language was crucial to Croat identity. Three dialects were spoken: *kajkavski* in the vicinity of Zagreb; *stokavski* in Dubrovnik and much of Dalmatia and Herzegovina; and *cakavski* in Istria, the Adriatic islands, and in other parts of Dalmatia. The Illyrians embraced the *stokavski* dialect for a number of reasons, not the least of which was that it was used by Gundulic and other notable 16th- and 17th-century writers from Dubrovnik whose works were steadily gaining popularity among Zagreb's intellectual elite. In addition, the Illyrians preferred *stokavski*, as many Serbs and Bosnians spoke the dialect, and it was comprehensible to Slovenes and Bulgarians, making it appropriate for a pan-Slavic movement.

Gundulic's vision of Slavic unity and freedom as expressed in "Osman" made him an iconic figure to the 19th-century Illyrians. His epic poem was the first work published by *Matica hrvatska* (Croatian Queen Bee) in 1842, a press established by members of the Illyrian movement for the printing of Croatian literature. "Osman" remained popular even as the notion of Slavic unity was replaced with a more exclusively Croatian orientation by the early 20th century. In light of Croatia's recent independence it is not surprising to find a picture of Ivan Gundulic on the 50 kuna banknote and as well as on numerous post stamps.

As for the *stokavski* dialect, it is still the foundation of the Croatian language in the 21st century, but it is too simple to say that the standardization of the language was based only on the selection of a primary dialect. Croatian territory had long been governed by various foreign powers and, as a result, the educated classes and ruling elite did not necessarily speak Croatian, which was known as a language for peasants and the working class. As mentioned earlier, Croatian was the official language of Dubrovnik, but this was the exception. Because of centuries spent under Venetian rule, Italian was the official language in the rest of Dalmatia and Istria. In the north, both German and Hungarian were used in schools and for official purposes.

Among those intellectuals who were interested in creating a Slavic identity, the notion of a standardized language was a critical pursuit from both an academic as well as political standpoint. In 1830, shortly before the creation of a formal Illyrian movement, Ljudevit Gaj (1809–1872), a 21-year-old student, published his book, *Brief Basics of the Croatian-Slavonic Orthography* (*Kratka osnova horvatsko-slavenskog pravopisanja*), which became a true milestone in the development of the Croatian language. *Brief Basics* established an alphabet for the language as well as rules for spelling and grammar. Croatians were already using the Latin alphabet, but certain sounds were not easily represented, so Gaj included letters such as ć and đ. Gaj soon went on, with the help of other like-minded intellectuals, to establish the Illyrian movement, and used his linguistic accomplishments for political purposes, namely, the unification of Croatian territories as well as the broader goal of Slavic unity. In addition to *Matica hrvatska*, the Illyrians established the first Croatian newspaper called *Danica Ilirska*, which included a cultural segment and published a number of significant poems, satirical works, and short stories. Most important, in 1835, *Danica* published a poem called "Croatian Homeland" (*Horvatska Domovina*) by Antun Mihanovic (1796–1861), which eventually became the lyrics of "Our Beautiful Homeland" ("*Lijepa Nasa*"), the Croatian national anthem. The Illyrian movement generally is linked with Romanticism in Croatian literature, characterized by both patriotic and personal themes often intended to promote an emotional response. In this sense, the movement paralleled that of Romanticism in Europe.

In the process of standardizing their language, Croatian writers hoped to create a Slavic literary canon. Politician, writer, and linguist Ivan Mazuranic (1814–1890) wrote the poem "Death of Smail aga Cengic" (*Smrt Smail age Cengica*) that captures the spirit of the period as he relies on the traditional form of epic poetry to tell a story of tribal animosities between Muslims and Christians while promoting the virtues of loyalty, justice, and ultimately freedom from tyranny. Mazuranic is remembered for his accomplishments in linguistics, including his coauthored *German-Illyrian/Croatian Dictionary* published in 1842 in which he coined words that have become a permanent part of the Croatian language. He currently is pictured on the 100 kuna note.

THE FOUNDATIONS OF MODERN CROATIAN LITERATURE

Following in the footsteps of the founders of the Illyrian movement, August Senoa[4] (1838–1881) is considered the first modern Croatian writer, who transitioned out of the Romantic period with the realism that swept through Europe during the mid- to late 19th century. His poems, plays, short stories, and essays are still studied today and are familiar to all educated Croatians.

Exposed to the Illyrian movement at an early age, when Senoa was a high school student in Zagreb his academic abilities led him to a position as tutor to Ljudevit Guj's son. Following an attempt at medical school in Vienna, he completed a law degree in Prague. By 1866, he returned to live in Zagreb permanently. By the time Senoa completed his studies, he had become politicized. He began writing poems while in high school and upon his return to Zagreb began publishing articles and theater reviews, all along promoting a pan-Slavic philosophy, encouraging Croatian politicians to stand up to the imperialism of the ruling Austro-Hungarians. Because he could not live from his writings alone, he took a job in the city magistrate's office where he was exposed to struggles faced by members of all social classes and he developed a particular sympathy for Croatian peasants.

By the late 1860s, Senoa became a significant figure in Zagreb's cultural scene although he was quite critical of his milieu from both a social as well as political perspective, viewing literature as a means of heightening awareness of issues that otherwise might be conveniently ignored. His comedic play, *Ljubica,* closed after only one night on the Zagreb stage, as the greed and hypocrisy revealed in his characters hit too close to home for the theater-going audience. The plotting and scheming, particularly among the female characters whose primary goal was the entrapment of a husband by whatever means necessary, might have reflected a common mentality, but it was not the sort of material that his audience appreciated.[5]

Senoa remained faithful to his own standards while using a combination of romance and reality to attract an audience. Aware that upper-class women accounted for a large part of his readership—after all, they were as educated and had more free time than their male counterparts—he generally included a love story with a dashing, brave hero and a beautiful, deserving heroine. Although some of his most important works were historical novels— *The Goldsmiths' Gold* (1872), *The Peasant Uprising* (1877), and *Diogenes* (1878)—he never sacrificed fact for poetic flare. Each of these novels was the product of extensive research, providing readers with a truthful view of life in the 16th and 18th centuries, and Senoa went so far as to describe his research in the forward of each book.

Senoa was influential in moving Croatian literature beyond the repetitive patriotic dramas about battles against the Turks, which typically were told using the romantic rhetoric embraced by the members of the Illyrian movement a generation earlier. (Ivan Mazuranic's aforementioned "Death of Smail aga Cengic" was an exception in this dreary canon.) Senoa focused on his observations and experiences as well as hardships faced by himself and those around him. "Friend Lovro" (1873), "Luka the Beggar" (1875), and "Baron Ivica" (1875) are among the contemporary stories and novellas he wrote that were inspired, in some cases more directly than others, by people he met. Throughout his career, he wrote short vignettes and sketches of daily life in Zagreb and, ever the realist, he encouraged other writers to look around themselves for inspiration and drama as he did. For example, "Baron Ivica" includes a character based on the true story of an uneducated peasant who was forced to become a street sweeper in Zagreb after his mother's lover took his land. "Luka the Beggar" is about a moneylender who takes revenge on those who abused him earlier in life. Stories of theft and exploitation, even between families and friends, were common is Senoa's work, but they were not always popular among his audience. Nonetheless, his honest observations and fluid, elegant storytelling not only earned him recognition as the father of the Croatian short story, but have also kept his work in the popular consciousness for well over 100 years.

By the 1900s, the notion of "Yugoslavism" had become a favorite topic among the Zagreb literati. Dissatisfaction with Austro-Hungarian control,

Statue of Marija Juric Zagorka located in Zagreb. (Courtesy of Risha Cupit, Risha Cupit Photography, Milwaukee, WI.)

coupled with greater social mobility and the declining economic power of the aristocratic class provided a backdrop for the work of Croatia's first prominent female writer, Marija Juric Zagorka (1873–1957). Zagorka's works are still read and, in a 2005 survey by the daily newspaper *Vjesnik*, she was named the second most popular Croatian writer. During her lifetime, however, she was the target of both admiration and scorn. Cultural and political leaders, such as Bishop Strossmayer, applauded her skills as a journalist and her fiction was popular. Her novels were first published in serial form in the Zagreb newspapers and her readers always waited impatiently for the next installment, guaranteeing strong sales for the publishers and attention for the controversial author. But much of that attention came in the form of personal attacks from those who found outspoken women offensive; her most vociferous critics were men with strong conservative political convictions. Zagorka was a socialist who opposed the Austro-Hungarian leadership and was a vocal advocate for women's rights, both notions that challenged the status quo in Croatia.

Her most popular work is a series of seven novels, The Witch of Gric (*Gricka vjesica*), which take place in the 18th century and revolve around a noble and beautiful countess whose popularity in Zagreb society make her the object of envy, especially among a particular group of aristocratic women. When the countess tries to save several poor women convicted of witchcraft from being burnt at the stake, she, too, is accused of witchcraft and is left to the mercy of corrupt forces. At the end, of course, she is heroically rescued by her love interest, providing an interesting metaphor for Zagorka's own life. The admiration the writer received was counterbalanced by scorn, and her redemption came not in the form of a heroic man but in her legacy as an enduring figure in Croatian literary history.

THE 20TH CENTURY, A LEGACY OF WAR, AND A YUGOSLAV STATE

Miroslav Krleza (1893–1981) is considered the most important Croatian writer of the 20th century. His work is colored by his experiences of war and political instability. By the time he was 20, he had completed his studies at the military academy in Budapest to become an officer in the Austro-Hungarian army. However, in 1913, he defected to serve in the Serbian military in the war against the Ottoman Empire Turks as he, along with many other Croatians, felt that a Serbian victory might lead to greater independence for Croatia. This was an unfortunate decision as the Turks quickly suspected Krleza was a spy and forced him to return to Austria-Hungary, where he was arrested and demoted to the rank of private in the Austro-Hungarian army. In a cruel twist, when World War I began in 1914, Krleza was sent to the front to fight against the Serb forces. During the war, he found himself sympathizing with the Croatian peasants with whom he fought side by side. They died in large numbers for the sake of the Austro-Hungarian Empire, which as Krleza saw it, only sought to exploit them.

He began establishing his reputation as a writer with leftist political leanings after the war by editing a number of short-lived literary and political journals in Zagreb. He also joined the Communist Party in 1918, although he was forced to leave in 1939 because his strongly held views regarding the importance of artistic freedom in the face of Soviet Union's dogmatic insistence on a socialist-realist approach to the arts. Krleza's conflicts with the Communists continued during World War II when he refused to join the Partisans. Although he continued writing during the war, his work remained unpublished until after Secretary General Tito restored his reputation in 1945 and, by 1955, he was given the prestigious position of director of the Lexicographic Institute of Zagreb and editor of the *Encyclopedia of Yugoslavia*, posts that he held until 1977 when illness forced him into retirement.

Through his plays, short stories, novels, and poems, Krleza often returned to the theme of the exploitation of the common person by the aristocratic or politically privileged classes. He frequently questioned the ability of humanity to rise above greed and selfishness and behave according to higher moral principles. Although generally held in high esteem by the Communist leadership in Yugoslavia, Krleza also was a controversial figure who advocated the rights of the individual and creative freedom for artists. Early in his career, he began writing about historic figures whose heroic endeavors were often clouded by doubt. For example, his first published work, *Legenda* (1914), was a play in which Jesus Christ questions his renunciation of earthly pleasures in the name of the loftier spiritual tenets that formed the foundations of Christianity. Ultimately, Christ does not view his own death as instrumental in the salvation of humanity, rather he knows that although he will always be remembered, he has suffered in vain and that humanity would never truly embrace his teachings. The play was labeled "antireligious" and certainly put Krleza at odds with prevailing religious and governmental institutions in Croatia. Krleza continued writing about conflicted historical figures in his 1917 play *Cristoval Colon* about Christopher Columbus who realizes that his discovery of the New World will only lead to an expansion of the same flawed society full of the avarice and exploitation that dominated Europe.

His experiences during World War I left Krleza disgusted. He, along with many other Croatians, did not believe the defense of the Austro-Hungarian monarchy at all, as they envisioned the possibility of a unified South Slavic state. Krleza could not find any justification for the horrific suffering and enormous loss of life that he witnessed. He expressed his abhorrence of war through a collection of short stories based in his experiences on the Galician front in Poland entitled *The Croatian God Mars* (*Hrvatsk Bog Mars*) published in 1922. The writer portrayed common foot soldiers like himself with dignity and sympathy. The Austro-Hungarian officers, on the other hand, are pompous oafs who enjoy contrived titles and spend most of their time eating and drinking, oblivious to the suffering of the troops under their command. In his story "The Battle at Bistrica Lesna" (*Blitka kod Bistrica Lesna*), Krleza writes about a group of Croatian peasants who die tragically at the front while their families are suffering at home with children starving and wives driven to drink. Such stories resonated with readers in the postwar years as they reflected an all-too-common reality.

Krleza's most popular works were published between the wars, and of those, the best known is the Glembay Series (or The Glembay Lords) (*Gospodina Glembajevi*) of three plays and 11 stories. These works are based on the rise and fall of a bourgeois family who grow more and more corrupt as they become wealthier and wealthier, cultivating the appearance of civility and propriety while their fortune was actually built on exploitation and theft. The family represents the hypocrisy that Krleza believed was a product of capitalist values that became an integral part of the Austro-Hungarian Empire. The Glembay family's downfall coincides with that of the fall of the Austro-Hungarian Empire, the state that they have faithfully served and that made their social ascent possible. As the empire crumbles, we see the Glembays for who they really are, weak willed and corrupt to the bone, nothing more than common criminals.

In Cecilia Hawkesworth's book *Zagreb: A Cultural History*, she observes that Krleza's literary works provided us with rich insight to life in Zagreb during the first half of the 20th century. The writer describes his characters in great detail and specifies the costumes they should wear as well as the nuances of the staging of his theatrical works. Krleza's audiences are drawn into a time and place with specific social and political values, which he eloquently questions. Hawkesworth also notes that some of his most powerful works defy translation, including his six-volume novel *Flags* (*Zastave*), which although written in 1967, deals with life in Croatia between 1912 and 1922, transitional years for the region during which Croatia is finally liberated from Austrian and Hungarian domination. Like many other intellectuals of his time, he valued the Croatian peasant's needs above the interests of the Austro-Hungarian elite, and this period represents at least a partial realization of his ideals, albeit at a high price. Hawkesworth also cites his 1936 collection of poems, *The Ballad of Petrica Kerempuh* (*Balade Petrice Kerempuha*) as a significant work defying translation. The poem is essentially a dark but humorous narrative account by Kerempuh, a Croatian peasant, of his life and that of his fellow peasants. For Krleza and other writers and artists of the time, the peasant represents a link to traditional Croatian culture as exemplified by a revival of poetry written in regional dialects as well as the interest generated by the artists' group called Earth Group (*Zemlja*), best known for the so-called naïve paintings produced by farmers in the rural village of Hlebine.

Although some of Krleza's most complex writings are not translated into English, several significant works are available. *Banquet in Blitva*, his satirical novel about the leadership of a fictitious Balkan country between World War I and II was published in English most recently in 2004. An English translation of *On the Edge of Reason*, another satirical novel poking fun at bourgeois values, was published in 1995, and the *Return of Philip Latinowicz*, a novel about an artist whose struggle for inspiration is only satisfied when he leaves his urban existence to spend time in a small village, also has been translated into English. The Glembay Lords is available in English and has been performed in the United States, including a run in New York City in 1982.

Ivo Andric (1892–1975) is one of the most famous writers from the former Yugoslavia, having achieved international recognition upon winning the Nobel Prize in Literature in 1961. Born into a Bosnian Catholic family, Andric lived in Croatia only for a short time, primarily in Zagreb, and identified himself as a Yugoslav. Croatians, however, often recognize Andric as a national literary icon claiming that his family was of Croatian origin. At the same time, he often is referred to as Serbian since he spent many years living and writing in Belgrade, which was the capital of Yugoslavia during his lifetime but is now the capital of Serbia. More significant, his works, including poems, short stories, and novels, remain popular in Croatia and his themes are drawn from historical events that defined Croatia as well as the rest of the former Yugoslavia.

Like Krleza, Andric was born into a generation of youth who defied Austro-Hungarian authorities to push for the creation of a South Slavic state, and then went on to survive two world wars as well as the political turmoil and violence associated with the creation of Yugoslavia, which was formed as a result of a civil war that took place in tandem with World War II.

Andric had a career in the diplomatic service both before and after World War II, and the suffering he witnessed and personally experienced colored his literary accomplishments. For example, *Ex Ponto* (1918), a memoir based on his three-year stint in an Austrian prison during World War I, deals with the theme of isolation and loneliness, which he would revisit throughout his career. In later works, he turned to Bosnian history, which inspired his most famous work, *The Bridge on the Drina* (*Na drini cuprija*), the novel that won him the Nobel Prize. *The Bridge on the Drina* is one of a group of three novels known as the Bosnian Trilogy because they were written, one right after the other, during World War II and published in 1945.

The Bridge on the Drina begins in the 16th century with the construction of a bridge over the Drina River by the Ottoman Turks in the town of Viesgrad where Andric spent his childhood. The story continues until the beginning of World War I, describing the political and social changes along the way with the bridge functioning as a symbol of stability while all else is shifting, sometimes violently. Most significant, the stone bridge, which attains a sense of permanence, is a unifying force for the diverse ethnic groups living in the region, including Muslims and Christians, as well as Jews and Roma (Gypsies). But just as the political conflict of the early 20th century inevitably leads to ethnic conflict and war, so too the bridge eventually is compromised by violence.

Critics have praised Andric for his even-handed representation of the human condition, particularly with respect to the brutality of war. He writes about a specific part of the world, yet the result is universal, thereby giving his work relevance beyond the former Yugoslavia. The strength of his prose is further enhanced by folkloric elements in his storytelling. In Mateja Matejic's essay discussing this theme,[6] she states that Andric's prose incorporates "the legendary, the mythical and the realistic" as typically is found in oral narration and the epic folk poetry common to Slavic cultures. She also states that Andric's work is not always historically factual, and yet, like folklore, it is "more true than the actual truth." Through his use of legends, he illuminates reality in a way that mere historical and biographical facts cannot. That Andric expresses essential truths contributes to the universal and enduring appeal of his writing and certainly transcends any debate over his ethnic origins or nationality.

Although he died more than 50 years ago, Augustin "Tin" Ujevic (1891–1955) is considered one of the greatest modern Croatian poets and has been called the greatest Balkan poet since Homer.[7] His name is familiar to all Croatians and his likeness is commemorated in statues throughout Croatia, most notably in Zagreb where a life-size statue of Ujevic is prominently placed in the center of town on Varsavska Street. Several schools and bookstores are named after Ujevic and as well as the bar at the Zagreb airport. Although primarily remembered for his poetry, Ujevic also wrote many essays and was recognized for his breadth of knowledge with respect to languages and literature. Fluent in at least six languages, Ujevic translated many English and French literary works into Croatian, including those of Walt Whitman and Marcel Proust.

Like his contemporaries, Ujevic was a politically oriented young man, involved in the cause of Yugoslav nationalism before World War I. He became disillusioned before the war's end and renounced politics, living the rest of his life as the consummate Bohemian vagabond, residing in Paris, Split, Belgrade,

Cars lined up for the ferryboat named after poet Augustin "Tin" Ujevic. (Courtesy of the author.)

Mostar, Sarajevo, and finally Zagreb, where his reputation as a writer and translator was matched only by his notoriety as a drinker. According to local lore, he spent many days getting drunk in a local tavern called Blato and just as many nights sleeping on park benches. The true extent of his debauchery is difficult to discern, but drunk or not, Ujevic created the most significant body of poetry in modern Croatia.

As Ujevic became increasingly disappointed with politics, he turned inward and devoted himself to literature and poetry. In 1916, he wrote "Daily Lament" (*Svakidasnja jadikovka*), one of his best-known poems, inspired by his disillusionment with the political movement to which he devoted enormous time and energy. During this period, he experienced a personal transformation, going from an idealistic young intellectual engaged primarily in politics to a bohemian who had little concern for his appearance or the world around him. He found his inspiration internally and paid minimal attention to political movements that previously had captivated him. According to biographical accounts, by the time a Yugoslav state was created, Ujevic could not care less.

Ujevic's poems are primarily about disappointment, loneliness, and love, yet for all of the darkness of his themes, the eloquence of his language still inspires the reader. In 1919, while living in Belgrade, Ujevic first received critical recognition for his collection of poems titled *A Serf's Lament* (*Lelek Sebra*). The title conveys the mood of the work as well as Ujevic's frame of mind, which remained focused on the tragedy of war and the emotional suffering that reflected his own psyche as well as that of postwar Europe. Also in 1919 his translation of Gustave Flaubert's *Novembre* was published; however, the recognition he received for his literary accomplishments meant little to Ujevic as he pursued a lifestyle characterized by heavy drinking and bar brawls with little regard for personal appearance or social niceties.

After scandalizing Belgrade society, Ujevic moved to Croatia in 1925, just as one of his most popular and critically acclaimed collections of poems, *Necklace* (*Kolina*), was published in Belgrade. In *Necklace*, as in other works, Ujevic used standard metric forms and often wrote sonnets. The originality of his metaphors, the engaging musicality of his language, and the universality of his themes transcended any limitations of form as well as generational and cultural barriers. Although his work cannot be fully appreciated unless it is read in the original Serbo-Croatian language,[8] fine English translations are available that convey the heartfelt elegance and evocative imagery of Ujevic's poetry.

With respect to Croatian poetry after World War II, Vesna Parun (1922–) and Jure Kastelan (1919–1990) are the two writers credited with introducing a more expressive and free-verse poetic style. Parun, in particular, has been cited as the "Grande Dame" of contemporary Croatian poetry, although both writers are recognized as defining forces in 20th-century Croatian literature.

Ujevic influenced Parun and Kastelan, but they moved beyond traditional poetic forms to delve into free verse. Their unconventional approach was not well received initially. Kastelan's earliest work, *Red Horse* (*Crveni konj*), was published at the beginning of World War II and dealt with the death and destruction of war, a sentiment that was not appreciated by the authorities. His work was censored and copies of *Red Horse* were destroyed. Parun faced scathing criticism for her first book, *Dawn and Storms* (*Zore i Vihori*), which was published in 1947 while the new Communist state of Yugoslavia was still under the influence of the Soviet Union. At that time, acceptable literature was limited to stylistically conventional works and politically acceptable themes. Parun's untraditional approach and emotional response to war, however fresh and honest, was labeled "decadent" and "sick." By the time she published her third collection, *Black Olive Tree* (*Crna Maslina*), in 1955, Marshal Tito had broken ties with the Soviet Union and Parun's work, like Kastelan's collection *To Be or Not to Be* (*Biti ili Ne*), gained critical and popular acclaim.

As Dasha Culic Nisula noted in her essay on Parun, both poets were influenced by their personal experiences during World War II, but their approaches differed. Kastelan, who had joined the Partisans, focused on the suffering and sacrifice associated with war, while often using a horse, an animal capable of simultaneous nobility and vulnerability, as a symbol for humanity. Parun was traumatized by her own wartime experience, yet she confronts fear, impending danger, and loss with greater optimism while infusing her work with themes associated with an awareness of her femininity. Love became a common theme in Parun's work, and over the years, she often ventured beyond more conventional imagery and into erotic territory. As for Kastelan, as his work matured, themes of nature appeared more often, in particular the sea and olive trees of his native Dalmatia, as he explored the human condition and modern realities employing occasional surrealistic imagery.

Both writers were known for their break with standard poetic form, but they also employed a traditional approach when the occasion called for it. In his 1950 collection, *The Rooster on the Roof* (*Pijetao na Krovu*), Kastelan writes about war and revolution, although the poems are infused with a hope for a more peaceful world. The book includes nine cycles of poetry and in the Sick with Typhus (*Tifusari*) cycle, the structure and imagery is reminiscent of traditional Croatian epic poetry. Although Parun is best known for free verse, she also wrote sonnets, many of which were published in her 1972 collection simply titled *One Hundred Sonnets* (*Sto Soneta*). She continued to write sonnets and by her own count has written more than 500.

Kastelan's and Parun's literary accomplishments are not limited to poetry. Parun, whose most recent collection was published in 2002, also wrote journalistic essays, short stories, and plays, as well as books of stories and poems for children. While English translations of several of her poems are readily available on the Internet, most of her other work still awaits translation. Kastelan also wrote essays, short stories, and lyrical dramas, but even less of his work is available in English. Croatia's growing popularity as a tourist destination, however, has spurred interest in Croatian culture and, as a result, translations of Croatian literature are becoming increasingly available.

THE HOMELAND WAR AND BEYOND

The finest collection of recent English translations of contemporary Croatian poetry can be found in the June 2009 edition of the Croatian poetry journal *Poezija*. The issue is titled "If We Crash into a Cloud It Won't Hurt" and features works from 1989, the year the Berlin Wall fell and Yugoslavia began to crumble, through 2009, representing the period during which the prospect of a sovereign Croatian state became a possibility and then a reality. Parun's recent poems are presented along with many younger poets such as Marija Andrijasevic (1984–), whose work is based in raw emotion and contains contemporary references to mobile phones, television remotes, sexual identity, and cybersex.

Throughout the 1990s and into the beginning of the 21st century, much contemporary Croatian literature has reflected the violent and disorienting Homeland War and writers often were caught up in the personal and political turmoil associated with military conflict. Serbs, Croatians, and Bosnians who once lived side by side began slaughtering each other, and Croatian nationalist rhetoric reached a fever pitch. In 1992, after the establishment of a Croatian state, but while hostilities were still under way, five female writers were castigated in the tabloid press for their antiwar stance and opposition to the right-wing hyperbole that swept through the country. The group was labeled the "Zagreb Witches," and each of the women suffered severe harassment, including death threats. From this group of "witches" emerged one of Croatia's most prominent literary figures, Slavenka Drakulic (1949–).

Before the Homeland War, Drakulic attained recognition as a gifted journalist who addressed women's issues from a feminist perspective while advancing the role of women in the Croatian media. Drakulic was first introduced to a Western audience in 1990 when she wrote a feature article for *Ms.* magazine discussing the role of women, feminism, and reform in the Soviet Union. The writer's first novel, *Holograms of Fear* (*Hologrami straha,* 1987), was published soon afterward and the English translation was short-listed for the Independent Foreign Fiction Award in Great Britain. The novel is an early example of the author's ability to link the personal with the political. She tells the story of a young woman's experience with kidney failure, dialysis, and finally, a successful transplant, all the while using the deteriorating body as a metaphor for the state under Communism.

Once the Homeland War broke out and Drakulic protested the political establishment's nationalistic rhetoric, she was publicly ostracized and found it impossible to publish in Croatia. She then turned to European and English language publications such as *The Nation* and the *New York Times* and eventually published a critically acclaimed compilation of articles detailing her observations of life under Communism entitled *How We Survived Communism and Even Laughed* (1991). Kirkus Reviews described the book as "[a] sometimes sad, sometimes witty book that conveys more about politics in Eastern Europe than any number of theoretical political analyses." Reviews of this sort attracted attention in the United States and set the stage for her next book, *The Balkan Express: Fragments from the Other Side of War.* Published in 1993, *The Balkan Express* featured a series of essays describing the early days of the war during which time ethnic tensions fueled by jingoistic sentiments pitted neighbor against neighbor and spurred unfathomable atrocities. Another edition of the book that included additional essays was published in 1994, but Drakulic's work did not reappear in Croatia until 1995 when her novel *A Taste of Man* (*Bozanska Glad*) was published and, as the public grew tired of the political regime that ostracized her, she redeemed her reputation domestically. From an international perspective, her 1996 collection of essays, *Café Europa: Life After Communism*, stands out as an account of attempts by Central European countries to reinvent themselves after years of Communism and the identity crisis that emerged. She returned to writing about the effect of war on the individual psyche in her book *They Would Never Hurt a Fly*, based on her coverage of the International Criminal Tribunal in the Hague, in which she examines how law-abiding people lose their sense of morality and commit unthinkable acts of violence, including genocide, during wartime. In 2007, Drakulic returned to fiction once again in her novel about Mexican painter Frieda Kahlo entitled *Frida ili o boli Frieda; or, On Pain,* translated into *Frieda's Bed* for the English edition (*Frida ili o boli*). As in her first novel, Drakulic revisits the subject of the body as she examines the relationship between the artist's psychology, creativity, and the chronic physical pain that Kahlo endured stemming from a debilitating accident during her teens. The novel won Drakulic the 2007 Kiklop Award, a major Croatian literary award, which has placed her reputation on solid footing in her native Croatia.

The aftermath of the Homeland War saw the publication of autobiographical accounts of the war and other sorts of literature related to the conflict. Miljenko Jergovic's book of short stories, *Sarajevo Marlboro*, stands out as a particularly powerful work based on his experience of the war in Sarajevo, Bosnia. The author, whose reputation as a gifted storyteller was firmly established by this book, was born in Sarajevo in 1966, moved to Zagreb in 1993, and figures significantly in both the Croatian and Bosnian literary scenes. He is one of the most popular writers in Croatia today and his books and journalistic efforts are widely read and translated in Europe.

English editions of some of Jergovic's book are available, although translations sometimes take years to appear. *Sarajevo Marlboro* originally was published in 1994, but the English translation became available only in 2004. In addition to short stories, Jergovic has gone on to write two novels. The first, entitled *Walnut Castles* (*Dvori od Orahi*) is not available in English. His 2002 *Buick Riviera,* a novel about the relationship between a recently emigrated Serbian refugee from Bosnia and a more established Muslim refugee, is set in North America; an English translation was published in 2007 and it was made into a film in 2008. Other significant contemporary figures in Croatian literature include Zorap Feric, known for his politically incorrect and darkly funny view of the world, and Pavao Pavlicic, who is recognized for his detective novels and an autobiographical account of his childhood in Vukovar.

Before concluding this section on Croatian literature, we must return to the question of language. The language spoken in the former Yugoslavia often was referred to as Serbo-Croatian. Although there were minor differences in the dialects spoken in parts of Croatia, Serbia, and Bosnia, communication was smooth and a standardized Serbo-Croatian language existed. After the Homeland War, an effort was made to differentiate the Croatian language from that spoken in Serbia. Words that were identified as Serbian were replaced either with terms that were resurrected from the pre-Yugoslav era or with entirely new words that were invented for the occasion. This led to confusion, which at best was funny but also could be disturbing. In Hawkesworth's book *Zagreb: A Cultural History*, she mentions the difficult but humorous position of television commentators who tripped over their tongues as they were forced to navigate around common terms that suddenly were politically incorrect. But she goes on to mention the accusations against refugees from the heavily shelled town of Vukovar who, upon their arrival in Zagreb, were accused of speaking "Serbian." During the early years after the war, political leaders as well as academics pushed the notion of a purely Croatian language. Over time, this fervor has died down, and although Croatian is today regarded as a unique language, it is easily understood by Serbs, Bosnians, and others living in the region that was once Yugoslavia.

NOTES

1. Bogdan Rakic, "Subverted Epic Oral Tradition in South Slavic Written Literatures, 16th–19th Centuries," University of Chicago, Project Muse, http://muse.jhu.edu/journals/serbian_studies/v001/1.1.rakic01.pdf (retrieved December 30, 2008).

2. Rakic, "Subverted Epic Oral Tradition."

3. John V. A. Fine Jr., *When Ethnicity Did Not Matter in the Balkans: A Study of Identity in Pre-Nationalist Croatia, Dalmatia, and Slavonia in the Medieval and Early-Modern Periods* (Ann Arbor: University of Michigan Press, 2006), 288.

4. For more information on August Senoa and other 20th century Croatian writers, see Celia Hawkesworth, *Zagreb: A Cultural History* (New York: Oxford University Press, 2008).

5. Maria B. Malby, "August Senoa (November 14, 1838–December 13, 1881)," in *South Slavic Writers before World War II*, ed. Vasa D. Mihailovich, *Dictionary of Literary Biography*, Vol. 147 (Detroit: Gale Research, 1995), 215–221.

6. Mateja Matejic, "Elements of Folklore in Ivo Andric's *Na drini cupria*." *Canadian Slavonic Papers: An Interdisciplinary Quarterly Devoted to the Soviet Union* 20 (1978): 348–357.

7. Dubravka Juraga, "Augustin ('Tin') Ujevic (July 5, 1891–November 12, 1955)," in *South Slavic Writers before World War II*, ed. Vasa D. Mihailovich, *Dictionary of Literary Biography*, Vol. 147, (Detroit: Gale Research, 1995), 241–247.

8. Because Ujevic lived in Serbia, Bosnia, and Croatia during the Yugoslav era, his poems contain terms that are considered uniquely Serbian today.

8

Media and Cinema

Freedom of the Press

Freedom of the press is a key component in any democracy and is an especially important issue in Croatia. Ideally, as a country transitions from having a strong centralized government that tolerates little dissent into a truly open, democratic state, the media also evolves into a watchdog, ensuring that all voices are heard, even those critical of the parties in power. The process of creating a free press in Croatia has been challenging. Considering the restrictions of the past, a perfectly smooth transition would have been unlikely.

The Croatian news media, including the Internet, print (newspapers and magazines), television, and radio, have moved steadily away from years of government control into an era of independence and free expression. During the 45 years of socialism after World War II, the press was heavily regulated and censorship was the norm. Yugoslav journalists were expected to act as mouthpieces for the Communist Party, although they were not as restricted as their colleagues in the Soviet bloc. The government urged the media to be "responsible" by limiting any less-than-enthusiastic commentary about the party to "constructive" criticism. At the same time, "soft" news was discouraged; however, by the 1960s, the public demand for more entertaining articles and television programming was increasingly met. The government's attitude toward lighter news fluctuated during the 1970s, and the media was constantly forced to balance the expectations of the leadership with the preferences of the public who continued to demand increasingly forthright and engaging reporting.

Once Croatia achieved independence in the early 1990s, the media responded to the overall shift toward democracy with somewhat more objective coverage of current events. The new Croatian constitution guaranteed freedom of expression and freedom of the press. The evolution toward a truly free press was fraught with obstacles. Many state-run newspapers were privatized only to end up in the hands of those sympathetic to the new government. As a result, powerful politicians continued to influence the headlines both on television and in newspapers. When Franjo Tudjman's Croatian Democratic Union Party won the 1990 elections, the new leadership introduced the strong ultranationalist mentality that would define the earliest years of the nascent Croatian state. Serbians, in particular, were marginalized and both television and print media reflected an anti-Serbian ethnocentric perspective.

Having just fought against Serbia in the bloody Homeland War, lingering hostilities against former Serbian residents of Croatia was predictable. According to EU human rights guidelines, as well as the basic precepts of civil society, Croatia was expected to grant its Serbian population certain fundamental rights. Most significant, Serbian refugees who were forced to vacate their homes in Croatia during the war were entitled to a peaceful return. Many of those who tried to do so were met with intolerable hostility and intimidation. The media exacerbated the situation by fueling progovernment nationalist sentiments and rarely providing an alternative viewpoint, even though a more tolerant attitude toward these refugees would have enhanced Croatia's standing in the international community.

The myopic response of otherwise well-educated members of the media was not surprising because Croatia lacked a tradition of a free press. Most journalists were trained under the Yugoslav regime and defined their professional standards accordingly. Even after the Homeland War, they still saw themselves as promoters of the party line. Consequently, the press was vehemently nationalistic and hate speech (which President Tito had adamantly opposed) was considered politically acceptable. Although censorship was prohibited by the Constitution, journalists who dared question the new patriotism were severely edited, faced difficulty getting published, and in some instances, were fired.

Eventually the public grew disillusioned with the Tudjman government (and Tudjman died in 1999) and by 1997 the government called on the media to tone down ultranationalist rhetoric in favor of a more tolerant tone. Over the next decade, major publications and television networks became more sensitive to the rights of ethnic minorities and began to embrace a more clearly defined set of ethics. As an EU candidate, Croatia is expected to foster an atmosphere of openness and transparency with respect to its media, and to reduce political interference regarding content as well media ownership. In 2004, Croatia established a Law on Media and a Law on Electronic Media designed to diversify ownership of print and broadcast outlets while also increasing transparency in reporting.

In spite of changing attitudes and new laws, Croatian media is subject to political meddling. In 2008, Denis Latin, an established figure on HRT (*Hrvatska Radio-Televizija* or Croatian Radio-Television), the state-run news organization, lost his contract and was barred from all HRT programs after he objected to management's decision to prohibit a controversial investigative journalist from appearing on his show. In 2009, Croatia's interior minister, Tomislav Karamarko, brought slander charges against journalist and blogger Zeljko Peratovic who accused the interior minister of obstructing an investigation into the death of a witness in a war crimes case. That case is still unresolved.

Threats of physical violence against journalists also compromise media freedom, especially since the high-profile murders of Ivo Pukanic, the editor of *Nacional*, and his marketing director, Niko Franjic. Pukanic was known for aggressively investigating corruption and crime in the upper eschelons of Croatian society, was well known to organized crime bosses and government officials, and was uniquely close to powerful individuals in both of these circles. Pukanic became the object of repeated death threats that were carried out in October 2008, when he and Franjic were killed, mafia-style, by a car bomb in the center of Zagreb. The public, as well as govenment officials, were outraged by these murders and ultimately Croatian and Serbian law enforcement arrested and indicted several individuals for the crime. Their trials began in the spring of 2010. In the meantime, threats and physical attacks against journalists have continued in Croatia to the point that, according to a 2009 report by Freedom House, investigation of organized crime has become "increasingly dangerous."[1]

On the positive side, many newspapers and magazines, as well as Web sites and blogs are published in Croatia without government interference. However, international watchdog agencies have expressed concern over the degree to which the current system allows for the government to manipulate the mainstream press by limiting transparency. For example, according to Freedom House and the Adriatic Institute for Public Policy,[2] the government controls a significant portion of both the economy and media and therefore has an inordinate level of influence over television, print, and Internet advertising revenues. Although the aforementioned Law on Media and Law on Electronic

Media are designed to limit the control that any single entity, public or private, has over the media, the laws are so vague that they have not been fully implemented. As a result, the U.S. State Department has reported that relationships between the government and private owners of media outlets are not obvious, allowing for insidious forms of government manipulation.[3] In the meantime, the country's four major daily newspapers—*Jutarnji List, Vecernji List, 24 Sata*, and *Slobodna Dalmacij*—have responded to declining readership and advertising by shifting their focus toward sensationalistic reporting, contests, and promotional schemes, at the expense of serious journalism.[4]

While many publications are struggling to survive, some of the most critical voices have been silenced. Rather than attempt to increase revenues by compromising its standards, the political weekly *Feral Tribune* ceased publication in 2008. Founded in 1984 by a group of young journalists as a satirical political leaflet, by 1993, it had evolved into a respected publication that covered sensitive issues, including war crimes committed by the Croatian military, government corruption, and questionable ties between the government and the Catholic Church. The government repeatedly sued the *Feral Tribune* for slander, driving the publication to rely on donations from abroad for its survival. By the mid-1990s the paper was internationally recognized as an important voice for democracy in Croatia and won a number of journalism awards, including the International Press Directory's award for freedom of the press. Ironically, Tudjman's death in 1999 and the decline of hypernationalism deprived the paper of its main source of inspiration. Although continuing with a highly skeptical view of the Croatian leadership, critics argued that the paper lost its focus and relevance. By 2007, the *Feral Tribune* faced serious financial problems due to a decline in advertising (although circulation was reportedly fine) and the pressure of numerous lawsuits. Both the Croatian prime minister and president acknowledged the *Feral Tribune*'s contribution to the development of democracy in Croatia, but the government failed to bail the paper out. The demise of the *Feral Tribune* is seen as a symbol of the difficulties Croatia still faces in creating a media environment that protects dissenting voices.

The Media Landscape

Like elsewhere in the world, Croatia's media landscape is changing, but television remains the dominant source of news. Only four television stations are licensed for nationwide programming: HRT1 and HRT2, which are state owned, and two private stations, Nova TV and RTL. In addition, at least 13 smaller, privately owned regional channels serve local interests. HRT1 and HRT2 are part of HRT, which also runs several radio stations and is funded largely by broadcast user fees that are paid by each household in Croatia, although advertising also provides revenue. Together, HRT1 and HRT2 have 80 percent of the television audience for news and political reporting. The country's main news agency, HINA, is also a public organization (its charter explicitly states that it is not state run and is an independent entity) and is composed of 20 specialized and general departments. HINA also has its own photo service (FAH) and audio service, as well as the electronic database called Eva. Privately owned NovaTV, founded by Central European Media Enterprises (or CPME) in 2000, has about 14 percent of audience share for news, and the German-owned RTL, has less than 7 percent.[5]

Croatia has several privately operated news agencies, including IKA, which covers the Catholic Church and is owned by the Croatian Episcopal Conference and STINA, a regional news services that focuses on diversity and minority issues. For English language news, one can turn to the Croatian Information Center Internet news portal,[6] which was founded in 1991 and is self-described as a "non-government, non-party and non-profit company."

As for entertainment programming, RTL has almost 50 percent of the television market, followed by HTV with 25 percent, and Nova TV with 20 percent. The range of programming is similar to what one finds in the United States, and many American programs are aired on Croatian television. For example, NovaTV introduced talk shows and reality television to Croatian audiences by showing such American programs as the *Jerry Springer Show* and *Survivor*. They also created a Croatian version of *American Idol* and produced their own sitcoms, while also showing popular American programs like *Lost* and *Desperate Housewives*. Reruns of *Seinfeld* are aired on NovaTV as well as newer shows such as *30 Rock*. American programs also make up a large portion of RTL's programming schedule, which includes *CSI:NY*, *The King of Queens*, and *Prison Break*. RTL has based a show on MTV's popular reality series *The Osbournes*, showcasing the family of the late Croatian pop musician Dino Dvornik. RTL also has produced its own version of the American programs *Big Brother* and *Wife Swap*.

A typical day of programming usually begins with news or cartoons in the morning, soap operas (including Latin American *telenovelas* and American soaps) and foreign sitcoms in the afternoon, and news, reality programming, and domestically produced shows as well as movies in the evening. Sports programming is always popular in Croatia and can be found on all major television stations and is always part of daily news shows. European soccer matches are popular, but tennis, water polo, and handball are regularly found on Croatian television.

As for radio, Croatia has plenty of stations to choose from. In total, the country has three national public channels and seven regional public channels run by Croatian Radio-Television, four national commercial channels, and 130 regional and local radio stations. Croatians take advantage of this variety by listening to the radio for an average of almost 250 minutes per day.[7] The large number of local stations keeps the radio market competitive and, on average, each of Croatia's 21 counties has at least two strong competing stations. Music stations are the most popular, with Narodni Radio broadcasting Croatian songs exclusively, although other popular stations play both foreign and Croatian music. Small regional stations abound, providing listeners with everything from classical music to hip-hop. Many larger stations follow a format familiar to U.S. listeners with hourly news programming coupled with humor and music.

Croatians increasingly rely on the Internet as a source of news, entertainment, communication, and networking. In 2000, only 4.6 percent of the population used the Internet regularly, but by 2006, that number rose to almost 33 percent.[8] By 2010, approximately 2.24 million, or about 50 percent[9] of the population used the Internet. All major newspapers and organizations have their own Web sites and thousands of other Croatian language sites have been created, usually with the ".hr" suffix. Internet users can search for these sites on Google.hr, which is the Croatian language version of the standard Google search engine.

CINEMA

Croatian movie theaters are filled with American blockbusters, and most Croatians are well versed in the latest news and gossip emanating from Hollywood. More than half of the population attends the cinema at least once in a given year[10] and visitors to Croatia will see plenty of advertisements for new films plastered across billboards, particularly in larger cities. Foreign films are a necessity as domestic production is limited. Croatia releases between six and nine features per year, leaving the country's 87 cinemas[11] to show movies imported primarily from the United States. That said, the country's small film industry is both diverse and accomplished, with roots in animation and avant-garde film as well as the world of commercially popular feature-length movies.

Early Film Production and the Yugoslav Era

The origins of film production in Croatia can be traced to the days just before World War I and the First Croatian Cinematographic Company. The company's initial purpose was the production of *Matija Gubec*, a silent film based on August Senoa's novel about a 16th-century peasant rebellion.

The movie premiered in 1919 in Zagreb and the company went on to make several additional films. Although copies of these early efforts have been lost, Zagreb's first generation of filmmakers, although primarily amateur, managed to plant the roots of a domestic movie industry in Croatia.

In the years after World War I, the First Croatian Cinematographic Company faltered, but Yugoslavia Films was founded in its place. Funding for production was minimal, so few domestic feature films were made, leaving Croatian audiences to turn to foreign movies for entertainment. During the 1920s and 1930s, films by major U.S. studios as well as French and Italian productions were shown in Croatia, which had about 100 movie theaters. By the time World War II started, the cinema was an established part of the Croatian cultural scene, and the stage was set for the creation of a Yugoslav film industry.

Croatian film first gained international recognition in the field of animation. The Zagreb School of Animated Film, founded in 1950, was a loose conglomeration of artists who went beyond traditional cartoon animation to develop a variety of idiosyncratic styles inspired by new developments in painting and graphic design. In 1953, Zagreb Film, a full-fledged production company, was established to further the achievements of the school. The artists had minimal funding, some were self-taught, and few traveled abroad, yet they still garnered attention in a field dominated by larger countries such as the United States and the former Soviet Union. In 1963, Dusan Vukotic, a Montenegrin-born member of the Zagreb School became the first non-American to win an Oscar for animated film with his short called *Surrogate* (*Surogat*, 1963) in which he created a world of abstract forms whose actions illustrated a series of human foibles in a humorous but thought-provoking fashion. Over the years, Zagreb Film has gone on to produce hundreds of animated films as well as commercials, documentaries, education projects, and a few feature films.

Beginning in the 1950s, filmmakers embraced avante-garde cinema, which, in Croatia at least, led to a wealth of small, idiosyncratic projects based around abstract ideas rather than the narrative or conventional cinematic qualities associated with feature films. This avant-garde approach complemented the rich conceptual nature of the best animation that already was coming from Zagreb. For example, in *K3 or Clear Sky without Clouds* (*K3 ili cisto nebo bez oblaka*,1962), Mihovil Pansini edited bits of transparent leader film together; Zlatko Hajdler in *Kariokinesis* (*Kariokineza*, 1965) filmed a static frame as it is burned by the lamp of a projector. This trend continued into the 1970s with Dalibor Martinis' *Open Reel* (1976) in which the filmmaker wrapped himself up in videotape as it emerged from the camera, which is recording him in the process. Each of these films challenged the notion of cinema at the most basic level, making the viewer aware of the fundamentally fragile physical quality of the film itself.[12]

From the 1950s through the 1980s, movies were made within the context of the broader statewide Yugoslav film industry. Some projects are identified as Croatian, including those by Dubrovnik-born director Branko Bauer (1921–2002), whose 1956 thriller *Don't Turn Around, Son* (*Ne Okreci Se Sine*) reflected the political turbulence within Croatia during World War II as it impacted a father and his sons. Croatian director Nikola Tanhofer (1926–1998) created one of the most memorable films of the 1950s with *H8* (1958), a suspenseful recounting of a real-life traffic accident between a bus and a truck in which several people died. In this classic of Croatian cinema, viewers know an accident will happen as the film reveals the dreams and disappointments of the potential victims who move about the vehicles in what has been called a "chessmatch with death."[13] Other significant Croatian directors include Kreso Golik (1922–1998), known for his comedies, including *Blue 9* (*Plavi 9*, 1950) and *He Who Sings Never Means Harm* (*Tko pjeva zlo ne misli*, 1970) as well as his television work, which included comedies as well as dramas. Zvonimir Berkovic (1928–2009), screenwriter for *H8*, is also remembered for his 1966 classic *Rondo*, a psychological drama.

Thanks to its dramatic scenery and skilled but relatively inexpensive labor, Croatia became a popular location for film production. Jadran Film Studios was founded in 1945 and gained an international reputation during the 1970s and 1980s as the company that facilitated the production of a number of films, including *Sophie's Choice*, *Fiddler on the Roof*, and *The Tin Drum*, as well as the television series *Winds of War* and *War and Remembrance*. Orson Welles even began the production of his 1962 cinematic interpretation of Franz Kafka's novel *The Trial* in Croatia. Scenes were shot in several European cities, including Dubrovnik, but most notable was a massive office scene shot near Zagreb, featuring 850 secretaries working at 850 desks. In the process, Welles also met the 21-year-old Olga Palinkas, whom he renamed Oja Kodar. She went in to become his partner, muse, and creative collaborator until his death in 1985. During their years together, Welles visited Croatia numerous times and appeared in several Croatian films, including *The Secret of Nikola Tesla* and *The Battle of Neretva*. In particular, Welles enjoyed visiting the city of Split where he became a prominent fan of the local soccer team, Hajduk. Split awarded Welles honorary citizenship in 2008 and installed a majestic statue sculpted by Kodar in front of a new shopping mall and Cineplex.[14]

Croatian Film in the 1990s

After the collapse of Yugoslavia, the Croatian film industry also found itself in serious trouble. With the country at war, the market for Croatian films

A statue of Orson Welles by Oja Kodar in front of a mall and Cineplex in Split. (Courtesy of the author.)

disappeared and the state funding that the industry depended on dwindled as well. To make matters worse, the new Croatian leader, Franjo Tudjman, and his political allies had little interest in cinema, except as nationalist propaganda. Under his watch, films were expected to serve his right-wing political agenda, thereby limiting their appeal both in the domestic and foreign markets. Clearly his predecessor, President Tito, also had used the cinema as propaganda, but as a film fan, Tito expected quality productions. Tudjman's standards were lower and thus many of the movies coming out of Croatia during the 1990s were of inferior quality.[15] The leadership's stand against cooperation with the International Criminal Tribunal created a political backlash that extended to its film industry. Most notably, Steven Spielberg refused to work with Jadran Films for the production of *Schindler's List*. The contract instead went to Polish and Slovakian companies.

Fortunately, the faltering movie industry was salvaged by an infusion of young, talented directors, cinematographers, and actors graduating from the

University of Zagreb, Academy of Dramatic Arts. Their projects included documentaries and short- and medium-length films inspired by the Homeland War. Hardly propaganda, their themes were dark, focusing on the human price rather than the heroic aspects of war. The perspective of these young filmmakers was summed up by up-and-coming director Nikolas Nola (1964) who stated that his generation had the war stolen from them.[16] Nola referred to the fact that the views of the younger generation, many of whom fought in the war, were not represented by the hyperpatriotic films made by the politically connected directors favored by the govenment, many of whom never donned a uniform. In his article on the subject, Ivo Skrabalo argued that the first credible films about the Homeland War were produced by the youngest filmmakers.[17] Skrabalo cites the work of Ivan Salaj (1969) whose notable documentary film, *Hotel Sunja* (1992), was made as a school project. The film provides an authentic portrayal of both the battlefield as well as individual soldiers. Salaj went on to produce *See You* (*Vidimo se*, 1995), a 70-minute movie about the camaraderie among five young men during wartime. His work received praise at numerous student film festivals and was recognized as presenting a fresh, new viewpoint in Croatian cinema. Other influential directors to emerge from the University of Zagreb include Jelena Rajkovic (1969–1997), who is remembered for her work documenting the psychological effects of war, and the previously mentioned Nikolas Nola, who gained recognition for his first medium-length film, *Dok nitko ne gleda* (*While No One Is Watching*, 1993).

The most unlikely director to be categorized as a voice for this younger generation of artists is Zrinko Ogresta (1958), as he was an open supporter of the Tudjman regime. His films, however, were dark social dramas, devoid of nationalistic hype.[18] Ogresta's second feature, *Red Dust* (1999), which critiqued the process of privatization of national industry by politically connected and corrupt tycoons, was Croatia's official submission in the category of Best Foreign Language Film for the 72nd Academy Awards.

The most famous filmmaker to emerge from this generation is Vinko Bresan (1964). His black comedy, *Kako je počeo rat na mom otoku* (*How the War on My Island Started*, 1996), was a domestic hit (even beating *Independence Day* at the box office) and was screened at 32 international film festivals. Bresan's next film, also a comedic satire, called *Marshall Tito's Spirit* (*Marsal*, 1999), was based on the premise of the appearance of Tito's ghost on a small Adriatic island. The characters range from old Communists who revered Tito to the new generation of capitalists who saw the former leader as an archaic relic of a bygone era. *Marsal* was screened at the 2000 Berlin Film Festival and won the special prize in the Junge Filme (Young Filmmakers) selection.

A New Era of Croatian Film

Following President Tudjman's death in 1999, his nationalist government was replaced in the 2000 election by a center-left coalition. Filmmakers were no longer pressured to produce the sort of right-wing cinema that the Tudjman government preferred. This current period of artistic freedom is often referred to as a "golden era" with the likes of Bresan and his colleagues gaining international recognition for their feature films, while small production companies and new technology became catalysts for the rebirth of avante-garde film and sophisticated productions for television.

Vinko Bresan's career as both an actor and director expanded to include several television projects, but he is best known, domestically and internationally, for his feature films. In 2003, the director approached the Homeland War from a somber and contentious vantage point with his production of *Svjedoci* (*Witnesses*) based on a novel by Jurica Pavicic. *Svjedoci* was the first Croatian film about war crimes committed by Croatian soldiers, in this case, the inadvertent murder of a Serbian smuggler. Although the movie won the Peace Film Award at the 2004 Berlinale, it remained controversial at home. In particular, Bresan was attacked by right-wing political groups for his choice of a Serbian actress in the role of a Croatian war widow. His next project *Nije Kraj* (*Will Not Stop There*, 2008) continued to deal with contemporary themes by providing an absurdist approach to, among other things, the continued tensions between Croatians and Serbs. The plot is narrated from the perspective of a cynical Serbian porn star (the Big Bad Wolf) who tells the story of a Croatian ex-sniper obsessed with the Wolf's costar, a young woman who plays an X-rated Little Red Riding Hood. While the domestic audience for Bresan's most recent projects is not as large as in the 1990s, he remains one of Croatia's most popular and critically acclaimed filmmakers. *Nije Kraj* was screened at numerous international festivals, winning the FIPRESCI (International Federation of Film Critics) prize at the Kalovy Vary International Film Festival in the Czech Republic as well as an Audience Award at the Pula Film Festival in Croatia.

Other prominent Croatian directors include Goran Rusinovic (1969–) whose first film, the black-and-white thriller *Mondo Bobo* (1997), originally brought him recognition, but his second feature, *Buick Riviera*, based on the novel by Miljenko Jergovic, was even more enthusiastically received. The film bears some similarity to Bresan's *Nije Kraj* in that both are based on humorously preposterous plots that become effective vehicles for the exploration of ethnic tensions. *Buick Rivieria* takes place in Fargo, North Dakota, and follows the story of a Bosnian Serb and a Bosnian Muslim who meet on a deserted road and proceed to psychologically torment one another for a 24-hour period. The film won best screenplay at the Pula Film Festival and was screened internationally.

One of the most engaging films of the postwar era is director Dejan Sorak's (1954–) *Two Players from the Bench* (*Dva igraca s klupe*, 2005). The darkly comedic film is a twisted buddy picture about a Serb and Croat who, against their will, are drawn into a convoluted plot to save a fictional Croatian general from prosecution by the War Crimes Tribunal. The Croatian secret service kidnaps the highly emotional Croat and the completely calm and fatalistic Serb, because they resemble a pair of missing Croats whose testimony can prove that the general did not commit the massacre of which he is accused. The movie explores ethnic tensions and the disturbing political and human aftermath of war in a way that makes us laugh in spite of the desperately sad nature of the situation.

Not all new Croatian cinema concerns itself with odd (and often comedic) characters dealing with ethnic issues in unlikely situations. Zrinko Ogresta (1958–) followed *Crvena prasina* with *Here* (*Tu*, 2003) and *Behind Glass* (*Iza stakla*, 2008), both psychological dramas that confirm his status as "one of the rare true craftsmen of Croatian film."[19] Another director known for high-quality drama is Arsen Ostojic (1965–), a graduate of the University of Zagreb who went on to get a master's degree in filmmaking at New York University. After several short films, Ostojic completed his first feature film, *A Wonderful Night in Split* (*Ta divna splitska noć*, 2004). The black-and-white movie artfully illustrates some of the social problems, such as the proliferation of illegal drugs, found in larger Croatian cities, especially Split. The mood is darkly compelling and the project won numerous awards, becoming the official Croatian candidate for the 78th Academy Awards. Ostojic's next film also dealt with societal problems in the post–Homeland War decade. *Niciji sin* (*No One's Son*, 2008) is the story of a disabled war veteran suffering from post-traumatic stress syndrome while his father runs for political office. The plot thickens as an exiled Serbian refugee returns to town with information that can compromise the family. This movie also was well received, winning best film and best director at the Croatian Film Festival in Pula, and became the Croatian submission for the 81st Academy Awards.

Croatian films have gained international recognition and routinely appear at festivals in the United States and Europe, but they typically are not screened at local movie theaters. In general, movie attendance in Croatia is down and audiences gravitate to the American blockbusters featuring world-renowned actors. Film festivals are the best place to see domestic movies and fortunately Croatia has at least 11 of them, six of which are international. The Pula Film Festival (originally known as the Festival of Yugoslav Film) is the oldest. Established in 1954, the festival has many screenings taking place in Pula's first-century Roman arena. Other prominent festivals take place in large cities, such as Split, Dubrovnik, and Zagreb, but one of the most interesting and intimate is located in the medieval Istrian town of Motovun. This festival was founded in 1999 with the explicit intent of screening the small independent films that were virtually impossible to see in Croatia. From the start, an informal atmosphere prevailed, and the yearly event became particularly popular with a younger audience. While Motovun's ambiance is relaxed, its film festival has become one of the most important and prestigious in the former Yugoslavia. The growing popularity of Motovun along with other festivals, coupled with international interest in Croatian film, bodes well for the country's motion picture industry. Ironically, its toughest audience is domestic, but eventually home-grown productions may actually succeed in attracting the attention of movie fans throughout Croatia.

NOTES

1. Petar Doric, Freedom House, "Nations in Transit 2009–Croatia," Freedom House, June 30, 2009, http://www.unchr.org/refworld/docid/ (retrieved April 11, 2010).

2. Freedom House, "2009 Study: Region Faces Biggest Drop in Press Freedom, Croatia's Journalists Murdered and Assaulted," Adriatic Institute for Public Policy, http://www.adriaticinstitute.org/?action=news&id=62 (retrieved April 11, 2010).

3. U.S. Department of State, *2008 Country Reports on Human Rights Practices: Croatia*, http://www.state.gov/g/drl/rls/hrrpt/2008/eur/119073.htm (retrieved April 11, 2010).

4. European Journalism Center, "Media Landscape–Croatia," http://www.ejc.net/media_landscape/article/croatia; Georgios Terzis, ed., *European Media Governance: National and Regional Dimensions* (Bristol, UK: Intellect, 2008), as excerpted on Intellect Web site, http://www.intellectbooks.com (retrieved April 22, 2010).

5. Zrinjka Perusko and Kresimir Jurlin, "Croatian Media Markets: Regulation and Concentration Trends" (Zagreb: Institute for International Relations, 2006), www.imo.hr/files/Media-Markets-in-Croatia.pdf (retrieved April 22, 2010).

6. Croatian Information Center, http://www.hic.hr (retrieved April 22, 2010).

7. Zrinjka Perusko, "Media and Civic Values," in *Democratic Transition in Croatia: Value Transformation, Education & Media*, eds. Sabrina P. Ramet and Davorka Matic (College Station: Texas A&M University Press, 2007).

8. Data from table "Internet Usage in Europe, Croatia" on "Usage and Population Statistics," Internet World Stats, http://www.internetworldstats.com/stats4.htm#europe (retrieved April 25, 2010).

9. Ibid.

10. Data from table "Cinema attendance (per capita) (most recent) by country," NationMaster.com, http://www.nationmaster.com/graph/med_cin_att_percap-media-cinema-attendance-per-capita (retrieved April 25, 2010).

11. UNESCO UIS Data, UNESCO Institute for Statistics, http://data.un.org/Data.aspx?q=cinema&d=UNESCO&f=series%3aC_F_220054 (retrieved April 22, 2010).

12. Andrew J. Horton, "Avant-garde Film and Video in Croatia," *Central Europe Review* 0, no. 6 (November 2, 1998), http://www.ce-review.org/kinoeye/kinoeye6old.html (retrieved April 22, 2010).

13. Program from "Beyond Boundaries," Croatian Film Festival, Film Society of Lincoln Center, 2008.

14. "Orson Welles Becomes 'Citizen of Split,'" *News and Views of Southeastern Europe*, January 17, 2008, www.SETimes.com (retrieved May 8, 2010).

15. Jurica Pavicic, "Moving into the Frame: Croatian Film in the 1990s," *Central Europe Review* 2, no. 9 (May 15, 2000), http://www.ce-review.org/00/19/kinoeye19_pavicic.html (retrieved April 22, 2010).

16. Ivo Skrabalo, "Young Croatian Film," *Central Europe Review* 1, no. 18 (October 25, 1999), http://www.ce-review.org/99/18/kinoeye18_skrabalo.html (retrieved April 22, 2010).

17. Skrabalo, "Young Croatian Film."

18. Pavicic, "Moving into the Frame."

19. Vladan Petkovic, "Serbia vs. Croatia: 2008 in Film—Vladan Petkovic Surveys the Scene," Neil Young's Film Lounge, August 11, 2008, http://www.jigsawlounge.co.uk/film/reviews/serbia-vs-croatia-2008-in-film-vladan-petkovic-surveys-the-scene/ (retrieved April 22, 2010).

9

Music and Performing Arts

THE CLASSICAL TRADITION

For centuries Croatia has maintained a rich and vital musical culture. Early on, the church was the primary repository of notated musical texts, the earliest dating back to 10th century, but music was always a part of daily life as well. A 12th-century manuscript described the visit of Pope Alexander III to Croatia, where he was serenaded by locals singing hymns in the vernacular language. Few Croatians studied Latin and illiteracy was common, so poems, which often were set to song, became a predominant part of Croatia's early oral and musical tradition. As mentioned in Chapter 7, Petar Hektorovic (1487–1572) was the first to chronicle two Croatian folk songs in his classic poem "Fishing and Fishermen's Talk."

The well rehearsed songs and dances that make up the repertoire of Croatian folk ensembles that perform at festivals around the world were not originally created for the stage. Rather, folk songs were played during village celebrations and other social gatherings. To find music that was composed for more formal occasions, we must look to the church where, in cathedrals at least, choirs and organists performed, the earliest being Gregorian Chants that span the 11th through the 15th centuries. Although a number of 16th- and 17th-century Croatian composers (most of whom were trained in Italy) still appear in the history books, Ivan Lukacic (ca. 1575–1648), a Franciscan monk who was the organist and choirmaster at the Split Cathedral, is best remembered. He was a composer of sacred music from the early baroque period and published at least 25 choral pieces characterized by elegant, clear melodies and harmonies. Meanwhile, the Hapsburg Counter-Reformation heavily influenced the northern part of Croatia (the coastal area was a Venetian province) and, in an effort to enhance piety in the population, music was reduced to simple religious songs sung in the local vernacular language. Some notable examples include Athanasius Georgiceo's "Songs for the Most Important Days of the Year" (1635) and the anonymous Pauline songbook (1644). The earliest symphonic works, however, were not composed by members of the clergy, but rather by a nobleman from Dubrovnik, Luka Sorkocevic (1734–1789). He wrote eight symphonies that contain both classical and baroque elements, representing a transitional phase between the two periods in European music. His son, Antun, also went on to compose several orchestral overtures and chamber music pieces.

By the early 19th century, the Illyrian movement created a patriotic fervor that was reflected in the Romantic music of the period. The most prominent composer was Vatroslav Lisinski (1819–1854), also a well-known member of the movement who is remembered as a talented but tragic figure. In addition to some patriotic songs that he composed, Lisinksi also wrote the first Croatian opera, *Love and Malice* (*Ljibav i zloba*, 1846), which coincided with the nationalist mentality of the day. After attending the music conservatory in Prague, Lisinski returned to Zagreb with a second opera, *Porin* (composed 1848–1851, first performed 1897), which also was sympathetic to the Illyrian cause and included clear musical references to the folk tradition. Eventually the Austro-Hungarian leadership suppressed the Illyrian movement and both *Porin* and Lisinski were nearly forgotten. Lisinsky died in 1854 in extreme poverty, but not before he wrote his own funeral march, *Jeder Mensch muss sterben*, which has since been lost.[1] *Porin* was not performed again until the early 20th century, and Lisinski has since been credited as one of the founders of modern Croatian and South Slavonic music.[2]

Italian-trained composer Ivan Zajc (1832–1914) was the most prominent Croatian figure in the later Romantic period. After a stint in Vienna composing operettas, he arrived in Zagreb in 1870 and became the first director of the newly founded Croatian National Opera (1870–1889) and director of the Glazbeni Zavod music school (1870–1904). He is remembered primarily for his patriotic opera, *Nikola Subic Zrinski*, based on the story of the Croatian general and viceroy who defended Vienna from the Ottoman Turks.

That some of the most significant developments in Croatian music occurred after World War I was at least in part due to a favorable shift in circumstances. First, Croatia was no longer part of the Austro-Hungarian Empire, and its writers and artists were able to express themselves without external political pressure. At the same time, music was changing on an international level, led in large part by Slavic composers such as Russians Igor Stravinsky, who challenged established musical forms, and Nikolai Rimsky-Korsakov, who incorporated folk elements with ethnic rhythms and harmonies. As Croatian composers followed these two courses, some were inclined toward late Romanticism and Modernism, while others turned to indigenous folk music for raw material.

The most popular composer to emerge from this period is Jakov Gotovac (1895–1982) whose composition *Symphonic Kolo* references the traditional Kolo dance in the title. He preferred relatively simple harmonies of the sort found in folk songs and created memorable compositions that appealed to the general public. *Symphonic Kolo* was performed internationally as was his most famous composition, an opera titled *Ero the Joker*, which has been staged in nine languages and in more than 80 European theaters.

Sometimes musicians begin their careers as performers but ultimately make an even greater impact as teachers and composers. Such was the case of Stjepan Sulek (1914–1986), a well-known concert violinist before World War II, who gained even greater fame after devoting himself to composition, producing works mostly in the late Romantic style, but eventually incorporating neobaroque, neoclassicist and neo-Romantic elements. He was a highly influential teacher of composition at the Zagreb Academy of Music, joining the faculty in 1948 and becoming the principal conductor of both the chamber and symphonic orchestras in Zagreb. During his years at the academy, Sulek mentored young musicians and composers, some of whom became leading figures in Croatian music during the postwar years.

After World War II, many Croatian composers moved away from folkloric sources and toward the modern, avant-garde themes that were gaining popularity elsewhere in Eastern Europe. Although Sulek rejected the avant-garde trends of the 1960s, several of his students, such as composer Stanko Horvat (1930–2006), eventually advanced these cutting-edge ideas. Horvat's earliest compositions, such as *Concerto for Strings* (1952), reflected the classical tradition but he went on to experiment with Arnold Schoenberg's 12-tone technique as well as serialism and other new modalities, all of which he eventually abandoned in favor of a "simple and traditional treatment of an instrument."[3] Horvat is best remembered for his compositions from the 1960s and 1970s, including his opera *Metamorphosis* (*Preobrazaj*), named after the story by Franz Kafka. He was also a professor at the Zagreb Academy of Music and became its dean in 1977. Like Sulek, Horvat was an important mentor for a younger generation of composers.

Milko Kelemen (1924–), certainly one of the most influential Croatian composers of the latter 20th century, is largely responsible for the development of avant-garde music in Croatia. Also a student of Sulek's (as well as Olivier Messiaen in Paris and Wolfgang Fortner in Freiburg), Kelemen began his career with a folkloric orientation, but he also experimented with 12-tone technique and, in later works, followed the so-called Eastern European sonorist style, an avant-garde approach popularized by Polish composers of the 1960s. In 1959, he founded the Zagreb Biennale, which has grown into one of Europe's most established festivals of new music. In the 1960s, Kelemen began to develop an international reputation and, by 1968, he was granted a Humboldt Scholarship to study at the Electronic Siemens-Studio in Munich, Germany, later going on to win numerous awards, including the French order of Chevalier des Arts et des Lettres. His more recent compositions are based on the philosophical works of C. G. Jung and the notion of "musical archetypes." In his book *Sound Labyrinth* he states, "The general concept of my judgment of works is based upon the fact that the influence of archetypes, or the effect of the 'most impressive chord,' remains present, starting with the imagination and extending into form, language and structure."[4] Kelemen lives in Stuttgart, Germany, where he is a professor of composition at the Stuttgart Academy of Music and the Performing Arts.

The contemporary music scene in Zagreb is diverse. Composers Davorin Kempf (1947–) and Marko Ruzdjak (1946–) both combine traditional motifs with modern technological innovations. Kempf's most relevant compositions integrate live performance and electronics. Examples include *Synthesis* (1979) for electronics and chamber ensemble, and *Spectrum* (1985) for orchestra and electronics. Ruzdjak's *Partita* (*La Gioconda*, 1993) written for solo violin melds the past and the present in a contemporary interpretation of a baroque form.[5] Composer Frano Parac (1948–) was a student of Horvat's and has produced a diverse body of work, but is best known for referencing the Eastern European sonorist tradition, while keeping to the midcentury modernist style exemplified by Dmitri Shostakovich. He is currently a member of the composition faculty at the Academy of Music in Zagreb.

The faculty at the Zagreb Academy of Music certainly has influenced many of Croatia's younger composers, but at the same time, new generations have defined their own direction. Like Parac, Ivo Josipovic, was a student of Horvat's, but he turned to non-European source material to create some particularly exotic compositions. He drew inspiration from Brazilian samba in *Samba da camera* (1985) and ancient Hindu texts with *A Thousand Lotus Flowers* (*Hiljadu lotosa*, 1987), which includes improvisation and jazz-inspired passages. Josipovic's career has been as unconventional as his compositions; he is also a highly respected legal scholar and politician and was elected president of Croatia in 2010.

Yet another one of Horvat's students, Srdjan Dedic (1965–) developed an international reputation while studying electronic music at the University of Strasbourg with François-Bernard Mache. In the late 1990s, he won a Japanese government fellowship to study composition and traditional instruments with the members of the Pro Musica Nipponia ensemble in Tokyo. In 1991, he returned to the Zagreb Academy of Music and has since focused on computerized music. In the meantime, his works have been performed by the Louisville Symphony Orchestra, Prague Symphony Orchestra, Ensemble Orchestral International, Korean Chamber Orchestra, and Zagreb Philharmonic Orchestra, and at the World Saxophone Congress in Montreal.

In addition to these composers, Croatia has produced some outstanding performers beginning with the illustrious soprano Milka Trnina (1863–1941). She performed in major European and American opera houses until 1906 when sudden facial paralysis forced her to abruptly retire from the stage. She never made any commercial recordings, but according to legend, the *Milka* chocolate bar, created in Austria in 1901 and available throughout Europe, was named in honor of the singer. Her legacy continued through her famous pupil, Zinka Milanov (1906–1989) who had a long association with the Metropolitan Opera in New York City. Other important figures include Lovro von Matacic (1899–1985) who is remembered as one of Croatia's finest conductors and founder of music festivals in Split and Zagreb, and Dunja Vejzovic (1943), a protégé of Milanov who also was considered one of Croatia's finest operatic sopranos.

Visitors cannot go to a major Croatian city today without seeing the name of pianist Maksim Murvica (1975–), either on placards advertising a concert or in music shops where his recordings are always prominently displayed. Murvica's rise to fame began in 1993 when he entered and won his first piano competition in Zagreb. He is known as a charismatic performer who has successfully integrated pop elements into a mostly classical repertoire. His first recording, *Gestures*, was released in Croatia in 2000 and became one of the fastest selling albums by a Croatian artist. Since then, Murvica has recorded several albums and toured Asia, where he has performed crossover shows as well as a classical concert with the Moscow Philharmonic. He divides his time between the coastal town of Sibenik, where he was born, and London.

The biggest Croatian name in 21st-century classical music is pianist Ivo Pogorelich (1958–) who has performed with the likes of the London Symphony Orchestra, the Boston Symphony Orchestra, and the Vienna Philharmonic, to name a few. After his debut recital at Carnegie Hall in New York City in 1981, he soon signed an exclusive recording contract with the prestigious Deutsche Grammophon. Pogorelich generated controversy from the beginning of his career, which was jump-started by losing the 1980 Chopin International Competition in Warsaw. Famed pianist and juror Martha Argerich resigned from the jury in protest, thereby immediately drawing attention to the young pianist. Over the years, critics have disagreed over Pogorelich's interpretations of well-known classical pieces, yet he has consistently succeeded in captivating audiences with his charismatic performances. In addition to performing, he has been involved with various charitable causes including the foundation he established in Croatia to further the education of young performers. Pogorelich performed regularly in support of UNESCO (United Nations Educational, Scientific, and Cultural Organization) and raised money for medical relief and the rebuilding of Sarajevo after the wars in the 1990s.

Croatia has several orchestras and opera companies, the Zagreb Philharmonic Orchestra being the oldest and most prominent. Founded in 1870, the orchestra regularly tours internationally, performing a mix of works by Croatian composers and standard classical pieces. The Croatian Radio and Television Symphonic Orchestra is an important cultural institution and, although their primary job is to record for radio and television, they also manage to appear at festivals and have performed pieces by every major Croatian composer. The Zagreb Soloists is a chamber orchestra that was formed by the Croatian Radio and Television Symphonic Orchestra in 1953. Over the years, this ensemble has performed throughout the world, and while their repertoire includes a range of baroque, classical, romantic, and contemporary works, they often focus on music written by Croatian composers. Croatia also has a national opera company and four national theaters, the main one being in Zagreb, with others in Rijeka, Split, and Osijek.

Music festivals have become significant venues for classical performances, and attract an international array of performers and composers. The Zagreb Biennale has evolved into a particularly prestigious event in the world of contemporary classical music with participants such as John Cage, Karlheinz Stockhausen, and Igor Stravinsky. Initially conceptualized as a festival to present innovative new works, it gradually expanded to include the occasional jazz or rock band. In 1983, the Biennale even hosted the Slovenian avant-garde band, Liabach, who, according to festival lore, pushed the boundaries of political acceptability by broadcasting a speech by the recently deceased Marshal Tito while showing a pornographic film.

Other popular festivals include the Dubrovnik Summer Festival, which has grown into a major tourist attraction with its multitude of performances in scenic outdoor venues. The program includes dance, theater, and classical music, and is weighted heavily toward domestic artists, but foreign performers appear on the bill as well. The coastal city of Zadar hosts Musical Evenings in Saint Donatus, a popular festival known for classical performances in the medieval Church of Saint Donatus as well as elsewhere in town. With its well-preserved baroque town center, Varazdin is the perfect location for its yearly festival of baroque music, which features both Croatian and international artists.

FOLK TRADITIONS

Twenty-first-century folk music is the culmination of centuries of tradition spanning the diverse cultural mix that makes up present-day Croatia. Across villages and cities, music was used to celebrate the changing seasons, harvests, religious holidays, and rites of passage, such as births, weddings, and death. An entire community would participate in a celebration by singing, dancing, or playing instruments and the notion of a formal performance by a select few trained musicians was the exception not the rule. In the 20th century, as more people left villages for city life, folk music was supplanted with the cosmopolitan notion of music as a performance-oriented art rather than a participatory one. At the same time, musical trends from Western Europe and the United States became a part of Croatian popular culture. Nonetheless, folk music has survived in Croatia as both an independent entity as well as an integral part of much of the popular music recorded by domestic artists and heard on the radio.

Traditional music reflects regional trends, but today geography rarely limits access to even the most obscure folk music. Folk festivals are popular and one always can hear old familiar songs, previously sung by one's grandparents, on the radio. The most popular type of folk music is referred to as "tamburica," a style based on the tamburica (or tambura) ensemble. The tambura is a type of long-necked lute of South Asian origin. The Turks introduced the instrument to the Balkans in the 14th and 15th centuries, and it appeared in the Slavoinian region of Croatia by the 17th century. Initially perceived as a solo instrument, the character of the tambura was forever changed in the mid-19th century when Croatian composer Pajo Kolaric founded the first of many tamburica orchestras in the Slavonian town of Osijek. Today, tamburica groups perform throughout Croatia and range in size from trios to orchestras. The instrument has evolved into various shapes and is played in a variety of tunings. The present standard combination of the tamburica ensemble includes the following: two *bisernica* (small instruments that play the melody), two *brac* (for melodic and harmonic parts), a *bugarija* (of medium size for accompaniment in chords), and the *berde* (the largest and lowest in pitch for the bass line).[6] Although the genre is based on a specific type of instrument, most Croatians do not consider tamburica as strictly

Folk dancers performing on an outdoor stage in Split. (Courtesy of the author.)

instrumental music. Love, village life, and humor are the main lyrical themes of this genre with *becarac,* a style that originated in Slavonia, being one of the most distinctive. *Becarci* (the plural form) are bawdy drinking songs, sung primarily by men in a teasing humorous manner that leaves lots of room for improvisation.

Although most types of folk music are readily available throughout Croatia, to make sense of the variety of styles and instrumentation beyond the typical tamburica orchestra, one must explore the regional origins of the music.

Love is a common theme of the folk music of the northern Pordavina and Medimurje regions, which typically combines the tamburica with violin, zither, and hammered dulcimer (also known as a cimbalom). The music from Medimurje is particularly melancholy and has been incorporated into Croatian ethno-pop music that is heard throughout the country today. Brass bands are part of the traditional culture of this region and still perform at major civic events as well as large weddings and funerals.

The traditional music of the Zagorje region includes small bands that feature violins, hammered dulcimer, tamburica, and accordion. Although Zagorje has a rich melodic tradition, the happier tunes in major keys are the most popular in Croatia today. During the 19th and early 20th century, a *gusle,* a type of fiddle with only one or two strings, was employed instead of the standard violin, and the *mih,* a type of bagpipe, also was common. These instruments rarely are heard in popular music, yet they are worth exploring because of their uniqueness and important role in traditional music of Croatia and south-central Europe.

The *gusle* has become a symbol of folk culture in Croatia. Like the tambura, it has a long history in the Balkans, probably coming from Asia as early as the eighth century. Throughout south-central Europe, one can find various types of *gusle* and, not surprisingly even in Croatia, the instrument is not standardized. It is difficult to master and creates a sharp distinctive sound that sets it apart from any sort of fiddle commonly heard in popular music. It is not a solo instrument, but rather is used to accompany a singer of epic folk ballads.

One of the most unusual indigenous instruments is the simple Croatian version of the bagpipe called a *mih* (also known as a *mjeh, mjesina, dude,* or *diple*). The bag usually is made of goat or sheep skin and the instrument includes a *kanela* or *dulca* through which air is blown, along with a single

Musician playing a *mih* (also known as a *dude*), a traditional bagpipe. (Courtesy of the author.)

or double (and rarely a triple) chanter that is used to create the melody. The chanter is often the most decorative part of the instrument as it is made out of wood and is covered with carvings, including traditional patterns, animals, and human figures. Unlike the bagpipes of Scottish origin frequently heard in the United States, the *mih* does not have a drone, so the overall sound is thinner and sharper than what most Americans have come to expect. The sounds created by this instrument vary: *mih* are handmade so each one sounds a little different to begin with, and the individual players who each have their own style create even more variation.

These instruments fell out of favor for most of the 20th century, but now are reappearing with the renewed interest in Croatian national identity and traditions. Wooden flutes, including *zvegla* or the *frula* (duct flute) and the *dvojnice* or *dvojke* (double duct flute), commonly were found in central Croatia. For decades, they primarily were sold as souvenirs that were decorated with traditional patterns or carved in the shapes of animals. The double-reed *rozenica* (or *sopila*) is similar to the shawm found in the Middle East as well as many other European countries and is still in use in Istria. The sound of this instrument is raw and powerful, and it usually is played in pairs.

The uniqueness of these traditional instruments is matched by the folk singing that originated in the rural Dalmatian hinterland (as well as Bosnia and Herzegovina). *Ganga*,[7] a type of solo singing initially associated with the lone traveler, took place in both Christian and Muslim communities. *Ganga* usually begins with one singer who is joined by others in a dissonant wail. The proper effect is created by at least two people singing in neighboring notes—for example, one might sing in C, while the other in B. The result is a sound that is extremely loose and emotional, which is surprising because the musical form is rather rigid. Both men and women perform *ganga*, but they do so separately. The text of *gangas* are sometimes improvised and usually stress regional identity, which, in the years since the Homeland War, also can carry a political connotation.

Guslari, as singers of epic poems and narrative ballads are known, also build on a tradition that originated in the Dalmatian hinterland and parts of Bosnia and Herzegovina. The tradition dates back to the 18th century at least, when Andrija Kacic Miosic's epic poem "A Pleasant Discourse about the Slavic People" (*Razgovor ugodni naroda slovinskog*) was memorized and sung by the largely illiterate population of the region. This type of folk singing is similar to *ganga* in that it has a narrow tonal range, but the *guslar* accompanies himself with a single- or double-stringed *gusle*. *Guslari* generally are held in high esteem by their community in part due to the fact that the songs they perform are long and often demand total concentration. The esteem of the *guslar* is further enhanced by his subject matter, which glorifies historic outlaws and rebels dating back to the days of Turkish invasions. More recently, *guslari* have found their inspiration in the form of heroes of the Homeland War.

In the past fifty years, *klapa* singing has become especially popular along the Dalmatian coast. The origin of this a cappella singing style, which resembles the traditional American barbershop quartet, typically is traced to the 1960s when *klapa* was first formally recognized in festivals and theater performances. However, some ethnomusicologists view formal *klapa* groups as the product of several converging influences, most of which precede the mid-20th century. The most obvious inspiration is simply spontaneous singing "for fun," a common practice in Dalmatia for celebrations or just an afternoon at the local tavern. This was coupled with the creation of folk choirs, various traditional singing groups, and tamburica orchestras that became particularly popular in the 19th century in response to the nationalistic consciousness associated with the Illyrian movement.[8] Some 21st-century *klapa* songs are modified versions of tunes originating during this era, which reminds us that *klapa*, like most folk art, evolves according to the tastes of the local population. Sacred music is also cited as an important influence, especially when hymns heard in church were sung with new secular lyrics. Other influences include Italian or Mediterranean melodies, songs from the Croatian interior, older traditional Dalmatian songs, and Croatian pop songs that are modified and sung in the *klapa* style. The theme of love predominates the repertoire although home, family, and the beautiful Adriatic also are popular. Many compelling songs have been written about the homesickness of sailors and immigrants who were forced to leave impoverished parts of coastal Dalmatia in search of a better life in Latin America or the United States.

In the 1960s, only men's *klapa* groups performed publicly, but female groups became increasingly popular in the 1970s. The typical *klapa* group includes two tenors, a baritone, and a bass for men and a similar vocal combination for female groups (mixed gender groups do not exist, yet). The melodic line of the first tenor is followed by a parallel melody in thirds below. Harmony and melody dominate *klapa* with less emphasis on rhythm. The size of a *klapa* group can vary, but most festivals limit the number of performers to eight. Many *klapa* festivals are held in Croatia, but the largest is held for several weeks every summer in the Dalmatian town of Omis, the location of the first festival in 1967. Today this event is a major attraction for tourists and locals alike and features performances throughout the town's plazas and churches.

Folk music usually inspires dancing. Croatia has a wide variety of traditional dance styles, but the *kolo*, or closed-circle dance, is the most popular and is performed at weddings and other celebrations, with guests spontaneously joining hands and dancing after a few drinks. Many variations of the *kolo* exist and the steps can be quite complicated, but the common versions are simple enough for the uninitiated to learn on the spot. With music performed by a tamburica orchestra, the dancers often sing, occasionally improvising lyrics as their mood and the circumstances inspire them. In northern regions of the country, the *kolo* dancers were accompanied by the singing of ballads, but this tradition faded by the early 20th century as couple dances, including the *polka*, became more popular.

The most unusual folk dance is the *drmes*, which traditionally is associated with the region around Zagreb and is rarely seen outside of formal performances by folklore groups. Usually danced in couples or small circular groups, the *drmes* is distinguished by the shaking of one's entire body. Another unique folkdance that originated in the Dalmatian hinterland is the *nijemo kolo,* or the mute *kolo* dance, which is performed without any musical accompaniment. The dancers create a rhythmic stomping, which is enhanced by the rattling of the coins that decorate their costumes. *Nijemo kolo* is quite memorable and dramatic, but like the *drmes,* it usually is performed by folklore groups and is not often seen at family or community celebrations.

LADO, Croatia's state-sponsored professional folklore group, relies on the talents of gifted musicians, singers, and dancers as well as the folklore experts who contribute to choreography, music, staging, and costuming. With a repertoire containing more than 100 choreographed dances as well as hundreds of vocal and instrumental works, the group has toured around the world and won numerous awards. Members of LADO's troupe are multitalented: the dancers also perform as a choir and the musicians play more than 40 different folk instruments. The company also boasts an exceptionally rich collection of folk costumes. Performances have been called "museum-like" with respect to the authenticity of the dancers' and musicians' clothing and accessories. The troupe emphasizes the preservation of traditional culture and does not attempt to fuse folk with contemporary trends in music or dance.

LADO was founded in 1949, but the performance of folk music outside of its traditional context dates back to the 19th-century Illyrian movement and the nationalism it inspired in the face of the Austro-Hungarian government. The notion of folk culture as a symbol of Croatian identity extended throughout the 20th century into the 21st century, as festivals have become a permanent fixture on the cultural scene. Today, more than 600 amateur folklore groups perform across Croatia, which, like LADO, include musicians, dancers, and singers, many of whom perform in their own costumes that have been handed down from generation to generation.

During the latter half of the 20th century, pop versions of folk songs were heard on Yugoslav radio along with so-called new folk songs, most of which originated in Serbia or Macedonia. Since the Homeland War, Croatians have gravitated toward music that clearly reflects their regional customs. While traditional music accounts for only about 10 percent of the Croatian recording industry's output, one can always hear folk-influenced songs on the radio. Many younger pop bands have reinterpreted traditional songs and melodies and incorporated these sounds into new contemporary recordings.

Musician and songwriter Miroslav Evacic has created some of the most interesting folk-inspired recordings in recent years. Growing up in Tito's Yugoslavia, Evacic's influences were an eclectic mix, listening to everything from ethno (traditional folk) music, to the rock and blues of Muddy Waters, Jimi Hendrix, the Beatles, Serbian guitarist Radomir Mihajlovic, and Goran Bregoni of *Bielo Dugne* (White Button). Proficient on guitar and the *prim* (soprano tamburica) Miroslav soon joined a folkloric band composed of 10 musicians with between 10 and 29 singers and dancers. The group was something of a traveling cultural emissary, playing folk music in Yugoslavia and Germany. While part of the ensemble, Evacic met his future wife, Gordana, a

Gordana and Miroslav Evacic play cimbalom and prim. (Courtesy of John Kruth.)

dancer who also played guitar and accordion but soon would become known for her powerful voice and virtuosity on the cimbalom (Eastern European hammered dulcimer). Although played by Hungarian Gypsies, the instrument was all but extinct in Croatia, and Gordana soon became its greatest proponent.

Inspired by the Podravina-based singer, bassist, and bandleader Blaz Lenger (1919–2006), the Evacics concocted an exotic cocktail of blues and ethno melodies they call *Cardas* (pronounced Chardash) blues, which they continue to perform and record together across Croatia.

POP MUSIC

Croatian popular music reflects a mix of traditional and contemporary influences. Most pop artists have made folk-oriented recordings at some point in their careers and have blended traditional instrumentation in their otherwise conventional easy-listening or rock-based repertoire. Certainly, popular musical styles reflect American and Western European influences, but the accordion, tamburica, and mandolin are heard in Croatian pop and remind us that folk traditions are deeply rooted in contemporary Croatian culture.

As in the rest of Europe, the biggest influence on popular music came from the United States. As early as the 1930s, American jazz in the form of big bands led by the likes of Benny Goodman or Duke Ellington could be heard on the radio. Yugoslavia was never as closed to Western influences as Soviet bloc countries and eventually crooners began striking a Sinatra-like pose and, by the early 1970s, Yugoslavia had its own rock stars. Ivo Robic (1923–2000) is remembered as one of Croatia's pop pioneers. He recorded his first album in 1949 for Jugoton, the newly established Yugoslav State record company and went on to perform throughout Europe and the United States, even appearing on the *Ed Sullivan Show*. Robic's biggest hit, a German song called "Morgen" was recorded in 1959 and had a distinctively American feel. From the saxophone solo to the backup vocals, it was reminiscent of Pat Boone's repertoire from the same period. If only the lyrics had been in English, the song would have fit into the rotation of any major U.S. pop radio station. Robic also has recorded in French, Italian, Spanish, and English as well as his native Croatian.

Many Yugoslavian pop artists performed in several other languages and made a serious effort to establish themselves in more commercially rewarding markets outside of their native land. One of the most successful is Tereza Ana Kesovija (1938–), a beloved diva of Croatian popular music, who has lived in Paris since 1965. Her discography includes releases in Croatian,

French, Italian, Slovenian, Russian, English, Spanish, Portuguese, and German, including 12 releases for Columbia Records. In 1999, she received the Chevalier des Arts et des Lettres, an award given by the French government to citizens who have "significantly contributed to the enrichment of the French cultural inheritance."

In the 1960s and 1970s, Croatian pop music followed an American easy-listening model, and singers did their utmost to create an image that matched the smooth contemporary sounds they heard on albums from the United States and the United Kingdom. While the recordings made in the former Yugoslavia never matched American production values, several artists from this era made a lasting impact on Croatian music and popular culture. Dalmatian singer Miso Kovac (1941–), a legend throughout the former Yugoslavia as well as in Croatia, mastered the art of image and the popular song. Kovac's first hits date back to the mid-1960s when he sold up to half a million copies of songs like "I Will Never Return" (*"Vise se Nece Vratiti"*) and "The Dawn Will Cry" (*"Proplakat se Zora"*), the sort of emotional tunes upon which he would build his career. Known for his fashionable suits, thick shoulder-length hair, and moustache, Kovac looked the part of an international pop star. In the early 1970s, he married a beauty queen and remained in the public eye with a continuous series of sold-out concerts, prestigious awards, and chart-topping hit songs. His song "Dalmatia in My Eyes" (*"Dalmacija u mom oku"*) draws on traditional folk melodies and Dalmatians' love of the sea to create a tune that is especially popular along the coast. Although he held a series of farewell concerts to celebrate his retirement in the early 1990s, Kovac continues to record and perform. He has maintained his trademark look, and in spite of a number of personal tragedies, including a failed suicide attempt, he remains one of the greatest legends of Croatian pop music.

Oliver Dragojevic (1947–) is another Dalmatian-born singer who has achieved legendary status. He first made his mark on the Yugoslav music scene in 1967 with the song "*Picaferaj*," but his career took off after his 1975 performance at the Split Summer Festival when he sang "Seagull and I" (*"Galeb i ja"*), which would become one of his trademark hits. Simply known as Oliver, he has performed and recorded consistently since the mid-1960s and is a household name throughout Croatia, but is especially beloved in Dalmatia. In 1994, he won a Porin Award (the Croatian music industry's version of a Grammy Award) for song of the year and in 1997 he won album of the year for a live recording of a concert in Zagreb's Lisinski Concert Hall. The influence of traditional Dalmatian melodies is apparent in his repertoire, but his performance style is reminiscent of that of American folk singers. Oliver's delivery is simple and unaffected and he often is pictured with an acoustic guitar. In 2008, he performed at Carnegie Hall in New York City and has scheduled a concert in London's Royal Albert Hall for 2010.

Like Miso Kovac and Oliver Dragojevic, Arsen Dedic (1938) is also a pop legend, and like his two generational counterparts, he initially established himself through a series of successful festival performances in the1960s. His compositions were influenced by Dalmatian folk tunes, although many of his recordings have a "soft adult contemporary" sound. To his credit, Dedic manages to transcend the pitfalls of this genre by creating elegant recordings that are neither overly emotional nor generic in their production. He is compared to French chanson singers, such as Jacques Brel, although many Americans might hear a bit of Neil Diamond in Arsen Dedic. Also a respected author, Dedic has published several popular books of his own poetry and has set the poems of famed 20th-century Croatian author Tin Ujevic to music. In spite of a serious battle with alcoholism, which led to a liver transplant several years ago, Dedic continues to perform and has established himself firmly as one of Croatia's most respected pop figures, while also enjoying a large following in Italy. He is married to Gabi Novak, a Croatian singer who also attained fame in the 1960s and has enjoyed a long career, culminating in several Porin Awards including one for lifetime achievement. Their son, Matija Dedic, is a well-known Croatian jazz musician.

During the 1960s, Yugoslavia distinguished itself from the rest of Eastern Europe by allowing its citizens relative freedom to travel and work abroad. As a result, Yugoslav youth culture was heavily influenced by pop trends in Western Europe and the United States. Much like their American counterparts, young people wore bell-bottom pants and blue jeans, the boys grew their hair long, the girls wore short skirts, and everyone listened to rock 'n' roll. Initially, the government did not approve of this fascination with Western pop culture, but Tito, ever the pragmatist, recognized that a full-blown crackdown would create an unnecessary strain on a country already dealing with serious economic and ethnic problems. Instead, the government approved and sometimes sponsored rock festivals, featuring Yugoslav bands and attracting fans from every corner of the country.[9] Such festivals were not political events per se, but they did exemplify the government ideology of "brotherhood and unity." Years later, after the country was divided by the Homeland War, rock musicians were among the first to defy nationalist tendencies and to bridge the ethnic divide that had been deepened by several years of violence.

A short tour of Croatian music Web sites illustrates the popularity and nostalgia for rock music and for the explosion of homegrown rock bands in the 1960s, 1970s, and 1980s. For example, the Web site Barikada.com provides a particularly detailed history of rock music in the town of

Koprivnica (population 25,776), located in the agricultural Podravina region near the Hungarian border. Although this relatively obscure town always had a strong musical tradition, the number of rock bands founded here is impressive, and worth briefly exploring as a case study of the evolution of rock music throughout Croatia (and the former Yugoslavia).

The influence of American and British rock was evident from the early 1960s and in the subsequent decades Koprivnica's music scene routinely reinterpreted songs and pop trends that came from abroad. In the 1960s, rock was rarely heard on domestic radio and albums were scarce and expensive. However, Yugoslavs traveled more than their fellow Eastern Europeans and consistently brought artifacts of American popular culture back home, including all sorts of recorded music. Thus, it is not entirely surprising that live rock music hit Koprivnica in 1963 with a band called *Abecesi* that played Elvis Presley and Duane Eddy covers. Although quality electric guitars were hard to find, by the late 1960s more and more young people in Koprivnica (and elsewhere in Yugoslavia) began forming their own bands. This initial generation of musicians and rock aficionados introduced younger siblings and friends to the music, creating an ever-expanding audience for the sounds that would have a permanent place in youth culture.

By the 1970s, young people in Koprivnica were listening to imported rock 'n' roll, playing in bands with English names like Quartet Panonia, and reacting to the early sounds of heavy metal with their own metal–influenced bands like *Nervni slom* (Nervous Breakdown). On the other side of the sonic spectrum, Koprivnica even had its own 1970s version of an acoustic protest rock band called *Prozor* (Window). It is unlikely that the censorship of the day allowed musicians to address specific grievances and *Prozor* probably was limited to Bob Dylan covers. While most local bands were limited to live performances, some did produce records. *Kap na Kap* (Drop by Drop, 1973–1976) and *Cmok* (Kiss, 1978–1989) were two of Koprivnica's most commercially successful rock bands, having at least one album and several singles to their credit. By the 1980s, the music scene in Koprivnica was diverse enough to support a popular dance band called E.T., a punk-influenced rock band called *Crni leptiri* (Black Butterflies) and the Lynyrd Skynyrd–inspired B. Pokus blues band. The popular teen new wave group *Fakini* (The Rascals, 1983–1985); the first death metal band in Koprivnica, Exploder (1983–1999); and the hardcore group called Overflow rounded out the scene. Overflow influenced the next generation of rockers who were decidedly passionate about punk and hardcore sounds. The local scene featured bands like Ganja (1995–1999) a death metal band; Hailstone (since 2004), a grunge punk band; and one cannot forget Bag of Assholes (2000–2001), also a death metal band. With this sort of constant passion and creative energy taking place in a small city, one can imagine the impact of rock music across the former Yugo-slavia and Croatia. Although recording budgets were small and relatively few albums were made, especially by current standards, rock music did permeate youth culture and Croatia produced a number of classic rock acts, which are still part of the contemporary consciousness.

During the 1960s, Croatian rock bands *Delfini* (the Dolphins), *Roboti* (the Robots), and *Cerveni Koralji* (Red Coral) achieved domestic fame while tak-ing their cues from bands like the Beatles, the Rolling Stones, the Animals, the Kinks, and the Byrds. Bob Dylan inspired an acoustic folk rock sound, which was adopted by Ivica Percl, the lead singer of *Roboti* who began a solo career playing in this style. Jospia Lisac (1950–) was the predominant female artist of the era who is still considered one of Croatia's most important pop acts. Her first solo album, recorded in 1973, *Dnevnik jedne ljubavi* (*Diary of One Love*) is considered a classic. Many of the songs on this album were writ-ten by her husband, Karlo Metikos, a pop star in his own right who lived in Paris during the early 1960s and toured under the pseudonym Matt Collins. Lisac continues to perform and has released more than 20 albums, the most recent being the 2009 *Zivim po svome* (*I Live According to My Own Rules*).

Rock diversified in the 1970s and so did the Croatian scene. By the 1970s, bands like Genesis, Yes, and Pink Floyd had defined a progressive rock (prog rock) sound that inspired Croatian musician Adolf Dado Topic to form Time, a band also remembered for its new jazz-rock fusion. *Atomsko Skloniste* (Atomic Shelter) is another unusual yet memorable group from the 1970s. Founded in 1977, when proto-punk bands like Television and the Ramones were playing at CBGB, the legendary New York City rock club, *Atom-sko Skloniste*'s sound was described as "hippie punk." The band's name was inspired by an antiwar play by poet Bosko Obradovic who also wrote many of the band's lyrics; ultimately, however, the band's overall sound was too esoteric for most of the mainstream audience. *Atomsko Skloniste* did develop a dedicated following and the band is remembered as a cult and critical favorite. Before the band broke up in 1992, the members exhibited their pacifist phi-losophy by becoming one of the few Croatian acts to perform in Serbia dur-ing the Homeland War. Both Time and *Atomsko Skloniste* perform reunion concerts for special occasions.

Of the bands formed in the 1970s, *Prljavo Kazaliste* (Dirty Theater) is one of the most famous today, and while their sound and lineup has changed, they continue to maintain a dedicated fan base. Originally inspired by the Rolling Stones and punk rock, they created an intense, energetic sound and their first recordings were featured on punk compilation albums that included cutting-edge bands from the former Yugoslavia, including the now legendary *Paraf* from Rijeka and the Slovenian band *Pankrti* (the Bastards).

Prljavo Kazaliste's self-titled debut album released in 1979 featured their logo, a punk homage to the Rolling Stones and a variation of the famous tongue-and-lips icon with a safety pin through the cheek and the tongue sliced into three parts. By the time *Prljavo Kazaliste* released its second album, *Crni bijeli svijet* (Black and White World), in 1980, the band's sound had mellowed to reflect the new wave and ska dance sensibility that was spreading throughout the United States and Europe. The band still tours and records, although their punk roots have all but disappeared behind the sentimental but tasteful ballads that the group and their fans favor.

Given the Croatians' love of rock, it comes as no surprise that by the late 1970s Yugoslavia, and by extension Croatia, had a vibrant punk scene. Open to Western influences, bands such as the Sex Pistols, the Ramones, the Clash, and the Buzzcocks were soon familiar to Yugoslav youth. That punk required relatively little musical skill and only basic equipment probably contributed to its popularity as did the fact that it was a musical genre born from frustration with the status quo. While the Yugoslav post-hippie generation may have enjoyed a better standard of living than their parents, they still had reason to feel disaffected. Ethnic tensions were constantly brewing below the surface, the threat of censorship loomed, and good jobs were hard to find. As with the advent of rock years earlier, the government did not approve of punk but did not suppress it either. As a result, Yugolavia was the first Eastern European country with a real punk scene.

Slovenia had the most vibrant punk scene in the former Yugoslavia but Croatia also made a notable contribution. *Paraf,* an early punk band founded by three teenagers from Rijeka in 1976, represented the Croatian punk mentality well. In the tradition of the Ramones, *Paraf* and their fellow punk rockers never took themselves too seriously. *Paraf*'s first album was titled *A dan je tako lijepo poceo* (*But the Day Started So Good . . .*) and was packed with humorous, suggestive lyrics. Their most famous track bears the ironic title "*Narodna pjesma*" ("Folk Song") and was included in the classic 1980 compilation album *Novi Punk Val* (*New Punk Wave*) released by the Slovenian label ZKP RTLJ. Also included on the album was a cut by *KUD Idijoti* (Society of Culture and Arts Idiots), a band that intentionally misspelled its name (*Idijoti* should be *Idioti*). Since its inception, the group, originally from Pula, has maintained a driving rock sound and an irreverent sense of humor. Although most punk bands from the early days of the genre have since broken up, *KUD Idijoti* still performs a repertoire worthy of New York City's famous (but closed as of 2006) venue CBGB. They have made at least 18 albums and, in spite of the fact that the band's members hold day jobs, *KUD Idijoti*'s performances retain the intensity and attitude of the early days.

Over the years, punk has merged with metal and, although purists may argue which category a particular group belongs to, it is fair to say that *KUD Idijoti* and newer bands like the relatively young *Debala Glava* (Fat Head) and the well-established *Hlado Pivo* (Cold Beer) straddle punk and metal genres in their performance and recording histories. As for absurdity and shock value, *Let 3,* a band from Rijeka, stands alone. Musically, the group draws from new wave, punk, and classic rock (including obvious Led Zeppelin references) to create an eclectic repertoire. The band's live shows are provocative and, according to its Wikipedia page, they have performed clad only in muzzles covering their penises. In 2000, *Let 3* staged a mock suicide in the middle of Ban Jelacic Square in Zagreb and repeatedly have satirized the political leadership and the ethnic allegiances that so many Croatians hold dear. In a feeble attempt to crack down on the band's irreverent tendencies, the authorities accused the members of *Let 3* of moral indecency during a 2006 open-air concert performance that included public nudity. Since the penalty was reportedly only 350 kuna per person (about €50 or $65), the enforcement action resulted in more publicity for the band rather than any real punishment.

Thompson, Croatia's most contentious rock act, has managed to elicit both love and hate, inside and outside of the country. Marko Perkovic (1966–) is the lead singer of the band who has been associated, fairly or not, with the extreme right-wing neo-Nazi politics that originated with the Ustashe movement during World War II. Perkovic was born in the town of Cavoglave, which was on the front lines of Serbian and Croatian conflict during the Homeland War. Like most Croatian men from this area, he joined the military where he acquired the nickname Thompson, derived from the old American-made submachine guns he and his battalion used. In 1991, Perkovic first gained fame because of his song "The Cavoglave Battalion" ("*Bojna Cavoglave*"), an anthemic number dedicated to the defense of Croatian territory against Serbian aggression. At the time, Perkovic was not a professional singer nor did he have a band, but the song appealed to the patriotic sentiments of a country beset by war. The controversy arose because the first lines of the song, "*Za dom – spremni!*" ("For the homeland, be prepared [to fight]!") was the popular salute used by the Ustashe, the Nazi puppet government that was defeated by the Partisans during World War II. In spite of the popular new context of the lyrics, any association with the Ustashe was bound to create problems.

While Thompson (Perkovic is now identified by his stage name, which is also the name of his band) recorded many apolitical songs, his career has been filled with controversy, some self-generated, some generated by his fiercely nationalistic right-wing fans. For example, in 2000 when a leftist government was elected, Thompson publicly and repeatedly made disparaging remarks about the new prime minister, Ivica Racan, and about President Stipe Mesic. In his 2002 concert before an audience of 40,000 in Split, he reserved seats for Gen. Mirko Norac, a Croatian war criminal on trial at the time (and later convicted), and Gen. Ante Gotovina, then a fugitive wanted by the ITCY (International Criminal Tribunal for the former Yugoslavia). At the same concert, just before Thompson's appearance on stage, the audience began singing a well-known Ustashe anthem, *"Evo zore, evo dana"* ("Here Comes the Dawn, Here Comes the Day").

In spite of the disturbing connotations of this and similar events, Thompson remains one of Croatia's top-selling artists, with his 2006 album, *Bilo jednom u Hrvatskoj* (*Once upon a Time in Croatia*) selling approximately 100,000 copies. The band's heavy metal sound has an appeal to a younger generation who may not be sensitive to or aware of the political connotations of the "U" (for Ustashe) that they wear on black t-shirts. Thompson, meanwhile, is a self-described patriot who has stated that he is inspired by God, family, and homeland and does not harbor any neo-Nazi sympathies or encourage fans to wear Ustashe uniforms to his concerts or raise their right arm in a fascist salute. Any Nazi connotations found in his music or performances were dismissed as "just teenage rebellion" by his manager, Albino Ursic, in a 2007 *New York Times* article[10] preceding a scheduled appearance in New York City. Thompson's supporters have argued that few fans actually display Usashe or Nazi iconography, but these claims have not quelled opposition to his appearances in New York, Australia, Canada, the Netherlands, and Germany. In recent years, he has tried to tone down his image and regularly records and performs songs that fall into the category of Christian rock. Whether one considers Thompson (Marko Perkovic) an anti-Semite or a Croatian patriot, the controversy has kept the band in the news, and does not appear to have a negative commercial impact as Thompson's recordings continue to sell and fans keep buying concert tickets.

Damir Urban (1968–) is another famous Croatian rocker who has courted controversy, although not of a political nature. Emerging in the late 1980s as the vocalist and creative force behind the popular early 1990s band Laufer, Urban has since enjoyed a successful career as a solo artist with his band, Urban & 4. His first album, *Otrovna Kiša* (*Poison Rain*, 1996), was both a critical and commercial success, topped only by his 1998 album, *Zena dijete* (*Woman Child*), which has been called the best Croatian rock album of the decade. His sound can be described as straight-ahead rock, reminiscent of the Irish band U2, although his repertoire certainly includes lighter pop material. Urban's first brush with controversy dates to the late 1990s video for his song *"Moja,"* which includes a violent depiction of a homosexual male encounter followed by a far more graceful lesbian scene performed to the sounds of Matija Dedic's jazz piano. Music took a back seat to the powerful and sometimes disturbing visuals, and the video was promptly banned from Croatian television. In 2004, Urban released *Retro*, an album that deals with infidelity—perhaps in reference to the dissolution of his own marriage and his devotion to a new girlfriend. This, at least, was the conjecture among many fans who viewed the album with skepticism, but purchased it anyway. Urban has toured internationally, including a 2005 performance at the rock club CBGB in New York City.

Pop music is alive and well with a younger generation of performers following in the footsteps of artists like Oliver Dragojevic and Arsen Dedic. Zlatan Stipisic Gibonni (1968–) is a household name in Croatia and popular throughout the Balkans. Known simply as Gibonni, the performer's first brush with fame came as a songwriter having penned Oliver Dragojevic's hit, "*Cesarica.*" His good looks and stage performance helped launch his solo career that now spans 14 albums, the most recent being the 2010 *Toleranca* (Tolerance), which includes performances by Damir Urban and Brooklyn Rapper Masta Ace. Throughout his career, Gibonni has employed elements of folk, recording traditional Dalmatian songs early on, although his most recent recordings have relied on generic rock production reminiscent of the 1970's California pop band, the Eagles. Tony Cetinski (1969) is another pop favorite whose popularity extends throughout the former Yugoslavia. His smooth rock sound encompasses 10 albums made between 1990 and 2008, and his 2009 concerts in Zagreb attracted more than 30,000 fans.

On the racier side, pop singer Severina Vuckovic (1972) has entertained Croatians with a string of hit songs and scandal. She established herself as a pop icon in the 1990s but the controversy generated by her 2004 recording, "*Moja Stikla*" ("My Stiletto"), which was Croatia's entry in the 2006 Euro Vision Song Contest, illustrates the narrow definition of cultural acceptability that still persists in certain academic circles. Several scholars, along with a segment of the public, claimed that the song was "too Serbian" leading to a temporary backlash against "*Moja Stikla*" and Severina (she is known by her first name only). Cowritten by Croatian pop singer Boris Novkovic, the song also drew from Croatian folk influences, including the *ganga* singing style of the Dalmatian hinterland. Prominent Croatian ethnomusicologists managed to quell the controversy by identifying this connection, and perhaps indirectly illustrating the similarities (rather than accentuating the differences) between Croatian and Serbian cultural traditions.

But this was only one episode in Severina's controversial career. In 2004, she was the focus of a sex scandal that put her in the international spotlight. Much to the singer's shock and dismay, a private sex tape featuring herself along with married businessman Milan Lucic surfaced on the Internet. The tape stunned her fans throughout the former Yugoslavia, especially since Severina presented herself as a devout Catholic and vocal promoter of abstinence. Somewhat predictably, the scandal only boosted her career by introducing her to a wider audience. She continued to court controversy with her 10th album, *Zdravo Marijo* (*Hail Mary*), largely written by famed Serbian musician and composer Goran Bregovic. The album was criticized for resembling Serbian turbo-folk, a genre that accents pop production with folk elements but that is associated with right-wing Serbian political sensibilities. Severina further irritated the more conservative elements of society by being pictured in a tight T-shirt featuring an image of the Virgin Mary. None of this dampened her popularity, and she has firmly established her status as Croatia's top female pop icon.

By the 1990s, rap and hip-hop appeared on the Croatian scene in the form of bands like the Ugly Leaders, Tram 11, and *Bolesna Braca* (Sick Brothers). Although most of these groups remained part of a youth subculture, The Beat Fleet (also known as TBF), and their eclectic and often humorous mix of rap, rock, and reggae has become part of mainstream pop culture. For a more straightforward rap and hip-hop sound, one can turn to Shorty (born Dalibor Bartulovic, 1980). In 1999, he began to make a name for himself by free-styling on a local radio show in his hometown of Vinkovce. In 2004 he released his debut album, *1,68*, which made him one of the foremost names in Croatian rap and hip-hop. His song "*Dodi u Vinkovce*" ("Come to Vinkovic") captures the essence of Croatian rap in that he identifies with his hometown, an ethnically mixed industrial city that was heavily affected by the Homeland War, by rapping over traditional Slavonian music.

The focus of this section has been on domestic artists, but the Croatian music scene always has extended beyond its own borders. American artists are especially popular, and over the years, acts ranging from Bob Dylan and Leonard Cohen to the Backstreet Boys and Beyoncé have performed in Zagreb before sold-out arenas. Perhaps even more significantly, after the Homeland War, Croatians continued listening to performers from the other Yugoslav states. Although some artists such as Thompson took a hard-line nationalist stance, many other musicians from the former Yugoslavia transcended politics to retain their prewar (now international) audience. This was not only a gesture of goodwill, but also an economic necessity. As individual countries, the states of the former Yugoslavia were too small to create a viable market for most domestic bands and, as described, Croatia's biggest pop stars have built a fan base well beyond their own country. Nor did Croatian audiences forsake their favorite Serbian performers after the Homeland War. Writing about Serbian culture in postwar Croatia, Gordana Crnkovic describes a 1998 concert by the Serbian ballad singer Dorde Balasevic that took place in Ljubljana, Slovenia.[11] The audience was full of Croats, most of whom traveled a considerable distance to hear Balasevic and to sing along to his litany of hits spanning two decades. Ironically, at the time of the concert, Balasevic's recordings were not available in Croatian record shops because Tudjman's ultranationalist government had encouraged the removal of items representing Serbian culture. Crnkovic notes that while it is easy to remove foreign—and in this case, politically incorrect—cultural influences, it is much harder to find a suitable domestic replacement. And besides, Croatia and Serbia have many cultural similarities, making Balasevic's music, for example, much more accessible than that of other European artists whom the government of the 1990s found acceptable. Generally, artists have been at the forefront of the reconciliation between Serbia and Croatia. Although the memories of war still persist, popular music has successfully forged a cultural exchange between Serbia and Croatia, leading the way to peaceful coexistence.

NOTES

1. *Grove Music Online*, s.v. "Lisinski, Vatroslav" (by Lovro Zupanovic), Oxford Music Online, http://www.oxfordmusiconline.com/subscriber/article/grove/music/16756 (accessed September 18, 2010).

2. Ibid.

3. "Stanko Horvat, Fellow of the Croatian Academy of Sciences and Arts," Croatian Academy of Arts and Sciences, 2007, http://info.hazu.hr/stanko_horvat_en_biography (retrieved May 15, 2010). The academy Web site has extensive biographical information on current and deceased members, including many of the composers mentioned in this chapter.

4. This quote is from *Sound Labyrinths*, a book by Milko Kelemen that is no longer in print nor available in English. The quote appears in the biography of Kelemen that is published on the Sikorsky Music Publishers Web site as a one-page PDF titled "Milko Kelemen Biography" at http://media.sikorski.de/media/files/1/12/190/241/308/1178/kelemen_milko_biography.pdf (retrieved May 17, 2010).

5. For a good, succinct overview of Croatian contemporary classical music, see William A. Everett, "Contemporary Music in Croatia, Traditions and Innovations," *Central European Review* 2, no. 19 (May 15, 2000), http://www.ce-review.org/00/19/everett19.html (retrieved May 17, 2010).

6. Grove Music Online, s.v. "Croatia" (by Stanislav Tuksar and Grozdana Marosevic), Oxford Music Online, May 4, 2010, http://www.oxfordmusiconline.com/subscriber/article/grove/music/40473 (retrieved May 4, 2010).

7. Ankica Petrovic, "Ganga, a Form of Traditional Rural Singing in Yugoslavia" (unpublished PhD thesis, Queen's University of Belfast, 1977), http://www.imota.net/html/ankica_petroviae.html (retrieved May 11, 2010).

8. Josko Caleta, "Klapa Singing, a Traditional Folk Phenomenon of Dalmatia," *Nar, umjet* 34, no. 1 (1997): 127–145, https://circle.ubc.ca/bitstream/handle/2429/5244/ubc_1994-0320.pdf?sequence=1 (retrieved May 11, 2010).

9. Dejdan Djokic, "Ex-Yu rock," openDemocracy.net, August 6, 2002, http://www.opendemocracy.net/arts-festival/article_546.jsp (retrieved May 20, 2010).

10. Nicolas Wood, "A Croatian Rock Star Flirts with the Nazi Past," *New York Times*, July 1, 2007.

11. Gordana P. Crnkovic, "Non-Nationalist Culture, Under and Above the Ground" in *Croatia since Independence: War, Politics, Society, Foreign Relations*, eds. Sabrina P. Ramet, Konrad Clewing, and Reneo Lukic (Munich: R. Oldenbourg Verlang, 2008).

10

Painting and Sculpture

ANCIENT ART IN A CONTEMPORARY CONTEXT

Contemporary life in Croatia is imbued with history. Just as centuries-old buildings are a vital part of Croatian culture, so too are the paintings and sculptures housed in timeworn churches and other historical structures. This section highlights the most relevant historical of works of art before moving on to a more detailed presentation of the paintings and sculpture of the last 150 years.

One of the oldest sculptures found in Croatia is the Vucedol Dove, an artifact of the Vucedol culture, which existed in the vicinity of modern-day Vukovar during the transitional period between the Neolithic and Bronze Age. Created between 2800 and 2500 BCE, scholars believe that this bird-shaped clay vessel was used in fertility rituals and perhaps represents a male partridge, a common fertility symbol of the period. The piece stands 7.7 inches (19.5 centimeters) high with several mysterious symbols engraved on its body, including three double axes and a necklace of sorts. It is covered with linear designs that appear to function simply as decoration. The relevance of this figure lies not only in its elegance and visual power but in its symbolic representation of the Vucedol culture, which was one of the most advanced civilizations in the region, having been credited by scholars with inventing one of the oldest European calendars. The figure captured the imagination of modern-day Croatians when it served as a symbol for peace in the town of

Vukovar after it was attacked brutally by Serbian forces during the Homeland War. This latter reference led to the incorporation of the Vucedol Dove into the design of the 20 kuna banknote originally issued in 1993 and then reissued in 2001.

Ancient Roman sculpture figures prominently in the history of Croatian art as well as in contemporary visual culture. By the first century BCE, the Romans settled the area around the modern-day city of Split along the Dalmatian coast, bringing with them classical art and architecture, including a number of sculptures that have made an enduring impression. Among these is a marble relief depicting a nude young man running, personifying the ancient Greek concept of "kairos," a fleeting moment of divine opportunity. This particular relief belongs to the monastery of Saint Nicholas in Trogir and has become a logo for the town to the point that copies of the relief are regularly sold to tourists in the form of plaques, postcards, T-shirts, and the like. Although the notion of kairos was adopted by Christians, it is unlikely that the popularity of this particular relief has much to do with its original meaning. Rather, it is an especially graceful and powerful image, which like the Vucedol Dove, captured the contemporary Croatian imagination.

Croatian art—as a product of the Croatian people as opposed to the Greeks, Romans, or Illyrians—began to develop in the seventh century when the Croatians first migrated into the region. The early Croats, however, were influenced by the aforementioned cultures as well as Byzantium to the east. By the ninth century, Croatians adopted Christianity and their artistic endeavors centered on ecclesiastical themes, including the production of illuminated manuscripts and both functional and decorative items for churches. Although much of this work is preserved in museums, perhaps the most common and recognizable visual theme from this period is the decorative plaitwork found on pre-Romanesque architectural reliefs. This ornamentation is similar to findings in other parts of the former Western Roman Empire and originated in ancient Greek and Roman art and architecture. In addition to the decorative abstract designs carved into the stone friezes and lintels in both Greek and Roman temples, geometric patterns, often called meander patterns, can be found on Roman floor mosaics as well as on ancient Greek vases. Scholars theorize that these designs, with their attention to proportion and composition, evolved over centuries into a pattern resembling a braid, hence the term "plaitwork."[1]

The plaitwork most commonly found in Croatia ranges from an ordinary braid composed of three long interlacing sections, to more complex geometric themes, including linked circles and knots. The extent to which plaitwork reliefs have been preserved along the Dalmatian coast is remarkable. Scholars attribute this to the fact that between the 17th and 20th centuries, the area experienced an economic decline.[2] The small pre-Romanesque churches that survived in Dalmatia would have otherwise been demolished by a wealthier society to make room for new construction. From the 7th through the 10th centuries, these geometric designs were far more commonly used in church decoration than were figurative images. This period also coincides with the earliest days of Croat identity and the establishment of the first Croatian state. For this reason, the plaitwork designs have gained popularity in the 21st century as a symbol of the rebirth of Croatia as an independent nation in the early 1990s.

The Diocletian Palace in the City of Split is one of Croatia's major tourist attractions. As mentioned earlier, tourism keeps historical art and architecture in the popular consciousness, and the details of this particular structure have attracted the attention of visitors for centuries. The palace itself is discussed in Chapter 11, Architecture and Housing. The doors of the Cathedral of Saint Duje, located at the heart of the complex, deserve mention here. The cathedral was founded in the seventh century and constructed over the Roman emperor Diocletian's mausoleum; the body had disappeared earlier, and according to legend, early Christian converts threw it into the sea. In 1214, Andrija Buvina (also known as Master Buvina) carved a 28-panel relief featuring the life of Christ from Annunciation to Resurrection for the gigantic double doors of the cathedral. With the exception of the lower panels, which were worn out over the centuries by worshipers passing through the entrance, the doors are in excellent condition and are one of the finest examples of relief sculpture in the Romanesque style.

Some of the most memorable examples of Romanesque, Gothic, and early Renaissance sculpture are integral elements of cathedral architecture along the Dalmatian coast. Radovan's Portal in the Cathedral of Saint Lawrence in Trogir and Juraj Dlamatinac's frieze of heads along the exterior of the Cathedral of Saint James in Sibenik are examples of historic sculpture that continue to fascinate scholars, tourists, and local residents.

Over the centuries, Croatian artists also produced illuminated manuscripts, wall frescoes, religious icons of note, and eventually secular portraits, all of which reflected the artistic trends in Europe at any given time. Generally, these works have not remained in the public consciousness to the same extent that the churches and other historical architectural achievements have. Since the focus of this text is contemporary culture rather than historical survey, we will skip ahead to more recent works of art and feature artists whose influence is felt in Croatia into the 21st century.

Juraj Dlamatinac's frieze of heads along the exterior of the Cathedral of Saint James in Sibenik. (Courtesy of John Kruth.)

MODERN EUROPEAN TRENDS IN CROATIAN ART

For centuries, the arts in Croatia were influenced heavily by European trends. Most Croatian artists studied and worked abroad, often in Venice, Vienna, or Paris, bringing ideas from these cultural centers back to Croatia. During the 19th century, young artists had little choice but to travel abroad since Croatia lacked any major institute of higher learning in the arts until 1907 when the Academy of Fine Arts at the University of Zagreb was founded.

Vlaho Bukovac (1855–1922) is generally considered the first modern Croatian painter to achieve recognition domestically and abroad. After finishing his studies in Paris, he went to London where he established himself as a portrait painter before returning to Zagreb in 1893. Initially, his style was greatly influenced by the impressionist work he saw in Paris, but he eventually developed a realist style with a distinct color sense and was known for the light tones of his palette and fluid brushwork. Bukovac's themes were unique as well. While his French contemporaries focused largely on modern Parisian life and the French countryside, he painted religious scenes and nudes, as well as scenes from traditional Croatian life, including figures dressed in the folk costumes that were quickly falling out of favor in cosmopolitan Zagreb.

During his four years in Zagreb, he made a lasting mark on the art scene, organizing exhibitions and initiating the construction of the Art Pavilion, which was originally designed for a millennial exhibition in Budapest.

Bukovac successfully argued that Zagreb should have its own permanent art museum. When the exhibition in Budapest was over, the pavilion was dismantled and rebuilt in Zagreb on what is now King Tomislav Square. The Zagreb Art Pavilion was the first large art museum in the region and still is one of the most important exhibition spaces in Croatia. While in Zagreb, Bukovac also founded the Zagreb Multi-Color School, which emphasized the use of lighter colors and looser brushstrokes than traditionally taught.

Bukovac was constantly at the center of a group of young artists who were interested in defining a Croatian cultural movement. One of his most famous works, *Croatian Revival,* is painted on the fire curtain at the Croatian National Theater in 1896 and features leaders of the Illyrian movement, whose focus was the creation of a pan-Slavic identity within the Austro-Hungarian Empire. This movement is sometimes referred to as the Croatian Revival because its members emphasized the importance of a standardized Croatian language and the promotion of Croatian literature and culture. Although the Illyrian movement had largely died out by the end of the 19th century, Bukovac's work still resonated with Zagreb's cultural leaders who continued to promote a Croatian, if not pan-Slavic, identity. Given Croatia's recent independence, *Croatian Revival* is more than just a historical painting; it also is a precursor to an idea that eventually became reality.

In 1897, Bukovac left Zagreb to live in Cavat, his birthplace just south of Dubrovnik, where he remained until 1903 when he was offered an assistant professorship at the Academy of Fine Arts in Prague. He became a proponent of modernist theories of painting and is credited with introducing pointillism, a style incorporating short abbreviated brush strokes, to the Academy in Prague. His work is represented in major museums and collections throughout Croatia as well as in numerous books and even on postage stamps.

Whereas Bukovac is considered the most relevant Croatian painter of the later 19th century, Ivan Rendic (1849–1932) is the sculptor with the strongest legacy. Rendic was raised on the Dalmatian island of Brac and retained an affinity for the region for his entire life. Although he was educated in Venice and lived in the Italian city of Trieste for a number of years, he took the politically risky position of openly supporting the annexation of Dalmatia (then part of Italy) with Croatia, which did little to advance his career in Italy, so he was forced to rely on commissions from Croatia. Rendic was sympathetic to the creation of a unified Croatia and the advancement of Croatian culture and, like Bukovac, was inspired by the Illyrian movement earlier in the 19th century. Working in a realistic style, Rendic is primarily remembered for his many portrait busts of culturally significant Croatians that are on display in public spaces throughout the country, including Zagreb's popular Zrinjevac Park. Not surprisingly, his subjects included Ljudevit Gaj, founder of the

Illyrian movement (see Chapter 1, Geography and History), and Ivan Gundulic, a 17th-century Croatian poet whose work greatly contributed to the standardization of the Croatian language, and who was depicted in of one of Bukovac's most famous paintings, *Gundulic's Dream*. Also of interest, although lesser known, are Rendic's mausoleums and elaborate grave markers which illustrate his compelling sense of design, incorporating art nouveau forms and elaborate mosaics. Most of his small memorial sculptures are located in the town cemetery at Supetar on the island of Brac and are included in guides for the many visitors who pass through in the summer months.

Rendic had the occasional opportunity to combine his affinity for decorative mosaics with portraiture. Such is the case with his monument to Croatian poet Andrija Kacic Miosic (1704–1760), a typical subject for Rendic as Miosic was an 18th-century Franciscan monk who wrote an epic poem reciting the history of the Slavic people called "A Pleasant Discourse about the Slavic People" (*Razgovor ugodni naroda slovinskoga*). With his use of a traditional folk form of poetry, Miosic's work became extremely popular, thereby promoting literacy and even influencing the development of the Croatian language (see Chapter 7, Literature). The statue, located in the coastal Dalmatian town of Makarska, includes a life-size sculpture of Miosic placed on a pedestal decorated with an elaborately colored mosaic. Numerous foreign tourists photograph this monument during the summer months with little knowledge of Miosic's accomplishments. They simply are attracted to the beauty of the monument with its compelling combination of Rendic's elegant monochromatic statue and vibrant mosaic.

While Rendic's legacy as a sculptor cannot be denied, his attempts at advancing the arts on an institutional level failed. Rendic spent the last 11 years of his life in Supetar, where he tried in vain to start an art academy. He exhausted his financial resources and died in poverty at the age of 82.

Rendic's successor, Ivan Mestrovic (1883–1962), is certainly Croatia's most famous artist and, almost 50 years after his death, he still is well known throughout the former Yugoslavia. Born to a poor family and raised in the Dalmatian interior, Mestrovic's early life was difficult. According to legend, he exhibited artistic tendencies at a young age, carving wood at the age of four and completing his first stone sculpture in his mid-teens. His family could not afford to send him to art school, but a display of his works at a local grocery store in Drnis brought him local fame and an apprenticeship with a stonemason in Split. By his late teens Mestrovic enrolled in Vienna's Academy of Fine Arts, where he embraced the ideals of the secessionist movement, leading him away from traditional academic realism and toward a style all his own. Throughout his long career, he carved distinctive figures, often dynamic and muscular with a fluidity characteristic of early 20th-century Viennese sculpture. His early influences are captured in his masterful sculpture *The Well of Life*. Completed in 1095 when he was still in his early 20s, the sculpture was purchased by the city of Zagreb and prominently placed before the Croatian National Theater where it remains to this day and has become a landmark.

Much of Mestrovic's work before World War I featured heroic themes from Slavic history in support of the idea, popular among young Croatian intellectuals, of a pan-Slavic state—that is, Yugoslavia, which did not yet exist. His ambitions culminated in his design for *The Vidovan Temple,* which was to include hundreds of statues of Slavic heroes. Only approximately 50 figures were ever completed, most just as plaster casts, but the design earned him first prize at the International Art Exhibition in Rome in 1911 and established his reputation in Europe. Interestingly, Mestrovic opted against including his work in the Hapsburg pavilion, even though much of Croatia was administered by Austria and he had been educated in Vienna. Instead, in an act of solidarity with the proponents of a pan-Slavic state, he exhibited under the Kingdom of Serbia. The sense of outrage among some of his Croat colleagues was symptomatic of the friction between Croats and Serbs, at least on the cultural level, but this did little to harm Mestrovic's career. He went on the exhibit his work in Paris and London and frequently was associated with the "Yugoslav Idea," which manifested itself as the Kingdom of Serbs, Croats, and Slovenes as a result of World War I.

After World War I, Mestrovic moved to Zagreb where he became a central figure in the local cultural scene and taught at the College of Arts and Crafts (later known as the Academy of Fine Arts). While his subject matter had diversified somewhat, his fascination with Slavic themes continued, inspiring him to create several monumental sculptures of historical figures that were virtually unknown to the rest of Europe. The most famous of these is the colossal statue of Grgur Ninski (Gregory of Nin, see Chapter 1, Geography and history), the 10th-century bishop who fought for the right to use the Croatian language rather than Latin in religious services. This gigantic statue (almost 25 feet high), completed in 1927, was originally placed in the middle of the peristyle in Split's Diocletian Palace in 1929 to commemorate the 1,000th anniversary of Ninski's successful efforts. During World War II, the Italian forces occupying the region removed the statue, and fortunately, opted against destroying it. After the war, it was placed outside of the palace's Golden Gate where it remains as one of Split's most distinctive landmarks. Visitors can be seen rubbing the statue's shiny big toe for good luck, a custom devoid of any known connection to local tradition or history.

Mestrovic's subject matter was not limited to historical figures. Throughout his career, he retained an interest in the female form, which he depicted as sensual but robust, elevating the stereotype of the Slavic peasant woman to one of primordial feminine energy and beauty. While his nudes are compelling, his most famous female figure is entitled *The History of the Croats,* in which he uses a strong, maternal form to represent the bedrock of Croatian culture and society. The sculpture depicts a woman clothed in simple peasant dress seated cross-legged and erect, eyes cast downward in a meditative fashion toward her hands, which rest on a tablet covered with the original Croatian Glagolitic script dating back to the ninth century. This statue is located in front of the University Rectorate in Zagreb. Copies also are found in the Mestrovic Gallery in Split and the Mestrovic Museum in Zagreb. The statue has attained iconic status, appearing on Croatian currency, and is reproduced in a souvenir-size version available in gift shops throughout the country.

Before World War II, Mestrovic engaged in a number of architectural projects, including the House of Visual Arts (1938), a distinctive circular structure with a continuous colonnade. Located in Zagreb, the building is recognized as a milestone of Croatian modern architecture. Despite its having functioned as a mosque during World War II, complete with the addition of three minarets that later were removed, the structure's basic design remains unchanged and it still stands out as one of Zagreb's most compelling 20th-century buildings. Mestrovic also designed relief sculptures for the facades of several structures in Zagreb and a stunning mausoleum for the Racic family in the Dalmatian town of Cavat. In his designs for the Church of the Most Holy Redeemer located in Otovac, his childhood home, he included a crypt for his family, thus the church is often referred to as the Mestrovic Mausoleum. Otovac saw significant fighting during the Homeland War and his relief sculptures, including portraits of the Mestrovic family, were looted. Much of the damage has since been repaired, and the church has retained its function as a monument and sacred structure. Mestrovic's familial home in Split is his best-known architectural accomplishment. The large austere structure, once known as the Mestrovic Palace, now functions as a museum where a large display of his work is on permanent view to the public.

World War II was a demarcation point in Mestrovic's life. After being imprisoned for four months by the Ustashe, he and his family left Yugoslavia for good, settling in Syracuse, New York, where he was offered a position at Syracuse University in 1946. His reputation preceded him in the United States, where his work already had been exhibited extensively since the 1920s, including a solo show at the Brooklyn Museum of Art in 1924 and a major commission for sculptures of two Native Americans called *The Bowman* and *The Spearman* (also known as *Indians*), which still reside at the entrance to Chicago's Grant Park. Having been warmly received in the United States, Mestrovic was honored with a solo exhibition at New York City's prestigious

Metropolitan Museum, marking the first time the museum had granted a solo show for a living artist.

Although he left Yugoslavia, Mestrovic's reputation as the country's foremost artist remained. He continued to accept commissions from the Yugoslav government and sent at least 50 pieces back to his homeland, but refused President Tito's offer to return. During the last 15 years of his life, he focused more closely on the biblical subjects that had always been a source of inspiration. In 1946, he created one of his most powerful pieces, *Job*, in which he distorted the human form to express a compelling combination of pathos and raw human strength. Today this piece is one of the highlights of the collection on display in his former home in Split. In 1955, Mestrovic went on to teach at Notre Dame in South Bend, Indiana, where he died in 1962.

Postimpressionist painter Emanuel Vidovic (1872–1952) was among Mestrovic's circle of friends in Split and, like Mestrovic, his work is permanently exhibited in a museum dedicated to his legacy. The Vidovic Gallery (*Galerija Vidovic*), as the museum is known, is located within the walls of the Diocletian Palace, making it an accessible destination for tourists and locals alike who are interested in viewing the work of one of Croatia's finest 20th-century painters. Like his contemporaries, Vidovic was influenced by European Postimpressionist painting, although his subject matter and color palette were distinctive. Vidovic studied abroad in Venice where he developed his dark, hazy interpretation of Adriatic towns on the verge of industrialization. The collection in the Vidovic Gallery features views of the Italian town of Chioggia, as well as Split and the neighboring town of Trogir. From a contemporary standpoint, Vidovic's work is particularly interesting as he captures locales that are primarily known today as scenic, quaint tourist attractions, but were once economically depressed and struggling to develop modern industries. Vidovic captures the futility of these efforts using his dark palette and light brushstrokes to create a perpetually foggy, oppressive, and yet enchanted atmosphere. His technique extends to paintings of church interiors and still lifes that simultaneously express the melancholy beauty of Dalmatia in an era in which poverty was common and electricity was still a luxury.

During the early years of the 20th century, Zagreb enjoyed a vibrant art scene that was fueled by the inspiration and experiences of a handful of young Croatian artists whose work remains relevant to this day. Most of these artists, after completing their studies in larger European cities such as Paris or Vienna, returned to work in Zagreb. One such group of painters, known as the Munich Circle, included Josip Racic (1885–1908) and Miroslav Kraljevic (1885–1913) both of whom studied in Munich and Paris.

They came back to Zagreb and experimented with Postimpressionist and expressionist techniques, each artist creating an influential body of work before their early deaths. Both men are credited with modernizing the course of Croatian art by replacing the staid, conservative approach of the academic art world with the more spontaneous and expressive style they found in Paris, where young artists such as Picasso and Matisse were redefining painting. Newspaper obituaries of Kraljevic and Racic name them as among the most influential artists of their generations and they are remembered as such into the 21st century. Kraljevic, in particular, has attained legendary status. His self-portrait is reproduced on posters promoting Zagreb's Modern Gallery, the city's premier museum for modern art, and one of the city's leading contemporary art gallery bears his name (*Galerija Miroslav Kraljevic*).

While creative movements elsewhere in Europe heavily influenced Zagreb's art scene, there was also a homegrown avant-garde movement. After World War I and the disintegration of the Austro-Hungarian Empire, artistic activity flourished in cities like Zagreb, which previously had been viewed as unsophisticated and irrelevant in comparison to larger cities in the Austro-Hungarian realm. In 1921, the avant-garde publication *Zenit* was founded in Zagreb and become the most important periodical of its kind in Yugoslavia (it was published in Zagreb until 1923 and then in Belgrade until 1925). At this point, most visual art produced by the domestic avant-garde was not exhibited in public museums or galleries. Like much of the European avant-garde, Croatian artists were motivated by the horrors of war and the rejection of the prevailing conventions of art and philosophy. By publishing these images, *Zenit* served as the primary means for viewing and disseminating experimental artwork both domestically and internationally. Along with local staff, the magazine established a large team of international contributors, thereby furthering its worldwide reputation. Today, remaining copies of *Zenit* offer the most important record of Croatian avant-garde art from the early 1920s as most of the actual works were lost.

Krsto Hegedusic (1901–1925) was one of the primary innovators on the Zagreb art scene in the 1930s. A painter and illustrator, he graduated from the Zagreb Academy in 1926 and continued his studies in Paris for two years, during which he was inspired by the peasant paintings of 16th-century Flemish artist Pieter Bruegel. Hegedusic's work reflected his fascination with Bruegel's unapologetic images of country life along with the surrealism he encountered in Paris and the expressive social commentary of German artist George Grosz. In 1929, Hegedusic, along with a group of artists, including the architect Drago Ibler and sculptor Antun Augustincic (1900–1979), founded the group *Zemlja* (Earth Group), which sought to liberate the arts in Croatia from dominant European trends. Their goal was to create work that was not isolated in intellectual circles but had broader social relevance. Although *Zemlja's* philosophy was influenced by Marxism, the group's inward-looking tendencies spared them from the socialist realism that became synonymous with leftist political ideals elsewhere in Europe and Russia. Instead, Hegedusic was interested in paintings created by farmers working in the Podravina region near Zagreb and became instrumental in introducing their artwork to the world.

NAÏVE ART: PAINTINGS OF THE RURAL WORLD

Within Croatia, the term "naïve art" applies to a specific style of 20th-century painting and sculpture created by self-taught artists, many of whom were poor farmers. Originally coined in 1932 by a Zagreb journalist in reference to paintings by these farmers, the term "naïve" has been used for lack of a more appropriate phrase; in many cases, the paintings included in this genre are sophisticated both technically and conceptually. The style is reminiscent of folk art with respect to the use of bold colors, strong lines, and relatively flat figures with little regard for perspective or other techniques of realism that one might learn in art school. In the United States or Europe, Croatian naïve art might fall under the broader definition of "outsider art" because these artists lacked formal training and had minimal contact with the mainstream art world. The best works of this genre are remarkable for their honest depiction of rural life as well as the attention to detail and, in some cases, surrealistic imagery. In Croatia, the popularity of naïve art has fluctuated over the past several decades, reaching its peak during the 1970s and retaining a smaller but dedicated following today.

The first naïve artists to be recognized as such include Ivan Generalic (1914–1992) and Franjo Mraz (1910–1991), both young peasants whose paintings captured the attention of Krsto Hegedusic. Because the original artists defining this movement were farmers by trade, their work epitomized the essence of *Zemlja*, capturing the traditions of farm life and fitting neatly into a growing Marxist consciousness celebrating rural life and peasant culture.

The earliest of these artists were living in the farming village of Hlebine. They painted on glass using tempera and developed a style that would characterize naïve painting to the present day. The finished work was usually two-dimensional, relying on clear drawing and minimal texture or brushwork. Painting on glass requires that the artist work from the foreground to the back of the final image, the reverse of the typical process. The naïves did not invent this technique; rather it was used by earlier folk artists primarily for ex-voto works created as a religious expression of thanks, for good luck, or survival of an injury or illness. The so-called reverse glass painting technique suited the naïves because it yielded the clear luminous colors that expressed the natural beauty of the countryside while also allowing the sort of detailed brushwork that eventually came to characterize paintings by Generalic and other naïve masters. Generalic states that he adopted the technique when "I realized that I could obtain fresher colors and put in more details. Colors on glass are more beautiful, more luminous. Canvas somehow swallowed up my colors . . . I found it impossible to do all those finer points that make naïve painting complete."[3] Although the main theme was peasant life, the artists' style was clearly modern and unique.

The artists' group *Zemlja* was short lived, but the naïve painters of Hlebine went on to exhibit their work and eventually gained international recognition. After World War II, Generalic and his contemporaries expanded the genre to include surrealistic visions of country life. These works, including larger-than-life flowers and animals, bright colors, and in some instances traditional religious themes, transported to the Hlebine countryside. Generalic's painting *The Tower* creates a fantasy landscape by placing the Eiffel tower in the middle of a rural village.

Sofija Naletilic Penavusa (1913–1994) was one of the most original artists working in a folk or naïve style. Naletilic generally is considered a Croatian artist, although she lived in the town of Siroki Brijeg in a region of Herzegovina, which is now part of Bosnia and Herzegovina. Croatian writer and art historian Dubravko Horvatic organized her first exhibition in the *Schira* gallery in Zagreb in 1982 after discovering her work by chance when visiting her hometown. Her hobby of "whittling" led her to create an incredible world of colorful wooden figures, both human and animal, most of which have an element of fantasy and a life of their own. Her work is on permanent display at the Museum of Naïve Art as well as the Gallery of Modern Art, both in Zagreb.

Other major artists from this genre include Ivan Rabuzin, Ivan Vecenaj, Ivan Lackovic, and Mirko Virius. These artists' works are represented in major galleries and collections throughout the world. The Museum of Naïve Art boasts an excellent small collection while the Museum of Naives in Hlebine not only exhibits the masters of naïve art but also shows works by lesser known local artists working in the naïve style. Currently, at least 100 artists in Croatia identify themselves as naïves and participate in festivals and exhibitions.

POSTWAR ABSTRACTION AND INNOVATION

In spite of the push toward socialist realism, the artistic movements associated with mid-20th-century Communist propaganda featuring muscular peasants and factory workers enthusiastically laboring toward a communal workers' paradise, Western European and American trends pervaded the Croatian art world in the 1950s. In Dubrovnik, a group of young painters formed what became known as the Dubrovnik Colorist School. The influence of their Dalmatian predecessor, painter Ignjat Job (1895–1936), whose colorful expressionist work captured the light and landscape of the Adriatic coast, led several young painters to develop a modern figurative style that remains relevant into the 21st century. Ivo Dulcic, (1916–1975), Antun Masle (1919–1967), and Duro Pulitika (1922–2006) are the most significant of this group, all of whom were born in Dubrovnik and, after studying at the Academy of Fine Arts in Zagreb, returned to work in their hometown. Dulcic, in particular, expressed an aversion to the socialist realism prevalent at the Academy and left before graduation. His style evolved from a blend of influences ranging from French painter Pierre Bonnard's vibrant Postimpressionist interiors to the abstract expressionism that was revolutionizing American and European art in the 1940s and 1950s. In spite of the hostility of the Communists toward the Catholic Church, Dulcic devoted substantial time and energy to religious subjects, creating stained glass windows and paintings for a number of churches. He brought an innovative, uniquely modern, and expressive approach to traditional scenes, such as the Last Supper and the Crucifixion. One of Dulcic's most spectacular projects is a massive fresco mural covering the entire wall behind the altar (9.5 by 19.5 meters, or approximately 31 by 64 feet) of the Church of Our Lady of Health (*Gospa od Zdravlja*), located near the Diocletian Palace in Split. Entitled *Christ the King* and painted in 1959, the mural dominates the church interior and features an elongated, distorted, and dramatic Christ in an azure blue sky presiding over the constellations and angels.

Antun Masle's subject matter focused more closely on domestic life, interiors, animals, and the female form. By the early 1950s, Masle employed loose, staccato brushstrokes and saturated colors that led critics to draw references to Vincent van Gogh.[4] Although his works are clearly contemporary, displaying an awareness of abstract expressionism, he never strays from figurative motifs. Duro Pulitika also painted domestic interiors but is best known for his Dalmatian landscapes that often are reduced to highly textured and nearly abstract curvaceous forms in rich blues and yellows. His scenes include small villages or isolated homes that become part of the organic composition of land and sky. All three of these artists' works have grown in popularity since 2000 and are displayed regularly in museums and galleries throughout the country, becoming reference points in the history of modern art in Croatia.

While Dulcic, Masle, and Pulitika left Zagreb to pursue their careers in Dubrovnik, another group of politically minded artists and architects took a stand against officially sanctioned emphasis on socialist realism at the Zagreb Academy of Fine Arts. Calling themselves Extat-51, the avant-garde membership rebelled against the government's denunciation of abstraction and other modern artistic trends that could be interpreted as Western or anti-Communist. They considered such limitations artificial and counterproductive to the development of a modern socialist society, which should use all types of fine and so-called applied arts as a means of visual experimentation and communication, although they had little interest in the work of artists, such as the Dubrovnik Colorists School, whose paintings had an overtly intimate sensibility. Painter Ivan Picelj, one of the founders of Extat-51, reflected the group's philosophy in his paintings of abstract geometric forms, which, while inspired by the Russian constructivist movement earlier in the century, have been interpreted as a response to the devastation of war, implying solidarity, construction, and the rebuilding of society on a physical as well as on the psychological plane. Even though the members of Extat-51 had few opportunities to exhibit their work as a group in Croatia or Yugoslavia, the organization is credited with helping to liberate Yugoslav artists from the politically motivated constraints they initially faced during the early years after World War II.

Edo Murtic (1921–2007) was instrumental in introducing abstract expressionism to Yugoslavia in the 1950s. Like almost every Croatian artist of note, he studied at Zagreb's Art Academy. A veteran of Tito's Partisan army, Murtic's early postwar work initially reflected both his political leanings and love of the Adriatic landscape. Once Tito split with Stalin, however, and freed Yugoslavia from Moscow's dogmatic approach to art and culture in general, Murtic began to draw on European and American influences. During a trip to the United States in the early 1950s, he visited New York City where he met abstract expressionist painters Willem DeKooning and Jackson Pollack. Murtic returned to Yugoslavia to produce new work combining abstraction and a lyrical appreciation of the landscapes that had continuously inspired him. His paintings from this period were controversial, but sufficiently innovative to earn him the honor of becoming the first Croatian painter to participate in the Venice Biennale in 1958. During the 1960s and 1970s, Murtic dominated the Croatian art scene with large abstract canvases, many of which were almost calligraphic in nature, featuring dramatic black brushstrokes similar to those typical of U.S. painter Franz Kline. His work reflected a physicality, reminiscent of Jackson Pollack's action paintings, in which the energy of the artist's sweep of a large brush across the canvas becomes essential to the completed painting. By 1980, Murtic's reputation as one of the leading artists in Eastern Europe was established and he began to deviate from the abstraction for which he was known to return to one of his earliest inspirations, the landscape. Murtic expressed concern over the public reaction to these new works, or his "conversion" as he called it,[5] but the artist's distinctive brushwork and sense of composition had remained consistent. His canvases from this period retain the same tension and dramatic energy as his purely abstract pieces, with the addition of rows indicating plowed fields and other visual references to vegetation, rolling hills, and trees whose branches appear to explode from the canvas. During the early 1980s, Murtic also illustrated Goran Kovacic's famed wartime poem *"Jama"* ("The Pit"), using symbols of aggression also found in Picasso's *Guernica*, including horns, bulls, teeth, and the like. For the remainder of his life, Murtic continued to convey inspiration drawn from the natural world in his recognizable abstract gestural style. He is acknowledged throughout Croatia as one of the country's premier modern artists and his paintings are widely exhibited. His original canvases are hanging in museums, galleries, and the homes of collectors, while reproductions are prevalent in almost every possible public place.

Dusan Dzamonja (1928–2009) was Murtic's counterpart with respect to sculpture in Croatia. Like his colleagues, he also studied at the Zagreb Academy of Fine Arts in the years immediately after World War II, but his earliest pieces remained free of any political influences. Initially a figurative sculptor, his work evolved toward abstraction during the 1950s. His most important early motif was that of a deer, which symbolized both fear and innocence. Dzamonja's figures eventually acquired narrower linear features with strong verticals and horizontals implying the violence of war, thus leading to an abstract style that was incorporated into monuments, usually memorializing victims of World War II and the Partisan victory, or revolution, as it was known. Characteristic of this period is his *Monument to the December Victims in Dubrava*, installed in Zagreb in 1960, a milestone piece, only about 13 feet high, but representative of a clear break in Yugoslav art, away from traditional representation toward purely abstract monuments. According to Andrija Mutnjakovic's 1961 essay referring to Dzamonja's model for a monument to victims of the Dachau concentration camp, artists no longer were interested in the physical attributes of the victims or their executioners, but rather the emotional, spiritual, and intellectual aspects of the Nazi crimes and the freedom that came with defeat of the enemy.[6] At this point, monumental sculpture in Croatia left the figure behind. Between 1960 and 1972, Dzamonja went on to design several large monuments, installed primarily in the Croatian region of Yugoslavia, commemorating the sacrifices of Tito's Partisan fighters as well as civilian victims of wartime violence, often characterized as martyrs of the revolution. In spite of the overtly political themes of his most prominent pieces, the abstract nature of Dzamonja's body of work, including his smaller sculptures and drawings, managed to transcend ideology and achieve international acclaim. In 1977, he was the recipient of the prestigious Swiss-based Goethe Foundation's Rembrandt Prize, which solidified his reputation as one of Yugoslavia's (and Croatia's) most influential contemporary artists. His two most important international exhibitions are the 1998 installation of a series of large sculptures in front of the Palace Vendome in Paris and his 1999 show at Lisbon's *Praça do Comércio* (Square of Commerce). In both instances, the sculptures on display, representative of his characteristic style, included pieces approximately 6.5 feet wide and almost 10 feet high. Made of welded metal, chains, and nails, each work was a conglomeration of large, organic curves juxtaposed against one another and echoing the sensuality of the human form without eclipsing the rough, inert nature of the materials themselves.

Dzamonja's name is synonymous with contemporary Croatian sculpture. In addition to a recent 2008 retrospective at Zagreb's Museum of Arts and Crafts, and frequent exhibitions elsewhere in Europe, his pieces are constantly on display in public spaces, as well as in museums throughout the country and abroad, including the United States, where one sculpture was installed at Brown University in Rhode Island in 1990 and another in front of the Trade Mart building in Dallas. The Museum of Modern Art in New York City also includes several pieces in its collection. A particularly inspiring display of Dzamonja's work is located in the sculpture park bearing his name in the town of Vrsar on the Istrian Peninsula. The park complex was designed by the artist and includes a gallery, a workshop, and the villa where he spent his summers. Built in 1965, the artist intentionally incorporated the ruins of an ancient farmhouse into his design, thereby tackling the question of how to combine the old with the new, an issue at the forefront of architecture in Croatia. Dzamonja's successful plan for his summer home and its surrounding gardens, gallery, and sculpture park epitomize a graceful synthesis of contemporary design with centuries old traditional stone architecture.

THE QUESTION OF MONUMENTS

Croatia's turbulent political legacy has constantly redefined the identity of its citizenry and their national allegiances. Freed from centuries of Hapsburg and Hungarian domination in the early 20th century, Croatia has since vacillated between the desire to establish a unique Croatian identity or to participate in a larger pan-Slavic federation. After World War I, ethnic tensions were temporarily submerged as Croatia joined the Slavic monarchy known as the Kingdom of Serbs, Croats, and Slovenes, and after World War II, Croatians were instrumental in establishing Tito's multiethnic Socialist Federal Republic of Yugoslavia. In contrast, by the 1990s, union with Serbia, Bosnia and Herzegovina, and Slovenia was no longer feasible and Croatians fought against the Serbian-dominated Yugoslav army to create the independent Republic of Croatia.

Shifts in leadership coupled with three wars in the 20th century created a complicated environment for the development and maintenance of public monuments, which often outlast the political sentiment they were intended to commemorate. Throughout Croatia, certain monuments, such as the statue of Ban Jelacic in Zagreb's main square, have been removed and then replaced, others destroyed and others simply ignored, left to the mercy of weather and vandals. The complications associated with the long process of fundraising, design, and installation of a monument is captured in the story of one of the city's most familiar landmarks, Robert Franges' (1872–1940) equestrian statue of King Tomislav located in front of the Zagreb train station. The statue was conceptualized in 1924 to simultaneously celebrate the end of Hapsburg rule, the unification of Dalmatia and northern Croatia, and the 1,000th anniversary of King Tomislav's coronation, which marked the origin of the Croatian state. As Celia Hawkesworth explains in her engaging cultural history of the city of Zagreb,[7] it made sense to name the first square in front of the rail station after Tomislav, the first Croatian king, with the following squares leading to Zagreb's main promenade also commemorating important figures in Croatian history. The middle of the three squares displays Ivan Mestrovic's statue of Bishop Joseph Georg Strossmayer, in solidarity with the bishop's promotion of Yugoslavism, with the third square named Zrinski, in honor of Nikola Subic Zrinski's victories over the Ottomans. Franges completed his statue in 1933, but in spite of initial enthusiasm for the project, *King Tomislav* remained in storage for 14 years. Approval for the project was given in 1925 when the political leadership, both in Zagreb and in Belgrade (the capital of Yugoslavia, located in Serbia), was particularly sympathetic to civic projects designed to replace the Hapsburg legacy with Yugoslav, or even Croatian, themes. The 1928 assassination of Croatian Peasant Party leader Stjepan Radic altered the political climate such that any emphasis on Croatian identity apart from the greater state of Yugoslavia was extinguished. Coupled with the country's economic woes, including insufficient funds for such basics as schools and roads, enthusiasm for the monument understandably diminished.

More complications arose among the small circle of prominent citizens attending the unveiling of the plaster cast of the statue in 1930. Which way should the equestrian monument face? Should the horse's derrière face the passengers exiting the train station, or should it face the other squares with all their references to Croatian history? How should the plinth be decorated? Which events should be pictured? Funding was not readily available for the purchase of bronze for the final cast so, thanks to a sympathetic general, the melting of two old cannons from World War I provided most of the bronze needed to finally complete the statue in 1933. Questions continued to arise regarding the decoration of the plinth and the location and position of the statue. Donations for the plinth were collected, although some prominent members of Zagreb society argued that it was inappropriate to erect a statue honoring King Tomislav when a proper statue of incumbent King Alexander did not yet exist. Franges died in 1940 without seeing the largest project of his career come to fruition. Amazingly, the plinth was completed during World War II, and the entire monument was finally erected in 1947, when Yugoslavia was a Communist state. A red Partisan star was placed on the plinth and the inscription emphasized Tomislav's role as a uniter of Slavic tribes, foreshadowing the alliance of Slavic people forming the state of Yugoslavia. Any reference to his Croatian identity was minimalized as Tito's government emphasized ethnic unity to downplay the racism fomented during World War II.

Artistic activity came to a halt during World War II and, given the victory of the Partisans and the establishment of a socialist state, it is not surprising that socialist realism dominated the art scene in the 10 years following the war. The legacy of this period is apparent in the various monuments to Partisan fighters that can be found in towns, both large and small, throughout Croatia. In contemporary Croatia, many of these monuments featuring muscular soldiers, sometimes barefoot and shirtless, are largely ignored, in part because of the disintegration of Yugoslavia and rejection of Marxist ideals embodied by Tito's Partisans. A second factor has to do with population shifts from rural to urban centers. During World War II, many Partisan fighters came from small rural towns. Soon after the war, monuments were installed to commemorate the sacrifices these communities made for the cause. But in the following years, before the bronze of the statues could tarnish, many citizens were forced to leave their hometowns in search of employment in larger cities. Eventually these rural hotbeds of Partisan support were little more than ghost towns with surprisingly large, well-crafted statues commemorating a bygone era. Unlike the bigger, more impersonal monuments erected in the 1960s and 1970s, most of these statues seem immune to vandalism, probably because each prominently displays a list of locals who died for the sake of the revolution. Although many families have moved away, they retain a sentimental connection, if not a physical one in the form of a house or land, to their familial hometown and to the great grandparents or distant cousins whose sacrifices are commemorated in these statues of young, defiant soldiers.

In the 1960s and 1970s, the trend in Croatian monumental sculpture veered toward abstraction and the government commissioned dozens of monuments, again commemorating Partisan victories and sacrifices. This new generation of public sculptures was remarkably adventurous. Gone were any traces of the brave Partisan soldier or portraits of local war heroes or even

Tito himself. These typically huge works were purely abstract, taking the forms of large science-fiction flora, hypermodern space stations, or monstrous crystalline formations emerging from a pastoral field. They are stunning statements of modernism, made of concrete, steel, or glass and speak perhaps more to Yugoslavia's independence from the cultural influences of the Soviet bloc than to the courage of the Partisans. The obscure locations of many of these monuments, which currently are referred to as *Spomeniks*, the Croatian term for monument, would have surprised anyone traveling through Yugoslavia in the late 1970s. They were erected on mountainsides, in fields, and outside of small towns, presumably wherever there was a battle worth noting. Before the breakup of Yugoslavia, these *Spomeniks* were the site of wreath-laying ceremonies, school field trips, and family outings. Now that the Yugoslav state inextricably linked to the Partisan legacy no longer exists, the fate of these *Spomeniks* is questionable in Croatia, as well as the other former Yugoslav republics. The most significant of the Croatian *Spomeniks* are the *Monument*

A *Spomenik* commemorating the "fallen fighters and victims of fascist terror." (Courtesy of the author.)

to the Revolution in Moslavina,[8] designed by Dusan Dzamonja in 1967 and located in Podgaric in northern Croatia; the *Jasenovac Memorial*, designed by Bogdan Bogdanovic in 1966; and the *Monument to the Partisans* at Petrova Gora, designed by Vojin Bakic in the 1960s and completed in 1981.

With the fall of Yugoslavia, each of these monuments suffered from neglect and, to some extent, vandalism. Representative of an era that many Croatians associate with economic exploitation and repression, there is little incentive to maintain these monuments, even though they are significant works of art. Dzamonja's *Monument to the Revolution in Moslavina* resembles a giant concrete bird in flight and was once pictured on a Yugoslav postage stamp. In the 21st century, it frequently is pictured without admiring onlookers and it is referred to as an "abandoned" monument having lost one of the aluminum plates originally attached to the center of the sculpture. The *Jasenovac Memorial* has fared somewhat better, perhaps because it was built to honor those killed in the Jasenovac concentration camp, giving the monument greater international significance. The massive sculpture was deserted during the Homeland War but in recent years substantial efforts have been made to renovate the entire site, beginning with the removal of mines from the surrounding area and the return of exhibition materials and documents, which were stolen from the nearby museum during the war. Research has begun with respect to restoration of Bogdanovic's stone creation, often referred to as the "flower monument" because of its giant floral shape. Vojin Bakic's *Monument to the Partisans* blurred the line between architecture and sculpture as one could walk into the glass and steel structure that housed a permanent exhibition dedicated to the Partisans. Located on the site of a Partisan hospital, it was in Serbian-occupied territory during the Homeland War during which the structure was partially destroyed. Now it serves as the inspiration for a video project entitled *Scenes for a New Heritage* by Croatian artist David Maljkovic (1973–). The series of three futuristic films, set between 2045 and 2060, shows the varying responses of a group of young people exploring the monument having no idea of its original function. The monument becomes a place for young people to socialize, thereby reinventing the significance and meaning of the structure.[9] Maljkovic's project has been well received in both the United States and England, although the monument remains in a state of partial ruin, functioning only as a signal-transmitter tower for Croatian State Television and the T-Mobile Corporation.

INTERNATIONAL TRENDS AND CONCEPTUAL ART

The Museum of Contemporary Art in Zagreb currently exhibits a combination of figurative, abstract, and conceptual pieces that reflect a Croatian interpretation of international art world trends. The complexity of the last 50 years of artistic development is matched by the heterogeneity of the country itself. As part of Yugoslavia, Croatia existed as a multiethnic entity with a nationalist Croat undercurrent. Between World War II and the Homeland War of the 1990s, the people of Croatia (and the rest of Yugoslavia), while commonly considered citizens of the Eastern Bloc, enjoyed far greater freedom to travel and gain exposure to other European cultural trends than their counterparts in countries such as Bulgaria, Romania, or Czechoslovakia. As a result, the art scene was vibrant and constantly evolving, with influences ranging from pop art, abstraction, surrealism, and most notably, conceptualism defined as an approach to creating art in which the ideas expressed take precedence over traditional concerns of materials, appearance, and taste. In Croatia and elsewhere, many of these conceptual pieces take the form of installations or performance art.

Working between the years of 1959 and 1966, the Gorgona Group was the predecessor of much of 21st-century conceptual art in Croatia. This was a conglomeration of painters, sculptors, architects, and even art historians and critics who used a variety of artistic means to explore the relationships between the individual, art, and society at large. Rather than rely on traditional painting and sculpture, they engaged in performances and published an "antireview" magazine, *Gorgona*, in which they challenged preexisting boundaries and definitions of artistic expression. According to the Gorgona Group, a work of art did not need to be an object. An idea alone, manifested as a verbal expression or physical action, was sufficient grounds for a work of art. Members regularly proposed projects and elevated the mundane activities of daily life, such as sending and receiving letters, into artistic events. For example, in a project called Thoughts for the Month, members selected quotes from philosophy, poetry, and prose literature and mailed them to each other. One of the group's founders, Josip Vanista, took the idea of a painting, as opposed to the physical painting itself, to its logical conclusion in his piece *Painting 1964*, in which he describes the physical attributes of a painting, such as scale and color, without ever creating the painting itself. Some members created paintings, but they were based on minimal gestural lines and shapes or works based on a narrow (monochromatic) color scheme. In 1966, Gorgona ceased to function as a group, although its members, including Vanista and painter Julije Knifer (1924–2004), continued to work and influence younger generations of artists. Interestingly, because of Gorgona's reluctance to participate in established art institutions, the group was virtually unknown until 1977 when the Museum of Contemporary Art in Zagreb exhibited their projects and published a catalog. It was only after that show that Gorgona became an influential force in Croatia's contemporary art scene.

A number of artists originally belonging to the Gorgona Group and other avant-garde communities in the 1960s and 1970s continued to create groundbreaking art for years to come. As previously mentioned, Julije Knifer spent his life at the vanguard of Croatian art, influencing generations of young artists along the way. He relied on the central motif of a meandering line, sometimes displayed as a thick angular form, which could be categorized as geometric abstraction, whereas other times his lines were thin and delicate. He frequently worked in black and white, eschewing the necessity of a broader palette, and for more than 40 years, he dedicated himself to repetition of the patterns, which became his trademark. Generally, Knifer disliked labels although his work often is compared to that of other artists whose work focused on repetition,[10] such as Ad Reinhardt, whose minimalist monochromatic paintings were based on subtle patterning. Knifer's paintings were consistent over the years, and it is not surprising that he considered the chronology of his work unimportant, stating that his later paintings carried the same "spiritual background and structure" as that of his earlier years.[11] Gorgona member Dimitrije Basicevic (1921–1987) was highly influential as well, working as curator of the Galleries of the City of Zagreb and as an artist under the name Mangelos, after a town near his birthplace. Rather than paint, he used text, in the form of poems or manifestos, often written in careful calligraphic cursive between two drawn lines on chalkboards, pieces of wood, and most famously, globes. Part of the visual attraction of his work is the combination of an intellectually complex (and sometimes obtuse) message expressed in the format of a young child's writing exercise. He combined English, German, and French and was as concise as possible when addressing the theme of the modern or machine age verses the manual or handmade age.

While Gorgona was a group with identifiable members, Red Peristyle (*Cerveni Peristil*)[12] was an informal crew of artists and activists from Split who were named after a project organized by Pave Dulcic, one of the few identifiable members of this group. Early in the morning on January 11, 1968, Dulcic and several others painted the peristyle (that is, the courtyard) of the Diocletian Palace in Split bright red, the color associated with Communist revolution. The act, referred to in art literature as an "urban intervention," was interpreted in numerous ways, ranging from a commentary about totalitarianism and the economic exploitation of Croatia by the Yugoslav government in Belgrade to simple vandalism of public property. Initially attacked in the press and hunted by the police, Dulcic and his fellow artists went into hiding. Eventually Dulcic was arrested, and according to local lore, suffered a beating from which he never recovered psychologically. He committed suicide shortly afterward, and the others associated with the act rarely spoke about it publicly. Over the years, the rumors surrounding the event grew with various people claiming to have participated in one way or another. As a result, we cannot be sure who the actual members of Red Peristyle were and what exactly motivated them toward their urban intervention, which more than 40 years later has attained legendary status. Not only is the Red Peristyle regarded as an important movement in contemporary Croatian art, but it also served as the inspiration for younger generations who have undertaken similar urban interventions in the name of art. The most notable of these is Igor Grubic's (1969–) *Black Peristyle* in which he reenacted the original painting of the peristyle 30 years later in 1998.

Film director and conceptual artist Tomislav Gotovac[13] (1937–2010) was one of the most fearlessly radical artists of his generation. In the mid-1990s, he collaborated with younger artists on at least one memorable project, *Weekend Art: Hallelujah the Hill*. Gotovac, who originally identified with the rebellion of the 1960's youth movement, was the first Yugoslav artist to organize a "happening" in Zagreb in 1967. This sort of provocative, counterculture, artistic public event typified Gotovac's work throughout the decades. He was famous for his unconventional approach, which often involved a public performance of some sort. Since his artistic statements usually contained timely critiques of Yugoslav society and politics, his projects were labeled subversive and he often was arrested. Whenever possible, he made sure that his projects were documented on film, which became part of the overall artistic act and remain as a lasting record of his work. In *Weekend Art: Hallelujah the Hill,* Gotovac collaborated with Battista Illic (1965–) and Ivana Keser (1967–) to create a project that ultimately was realized through a series of photographs, postcards, performances, and even billboards. The project revolved around a series of walks through a scenic area in the vicinity of Zagreb. The calm pastoral beauty of nature masked the reality of Croatia at the time, which was involved in the war in the nearby border region between Croatia and Bosnia. Illic describes the work as "not only a hymn to nature, the body and the simple life, but also an aesthetic repression of horror."[14]

Much of the contemporary art produced in Croatia during the 1990s dealt with political and social issues directly related to war. Once the violence subsided, artists broadened their scope, but social commentary was still at the forefront of contemporary art. In a 2006 article, art historians Maja and Reuben Fowkes present projects that dealt with issues of ecology and environmental sustainability.[15] The authors discuss *Hallelujah the Hill* as well as several other projects, including Dalibor Martinis's 2004 work entitled *Variable Risk Landscape*. Martinis bought 365 shares (one share for each day of the year) in an investment fund through the MAN (Man, Art, Nature)

Foundation. He periodically would climb an unspecified mountain range to an elevation matching the value of his shares. The final project included the artist's climbing log in which he included his observations of nature as well as the impact of global news events on the value of his investment. His language is neutral, mimicking that of the financial news media, and in accompanying photographs the artist appears to be hiking in the wilderness wearing a business suit. The project addresses the issue of sustainability by illustrating the disconnect between the motivating forces behind the global financial system and the values associated with environmental protection and sustainability. The Fowkes' observe that Croatian artists' focus on the natural environment and the threats posed by global politics and economic activity has signaled a return to the radical ideas of the artistic avant-garde of the 1970s. The Croatian art scene rarely has embodied the "art-for-art's sake" mentality that has prevailed elsewhere in Western culture. Because the country has been constantly in political flux, social issues have never been far from the consciousness of Croatian artists.

Notes

1. Radovan Ivancevic, *Art Treasures of Croatia* (Croatia: Iro Motovun, 1986), 54.

2. Ivancevic, *Art Treasures of Croatia*, 53.

3. For additional information on Ivan Generalic, see Nebojsa Tomasevic, *The Magic World of Ivan Generalic*, trans. John Shepley (New York: Rizzoli International Publications, 1976).

4. Antun Masle, http://antunmasle.com/bio.htm (retrieved January 6, 2009).

5. From an essay covering 1980–1990, Edo Murtic, http://www.murtic.com/ciklus05/txt-e.htm (retrieved January 6, 2009).

6. Fedor Dzamonja, ed., *Dzamonja; Sculpture, Drawings, Projects* (Zagreb: Kaligraph, 2001), 65.

7. For more details regarding the statue of King Tomislav, see Celia Hawkesworth, *Zagreb: A Cultural History* (New York: Oxford University Press, 2008).

8. Moslavina is the name of a county in Croatia located in southwestern Slavonia. Oddly, Podgaric is not located in Moslavina.

9. "David Maljkovic," *Frieze Magazine*, October 2007, http://www.frieze.com/issue/review/david_maljkovic (retrieved February 2, 2009).

10. Branka Stipancic, "Untitled," in *East Art Map: Contemporary Art and Eastern Europe*, ed. IRWIN (London: Central Saint Martins College of Art and Design, University of the Arts, 2006).

11. Ibid.

12. Ana Peraica, "A Corruption of the 'Grand Narrative' of Art," in *East Art Map: Contemporary Art and Eastern Europe*, ed. IRWIN (London: Central Saint Martins College of Art and Design, University of the Arts, London, 2006).

13. Stipancic, "Untitled."

14. Nada Beros, "Case Study: *Weekend Art: Hallelujah Hill*," in *Primary Documents, A Sourcebook for Eastern and Central European Art since the 1950s*, eds. Laura Hoptman and Tomas Pospiszyl (New York: Museum of Modern Art, 2002).

15. Maja Fowkes and Reuben Fowkes, "The Lure of Fresh Air: Sustainability in Contemporary Croatian Art," October 12, 2006, ARTMargins: Contemporary Central & East European Visual Culture, http://www.artmargins.com/index.php/archive/157-the-lure-of-fresh-air-sustainability-in-contemporary-croatian-art (retrieved February 2, 2009).

11

Architecture and Housing

Contemporary architecture is alive and well in Croatia. However, the cultural importance of newer buildings is often downplayed by the presence of many beautiful and historic structures that define the centers of larger cities and towns. Over the centuries, Croatia has constantly been subjected to various foreign influences, beginning with the Greeks and Romans who settled the area before the arrival of the first Slavic tribes, and later on, Hungarians, Venetians, Austrians, and Italians who dominated parts of the country. Each of these cultures have contributed to the fascinating and diverse architectural legacy that is a vital part of the contemporary Croatian cityscape. Buildings that are hundreds of years old still function as apartment houses, churches, and places of business. Tourism, a growing industry in Croatia, also helps to keep historical art and architecture in the popular consciousness.

The architecture of older Croatian towns illustrates the fact that various regions of the country developed at different rates and faced a range of cultural influences. Many larger municipalities have a historic "old town" defined by the original timeworn structures and passages around which newer buildings and streets were gradually added. The buildings in these older sections typically represent the cultural nucleus of the modern Croatian city. They are where the past meets the present; centers of history as well as commercial activity, including traditional business as well as trendy restaurants and retail shops. Especially along the coast, the historic sections of towns such as Split and Dubrovnik have attracted wealthy tourists who, in turn, created a demand

A panorama of Split with the towers of Split 3, a megacomplex designed in the 1960s, in the distant background. (Courtesy of the author.)

for high-end hotels, restaurants, and designer boutiques. As these businesses moved in, the demand and prices for historical real estate grew, creating an unlikely commingling of luxury businesses, their wealthy (often foreign) clientele, and the families who have lived there for generations.

The details of old stone buildings provide valuable insight into the history of older Croatian towns. Coastal cities of Roman origin, such as Split, usually contain centuries of infill, buildings that were expanded on or just rebuilt on the ruins of older structures as the population grew and architectural needs changed. For example, the foundation and walls of an old Roman palace might be incorporated into several residential structures as more families moved into the city during the Middle Ages. With respect to churches, pagan temples were either taken apart, their masonry recycled to build medieval Christian churches or they were transformed into Christian sanctuaries through the removal of pagan imagery and sanctification. In contrast, inland cities, such as Zagreb, which was founded in the 11th century, was not based on Roman foundations and tend to reflect Central European trends in city planning and architecture.

Whether one explores historical ruins or brand-new hotels and villas, stone appears frequently, either as a primary building material or as decorative surfacing. Croatia is rich in limestone and has approximately 50 working quarries and an unknown number that have been abandoned, some dating to Roman times. For example, limestone from Croatia's oldest quarry, located in the Istrian town of Vinkuran, was used to build the ancient Roman amphitheater in Pula approximately 2,000 years ago. Over centuries, quarries on the island of Brac have provided high-quality limestone both locally and internationally. Croatians are proud of the fact that, in 1824, Brac provided white limestone for the columns in the White House portico.[1] To this day, stone buildings ranging from humble old farmhouses to expansive villas are found all over Dalmatia and Istria, where limestone was, and is, plentiful. Many of these structures have been around for centuries, whereas others are much newer, reflecting Croatian's interest in preserving a traditional architectural aesthetic.

ROMAN FOUNDATIONS

The Diocletian Palace in the inner city of Split is the most captivating and historically relevant ancient Roman structure in Croatia. For centuries, this maze of alleys, medieval apartment houses, and Renaissance palaces has functioned as a central location for the citizens of Split (also known as *Splicani*) to meet for business and social purposes. It is also one of the best-preserved examples of a Roman imperial palace, and is designated a UNESCO (United Nations Educational, Scientific, and Cultural Organization) World Heritage Monument.

The palace complex was built in the early years of the fourth century as a home for Roman emperor Diocletian after his retirement from the throne. At that time, Split was just a small coastal Roman settlement called Spalatum, which was overshadowed by the much larger town of Salona several miles away. Originally the palace's 322,800 square feet (30,000 square meters) served as a combination imperial residence and military fortress that housed between 8,000 and 10,000 people. Built on the shoreline, Diocletian's private apartments were located on the southern side of the complex with a view of the Adriatic Sea and its many islands. Military quarters and the like were located toward the north. The entire structure was surrounded by massive walls, approximately 6.5 feet (2 meters) thick, and between 56 and 79 feet (17 and 24 meters) high, including 16 guard towers.

Much of the palace was built using the aforementioned local limestone from quarries on the nearby island of Brac. The marble and granite used for the columns were probably imported from Egypt along with several sphinxes, which remain to this day, including one that was placed outside of Diocletian's mausoleum to guard it. The palace had four gates, which today serve as landmarks and meeting places for groups of tourists. The most impressive of these is the northern gate, also known as the Golden Gate, through which travelers once passed on their way to the ancient city of Salona. The Sliver Gate faces east, and leads directly to an outdoor market. The Iron Gate faces west on to Split's town square, also known as the piazza. The Bronze Gate is to the south, originally providing access to the sea, but now functions as the entry to the palace basements, which house a museum and souvenir market.

After Diocletian's death, the imperial complex remained under government control until the seventh century when the inhabitants of Salona poured into Diocletian's Palace seeking protection from marauding tribes of Slavs (early Croatians) who eventually would dominate the area. The palace's huge walls protected the inhabitants from invaders and many of the refugees decided to remain within, abandoning the more vulnerable city of Salona for good. The palace interior began to take on the character of a medieval town. Diocletian's residence was divided into smaller housing units and other larger structures were modified to accommodate the newcomers. Construction and reconstruction has continued within the palace walls for centuries, creating an architectural patchwork that includes Renaissance and baroque elements, but that still retains a medieval character. The well-preserved remnants of Diocletian's original imperial palace, however, recall Split's Roman origins.

The peristyle is the most significant original part of the palace in terms of contemporary Split. A peristyle is typically defined as a courtyard surrounded by a colonnade or arcade. Today Diocletian's peristyle is a primary meeting place for locals and tourists, while also providing a wonderful example of late classical architecture, including one of the earliest examples of an arcade (a series of arches supported by columns). Of particular relevance to contemporary residents is the café located on the western side of the courtyard that serves drinks to patrons seated on the steps in front of the arcade. In the immediate proximity is a jewelry shop featuring traditional Croatian filigran designs, a visitor information center, cash machines, a camera shop, and other enterprises that keep the peristyle bustling with commercial activity. The palace basements, a series of large barrel-vaulted rooms, are quite busy during the summer tourist season as they house shops catering to visitors as well as a museum.

Just beyond the east arcade is the Cathedral of Saint Duje, which was built over Diocletian's mausoleum in the seventh century by Christians who wanted to transform Split's pagan legacy to suit the needs of the newly converted Christian population. Like many of the buildings within the palace, this structure combines a series of architectural styles. For example, the campanile (bell tower) was originally constructed between the 13th and 16th centuries and featured both Gothic and Romanesque elements. The rebuilding of the bell tower in the early 20th century led to the removal of many Romanesque elements, making the structure somewhat incongruous with its surroundings, but the two magnificent Romanesque lions at its base highlight the original architecture of the tower. The wooden doors of the cathedral are a true masterpiece of Romanesque sculpture, featuring 22 panels illustrating the life of Christ carved by the sculptor Andrija Buvina of Split in 1214. Between the columns around the octagonal base of the cathedral are early Christian and medieval sarcophagi, once again contrasting with the refurbished campanile.

Split is not the only city in which ancient Roman architecture is part of contemporary life. For example, a Roman arena, simply known as the "arena," is located in the center of the Istrian city of Pula. The well-preserved structure dates back to the first century and is used for summer film festivals and concerts. A number of other monuments are part of Pula's cityscape, including the Arch of the Sergii, a well-preserved ancient Roman triumphal arch that was once part of a series of gates leading into the fortified Roman city, and other original Roman gates, the Gate of Hercules and the Twin Gates.

Medieval and Renaissance Architecture in Croatia's Contemporary Cityscapes

The Romans contributed substantially to the development of cities like Split and Pula, but building slowed as the Roman Empire deteriorated during the early Middle Ages. It was not until the 9th and 10th centuries, when King Tomislav united Dalmatia with the interior of Croatia, that construction accelerated. By this time, the region was also under the jurisdiction of the Catholic Church. Not surprisingly, most of the significant surviving structures from this era are churches that were designed in a simplified Byzantine style, sometimes also called pre-Romanesque (although by the ninth century the region was free of Byzantine rule). These churches often were vaulted single-domed structures, many of which were quite modest in size. The Church of Saint Donatus in Zadar, however, is the exception. Like Split and Pula, Zadar was once a Roman town and Saint Donatus was constructed on the remnants of prior Roman structures. Two altar stones were originally inscribed to Jupiter and Juno, and other bits of Roman masonry are found in the foundation.[2] The building is circular, 85 feet (25 meters) tall, and has a gallery on the upper floor with some small traces of paintings remaining on the walls. Saint Donatus is no longer used for religious services, but it is a popular symbol of the city of Zadar and often is depicted on postcards and other materials used to promote tourism. The interior is known for excellent acoustics and functions as a concert venue for the annual International Festival of Medieval and Renaissance Music.

The finest examples of Romanesque architecture can be found along the coast, primarily in the form of churches with characteristic simple geometric forms, including a rectangular floor plan and either an internal or external altar area (also known as the apse), rounded arches, and barrel and cross vaults. These buildings reflect the architectural trends in Europe at the time, most specifically Italian Romanesque architecture.

Especially well preserved examples of Romanesque architecture are found in the town of Rab, located on the island of the same name. The Church of Saint Mary Major, a triple-aisled basilica, is one such structure, which was consecrated in 1177 and features a freestanding campanile rising 85 feet above the town. Like most churches built during this period, the fundamental Romanesque design is complimented by details added many years later, during the Gothic or Renaissance periods, for example, and ultimately resulting in a blend of architectural styles. Other fine examples of Romanesque architecture, including secular structures and private homes, are found along the coast from the northern city of Porec in Istria to Dubrovnik in the south.

Throughout Croatia, medieval churches still play an important role in contemporary day-to-day life. Historic churches are more than just monuments; they have a lasting personal significance for many Croatians. For generations, these landmarks have functioned as social gathering places where important family events such as weddings, funerals, and baptisms traditionally have taken place. Unfortunately, only those Romanesque churches constructed in populated areas have survived over the centuries. Churches that were built in smaller towns whose citizens left (usually due to economic decline) are now little more than ruins. Aside from the archaeologists who study what little remains of these structures, the general public has largely forgotten them.

Dubrovnik is one of the best-preserved medieval cities in Europe and provides a clear example of centuries-old architecture functioning in a modern capacity. In the early 12th century, when Hungarian kings gained control over Croatia, Dubrovnik managed to remain independent and developed more quickly than the rest of the region, ultimately becoming the first Croatian city to engage in urban planning. Dubrovnik still reflects its original city plan, which was designed in the 13th century and based on a series of streets extending from a central avenue known as the Stradun. At that time, regulations were established concerning the width of streets, stairways, sizes of buildings, and plots of land. In the 14th century, the streets were paved and a sewage and drainage system was built, some of which still function in the 21st century. These basic plans resulted in a city center that has not needed major modifications and still accommodates many of the needs of its current population. Profits from Dubrovnik's trading endeavors were invested in architecture and a public welfare program that included a medical service, a home for the elderly, and the oldest surviving pharmacy in Europe, established in 1317. The massive fortifications surrounding the city are still intact and provide an excellent tourist attraction with vantage points from which to view the cityscape's intriguing patchwork of architectural styles, including Romanesque, Gothic, Renaissance, and baroque influences.

Gothic architecture, characterized by large cathedrals with pointed arches, ribbed vaulting, and strong vertical lines, swept through Europe between the 11th and 14th centuries. Each region interpreted the style a little differently. Although the Gothic influence can be seen in numerous buildings still standing, there are a few notable churches and secular buildings that best represent the style in Croatia.

Because it could take centuries to construct a cathedral, several architectural styles might appear in a single structure. Such is the case of the Cathedral of Saint Lawrence in Trogir, a Romanesque building whose Gothic sculptural details are at least as significant as the architecture itself. The main entrance to the cathedral is known as Radovan's Portal, named after the sculptor who designed and carved much of the ornamentation that surrounds the doorway, which, like the cathedral doors in Split, are a major tourist attraction. (Radovan is known only by his first name, which he carved into the portal in 1240, although the entire project was not completed until the 14th century.) The portal is covered with both freestanding and relief sculpture, more than 100 figures in total, including both Old and New Testament scenes. The relief illustrates Christ's Nativity and the Adoration of the Magi along with scenes from daily rural life, such as a slaughtered hog and a shepherd in the fields. The signs of the zodiac are evident, which at that time represented the study of astronomy. Two majestic lions, symbolic of the church, stand on either side of the doors. Perhaps the most popular images of the entire complicated and overwhelming composition are Adam and Eve, representing original sin. They are freestanding nudes placed atop lions, one at each side of the doorway. As the largest figures in the portal, they are particularly compelling in their humanity. The realism of Radovan's figures extends beyond the Romanesque aesthetic and introduces the new Gothic style as characterized by the volume and vitality of his figures coupled with the attention paid to the relief details of everyday life. The result reflects the shift toward greater realism in sculpture, a Gothic trend that revived the highly realistic classical style of the Renaissance.

During the summer months, Trogir is packed with tourists. The cathedral and Radovan's sculptures are photographed repeatedly, always attracting a large crowd. For a small fee, visitors can climb the long staircase to the top of the tower that rises almost directly above the portal. The panoramic view from the top of the tower captures one's attention, but the tower itself is a fine representation of the evolution of architectural style in Europe from the 14th through the 17th century. The ground floor, with its simple Romanesque rounded arch, was built in the 14th century. The first story was built in the early 15th century and is characterized by its Gothic pointed arches. The second story was built soon afterward and represents a more ornate and mature Gothic style, whereas the third story, built in the early 16th century is reflective of Renaissance architecture. The four statues were placed at the top in the 17th century and exemplify a Mannerist aesthetic.

While Radovan was sculpting the portal figures, the Mongols were burning down Zagreb's Romanesque cathedral, which had just been consecrated in 1271. A new cathedral was begun in 1276, but progress was constantly interrupted, largely because of continued threats of invasion by Ottoman Turks, making the construction of defensive walls and towers a larger priority. Like the Trogir Cathedral tower, the Zagreb Cathedral was under construction for more than 300 years. Its original appearance was largely Gothic with a patchwork of other styles corresponding to later construction. The original Gothic influence is apparent in the nave (the area where the congregation sits) and aisles (the areas on the sides of the nave), which are all approximately the same height, a distinctly Gothic characteristic. The choir is another fine example of early Gothic design integrated with Renaissance and baroque elements that were added later. In the 21st century, much of the structure's current appearance must be considered neo-Gothic because it is the product of a 19th-century restoration effort. Viennese architects Friedrich von Schmidt and Hermann Bolle largely reconstructed the cathedral after a devastating earthquake in 1880. The restoration resulted in a fairly consistent Gothic look, but critics complained that the complicated balance of styles achieved through the gradual construction of the original building was lost.[3] Old tombstones were removed, the old portal was destroyed, and valuable baroque altars were moved to other churches. On the positive side, the architects put substantial effort and expense in the design and construction of the two large towers, which currently provide a distinct addition to Zagreb's skyline.

Saint Mark's Church is another one of Zagreb's most important architectural landmarks. Like the Zagreb Cathedral, it also lost many of its original features through fires, earthquakes, and 19th-century restoration. The church was constructed in the early 15th century at the highest point in the hilly Gradac section of town. This area is of particular historical interest as it retains its original urban Gothic layout with a central square and an irregular street grid plan.[4] Saint Mark's was built on the main square in the spirit of the late-Gothic style found in Central Europe, with nave and aisles almost the same height, giving the structure a hall-like look. Some historians have noted that Gothic hall churches of this sort did not differ much from the large halls of feudal castles of the period.[5] The interior was lit by light flowing through large windows framed by typically Gothic pointed arches. The bell tower, originally a baroque design, was added in the late 17th century. (The tower was altered in a 19th-century neo-Gothic restoration, losing some of its original character. Fortunately another restoration in the 1930s recaptured some of the structure's baroque features.)

The main entrance of Saint Mark's, also known as the main portal, includes one of the finest examples of Gothic sculpture in northern Croatia.[6] The Virgin Mary, Christ, and Saint Mark along with the 12 apostles are represented with a sense of movement and vitality characteristic of the best sculpture of the Gothic period. Although three of the figures were destroyed and have been replaced with wooden figures in the baroque style, the entire composition retains its original integrity. The portal sculptures are the most important from the standpoint of art historians, but the most famous feature of the church is its colorful tiled roof, constructed in 1880, and decorated with the coats of arms of Croatia, Dalmatia, Slavonia, and the city of Zagreb. The roof was restored in 2007 and is a major tourist attraction, pictured on postcards and on guidebooks, and it has become a primary symbol of the capital city of Zagreb.

Coastal Croatia, with the exception of Dubrovnik, came under Venetian rule by the early 15th century and the resulting architecture reflects a mature Venetian Gothic style that is evident in the building now housing the City Museum in Split. Designed by Juraj Dlamatinac (also known as George the Dalmatian or Giorgio da Sebenico) as a palace for the Papalic family, the structure features a beautiful courtyard and delicately decorated loggia clearly reminiscent of Venice where Juraj was educated. Born in Zadar, Juraj is the architect and sculptor most closely associated with the spread of the Gothic style along the Dalmatian coast in the 15th century. His aesthetic, however, was not purely Gothic. He was influenced by the Italian Renaissance and brought that mentality back to Dalmatia when he was summoned to Sibenik in 1441 to lead the construction and design efforts at the Cathedral of Saint James. He was responsible for the baptistry, sacristy, and the distinctive sculptural decoration, including a frieze featuring 74 individualized heads, which are a constant source of fascination to tourists and locals alike (see photo on p. 170). The faces have a portrait-like quality and, according to legend, were inspired by the residents of Sibenik, marking the first time so much purely secular sculpture was applied to a religious building. These "portraits" are reflective of Juraj's Renaissance leanings, marking a departure from the medieval notion of a world dominated by religion to one in which man's awareness of nature and himself allowed for a more scientific approach to the universe. The faces on the exterior frieze are the most distinctive sculptural work associated with the cathedral, overshadowing all conventional religious imagery.[7]

Juraj's style, ultimately, was a combination of both Gothic and Renaissance design. In the case of the Cathedral of Saint James, he is credited with placing Renaissance sculpture within a Gothic architectural framework, clearly straddling the transition from the Gothic to the Renaissance age. The cathedral baptistry features an interior space with rich Venetian Gothic ornamentation, and the base of the baptismal font is decorated with three putti (young naked child-like figures sometimes with wings) that are sculpted with the grace and naturalism of the Renaissance. After Juraj's death in 1473, building continued under the direction of Nikola Firentinac (1477–1505) whose contributions were a pure reflection of the newer prevailing Renaissance aesthetic. Firentinac certainly influenced the overall appearance of the structure, but his most notable contribution was the use of a barrel vault design for the cathedral roof, which also gave the interior ceiling the same semicircular shape, thereby unifying the interior and exterior of the structure and creating an overall harmony found in Renaissance architecture. By the time major construction was completed in 1536, it was fair to say that, while the early phases of the construction of the cathedral were begun in the Venetian Gothic style, the final phases and external appearance of the cathedral were dominated by Renaissance design.

This blending of styles was not unusual, and as can be seen in the case of the Trogir Cathedral bell tower, Renaissance elements often were added to Romanesque or Gothic structures as tastes and architectural styles progressed more quickly than construction. The challenge faced by architects working on later phases of construction was to combine these newer styles with the existing architecture of a building in a harmonious way. On occasion, however, the combination and contrast between old and new styles was intentional. Such is the case of the Sponza Palace, originally the Dubrovnik mint and customs house, built between 1518 and 1524. The semicircular arches and elegant pillars of the ground floor are classic Renaissance design. The first floor has three windows, all of which are decorated using a delicate Gothic motif featuring pointed arches. The second floor windows reflect a return to Renaissance design and the roof ornaments are Gothic. Historians believed that the building was constructed in two phases, but the discovery of the original contract and construction analysis reveal that the building was designed by a single architect, Paskoje Milicevic, who successfully integrated the two styles.

As a result of constant threat of Ottoman invasion, during the 16th century resources were directed toward the construction of military fortifications in

Northern Croatia. Instead of building Renaissance-style churches in Zagreb, for example, architects designed fortifications for the city and its surroundings based on the latest theories on defensive warfare. Between 1513 and 1521, a large wall with five round towers was built around the cathedral in Zagreb, which was still under construction after the Mongol invasions of the 13th century. The nearby city of Karlovac (which now has a population of more than 50,000) originally was built from scratch in 1579 as a military outpost. The town was designed according to the ideal model of a Renaissance citadel, with massive walls in the shape of a six-pointed star enclosing a grid of city streets. Karlovac lost its military relevance by the 19th century and the walls were torn down, but their remnants can be seen around parts of the city center.

Cities in Dalmatia also reinforced their walls in fear of Ottoman attack. Parts of Dubrovnik's remarkably well-preserved city walls date back to the 10th century, with major construction taking place in the 12th and 13th centuries. The city undertook more construction in the 15th and 16th centuries as a precaution against the Ottoman threat as well as possible naval attack by the Venetian fleet. Florentine architect Michelozzo di Bartolomeo was given the task of designing the Minceta Bastion, on the northern-most corner of the wall, in a modern Renaissance fashion. Although he certainly contributed to the final design, in 1464, Juraj Dlamatinac was called on to construct the battlement at the top of the tower, which is considered its defining feature. In a city full of monuments, the Minceta Bastion is one of the most majestic and, according to the local tourist board, is a popular site for weddings and other such occasions.

THE LEGACY OF HAPSBURG RULE IN ARCHITECTURE AND URBAN PLANNING

During the early 17th century, architecture in Croatia still retained both Renaissance and Gothic elements. Elsewhere in Europe, however, Renaissance architecture already had evolved into the baroque style, which substituted the harmony and symmetry of the Renaissance with dramatic asymmetrical forms and decorative flourishes. As a result of Hapsburg control over Zagreb and the northern region of Croatia, the baroque aesthetic that eventually appeared in this region reflects the Austrian interpretation of the style. In the meantime, coastal Istria and Dalmatia remained under Venetian control and architecture retained an Italian influence.

Once the danger of Ottoman invasion subsided in the 17th century, the Vienna-based Hapsburgs funded a rapid increase in building in the northern region of the country. (Because of the constant threat of war during the previous century, the nonmilitary population declined in the north and the restoration of civilian social structures took decades.) Although significant construction took place once the Ottoman threat declined, native-born Croatians are credited with few major artistic accomplishments during the early 17th century. Foreign architects designed most of the new structures. The painting, sculpture, and decorative work inside of these structures typically was done by foreigners who brought with them the new baroque aesthetic, which would prevail in Croatia until the late 19th century.

From a contemporary standpoint, the most relevant indigenous achievements of the 17th and 18th centuries do not lie in individual buildings or monuments, but rather in the creation of beautiful, well-organized urban environments. In northern Croatia, one can still find towns whose streets are lined with 17th-, 18th-, and 19th-century baroque buildings arranged in a picturesque fashion. The surrounding public spaces usually include a town square and carefully designed parks and gardens, creating a refined cosmopolitan atmosphere echoing that of the Hapsburg capital, Vienna. The town best exemplifying this new trend in urban planning is Varazdin, located northeast of Zagreb in a lush agricultural region near the Drava River. By the time the Turks retreated from the region, the local nobility had profited sufficiently from the war to finance the building of large homes, which survive in the 21st century as apartment houses and office buildings located in what has become the historical center of the town. When Croatia was part of Yugoslavia, funds were scarce for upkeep of these older structures, which suffered from problems ranging from cosmetic issues like severely cracked plaster and peeling paint to more serious structural decay. Today maintenance of historic buildings is a much greater priority and most of the older structures in Varazdin are fully restored and painted in their original pastel colors. The same is true of other villages that were developed into proper towns under Hapsburg rule, including neighboring Cakovec, and Koprivnica to the south, as well as the Slavonian town of Osijek. The center of each of these towns retains the unmistakably Hapsburg sense of order and design, including large public parks that are in use today.

In the 17th and 18th centuries, many churches in small villages were restored in the baroque style. One of these, the small Church of Saint Mary, is considered one of the most important examples of baroque architecture in Croatia. Off of the beaten tourist path, located in the village of Belec in the Zagorje region of the country, the simple exterior of the church provides no hint of its fantastic, heavily decorated baroque and rococo interior. Built by a local noblewoman in 1675 after she heard that the Virgin Mary had appeared nearby, the church became a popular pilgrimage site for other members of the local nobility who donated enough money for a restoration in the mid-18th century. The result is a church filled with dozens of winged cherubs poised to take flight, gold gilt, and at least five altars with lots of pink and green accents. The interior is also decorated by a late-baroque *trompe l'oeil* painting by Croatia's greatest baroque painter, Ivan Ranger, who intertwined biblical scenes with heavy ornamentation. Although the pulpit is considered one of the most beautiful in Europe, the entire space, with its opulent combination of painting, architecture, and sculpture defines this baroque masterpiece.

As the largest city in the region, Zagreb benefited from the new construction that came from Hapsburg interests, but the most famous baroque structure in Zagreb did not come from a Hapsburg patron. It is the Church of Saint Catherine, begun by the Jesuits in 1620 and modeled after the mother church of the order, Il Gesu, in Rome. The interior of the church is lavishly decorated with ornate stucco reliefs, a dramatic frescoed ceiling opening to portray the heavens, and a *trompe l'oeil* fresco behind the altar by Slovenian painter Kristof Andrej Jelovsek, who used a deep sense of perspective to create a detailed combination of painted architecture and landscape. The church interior is well preserved with additional paintings, six chapels, and a number of wooden altars, including one by Italian sculptor Francesco Robba. It also includes a number of tombs from the 17th through the 19th centuries, including those of several historic Croatian figures.

Baroque architecture is also plentiful in Dubrovnik, due, in part, to the damage inflicted on the city by a catastrophic earthquake in 1667. Houses all along the wide main promenade known as the Stradun needed to be rebuilt. The city commissioned Roman architect G. Cerruti to design a baroque prototype for the reconstruction of homes along the heavily damaged northern side of the street.[8] An even larger transformation occurred with the building of a new cathedral, a Jesuit center, and, most notably, at a later date, the rebuilding of the Church of Saint Blaise, which is located on the southern end of the Stradun at Luza Square, one of the most popular areas of the old city near the Rector's Palace and the Sponza Palace.

In addition to its prominent location, the Church of Saint Blaise is important, as the residents of Dubrovnik have traditionally prayed to the saint, also known as *Sveti Vlaho,* for protection. The church was first built in the 14th century to honor Saint Blaise, originally known as an Armenian martyr, but according to legend, appeared to a local priest in the 10th century warning him of an impending Venetian attack. Since then, images of Saint Blaise have been placed throughout the city in private homes and shops as well as on public buildings and the city walls. Although the original church was destroyed, it is not entirely clear how or when. Some texts state that it was destroyed in the 1667 earthquake, but according to UNESCO, the church survived the earthquake only to be destroyed by a fire in 1706. Apparently started by candles, the fire burned through the wooden interior and eventually engulfed the structure. The only surviving objects were the sacristy and a silver statue of Saint Blaise that stands on the church altar.[9]

Venetian architect Marino Groppelli, who also sculpted a number of statues for the original Church of Saint Blaise, built the new sanctuary in a baroque style between 1707 and 1715. The interior houses a rich collection of vestments, paintings, silver ornaments, and various other works of art that were donated in the 18th century, as well as number of 19th- and 20th- century pieces, including a sculpture of Saint Blaise by modern Croatian master Ivan Mestrovic. The powerful relationship of the local population to this church was expressed during the recent Homeland War when the saint was called on to protect the city as the Serbian army besieged it in 1991. Even though the church was severely damaged, residents not only asked local authorities to keep the statue of Saint Blaise in its place on the altar, but also to remove it from its protective case so that the saint's spirit could better guard the city and restore peace.[10]

In the 19th century, Zagreb's population finally exceeded that of Split and Dubrovnik, and the city came into its own as a European metropolis. With both Dalmatia and the northern regions of the country under Austro-Hungarian rule, Zagreb functioned as the capital of the entire Croatian state, which was finally governed by a single political entity. Unlike cities in more industrial parts of Europe, Zagreb was not faced with the pressures of rapid industrial growth. Croatia experienced industrialization at a slower pace, making planning easier than in other countries. As a result, some of Croatia's finest accomplishments in urban planning and architecture can be found in Zagreb, including the development of parks and green spaces, much to the benefit of the city's current residents.

Zagreb's popular Maksimir Park, opened in 1843, was the first major public park in Croatia. Designed according to the highest European standards of the day, Maksimir Park was originally conceptualized in the so-called French style with a large central avenue, but was landscaped like an English garden with pathways, small hills and wooded areas, ornamental sculpture, and artificial lakes. The park includes a number of pavilions, the most notable being the Bellevue Pavilion, which stands as one of the most popular locations in the park. Guidebooks often refer to this park as one of the most beautiful in the city, with no shortage of trails for walking, biking, or jogging. In addition, smaller parks and private gardens were created, including a series of tree-lined squares, such as Strossmayer Square located between the rail station and Jelacic Square, together forming part of a green belt surrounding the lower part of the town.

A similar phenomenon occurred in other Croatian towns in both the north and south, where parks were built in place of the medieval and Renaissance fortifications that were being demolished. The motivation behind this development was not urban expansion so much as sanitation. These fortifications and their old moats and trenches not only became unsightly makeshift garbage dumps but also created damp breeding places for mosquitoes and other vermin. Once these ditches were filled, they became prime locations for attractive parks and gardens. Varazdin, Osijek, Split, and Zadar were among the cities that transformed at least some outdated fortifications into green spaces.

The development of urban parks was accompanied by significant new construction. During the first half of the 19th century, neoclassical and Biedermeier architecture was popular. In the latter half, historicist tendencies prevailed with neo-Romanesque and neo-Gothic styles flourishing, especially when it came to church construction. The architect most closely associated with classicist Biedermeier style was Bartol Felbinger who, in addition to designing numerous buildings also participated in the design of Maksimir Park. Felbinger was known for imbuing classical elements with functional qualities. For example, columns were not just decorative, but also served a structural purpose. This approach freed his designs from superfluous frills and preserved a simple elegance. Felbinger's principal buildings in Zagreb are the residential palaces at Nos. 7 and 10 Ilica, both with courtyard pavilions; the Domotörffy Palace (1815), 32 Radiceva Street; Felbinger House (1820–1824), 15 Jelacic Square; and Alagovic Villa (1824), 87 Nova Ves. Perhaps the most outstanding is Karlo Draskovic (now Dvorana) Palace (1837–1840), 18 Opaticka Street.

In terms of the historicist architectural tendencies, Hermann Bolle, already mentioned with respect to the 19th-century neo-Gothic restoration of the Zagreb Cathedral, was the city's most significant figure. Born in Germany and educated in Vienna, Bolle worked primarily in Croatia. In addition to the Zagreb Cathedral, where he worked under his mentor Friedrich von Schmidt, he is remembered for his neo-Renaissance restoration of the main church in the town of Marija Bistrica (1878–1883) located in the Zagore region just outside of Zagreb. Bolle also designed Zagreb's Crafts School (now known as the Museum of Arts and Crafts) in a German Renaissance revival style reminiscent of buildings in Vienna, where Bolle completed his studies. The Croatian National Theater, still one of the most spectacular buildings in Zagreb, illustrates the historicist trends of the time. Unveiled with much fanfare in 1895, it was designed by Viennese architects Ferdinand Fellner and Hermann Helmer in a neobaroque style. This well-known team also designed theaters throughout Europe as well as in the Croatian cities of Varazdin and Rijeka.

While individual structures are of interest, art historians, along with most visitors to Zagreb, have observed that Zagreb's architectural charm is in its "unity of diversity,"[11] with rows of two- or three-story buildings with facades representing a variety of historical styles all lined up along streets in the central part of town. Some of the most distinctive structures in central Zagreb, as well as in other major Croatian cities, were built in the early 20th century and reflect the aesthetics of the Vienna secession. Several noteworthy buildings in the secessionist style can be found in Zagreb, including the Ethnographic Museum (1901) and the Croatian-Slavonian Bank both designed by the Croatian architect Vjekoslav Bastl for the firm of Hönigsberg and Deutsch. One of the most prominently placed secessionist structures in Zagreb is located on the corner of the city's busy Ban Jelacic Square and features beautiful monumental ceramic reliefs by prominent 20th-century sculptor Ivan Mestrovic. Another stunning example of secessionist architecture, also by Vjekoslav Bastl, is the Kalin House (1903), a residential apartment house only a few blocks away from Ban Jelacic Square. The Kalin House's exterior is lavishly decorated with glazed brick and art nouveau–style red flowers complemented by delicate metal balconies originally inset with glass.

Additional secessionist structures can be found elsewhere in Croatia, including the Nakic Palace (1902), a recently restored residential structure prominently located on the People's Square in the center of Split. Also located in Split is the much-photographed building housing Split's sulpher baths.

Traders' Casino, located in Cakovec, designed by Hungarian architect Odon Horvath and completed in 1904. (Courtesy of the author.)

This structure was designed by Kamilo Toncic, an architect who was born in Split but, like his colleagues in Zagreb, studied in Vienna and brought the secessionist style to his hometown. The most distinctive features of the building are the sculptures decorating the exterior featuring a series of elegant and dramatic art nouveau figures. One of Croatia's most compelling secessionist structures is located in the northern town of Cakovec. Designed by Hungarian architect Odon Horvath and completed in 1904, the building is most often referred to as the Traders' Casino, referring to its original function. It was also used as a trade union building after World War II and as a town library, although its function seems incidental given the unique details of the structure, including decorative brick work and relief images of girls with long braids.

MODERNISM AND THE YUGOSLAVIAN STATE

Before World War I, when Croatia was still part of Austria-Hungary, young Croatians who wanted to study architecture had to go to Vienna. At the conclusion of the war, however, Croatia became part of the newly established Kingdom of Serbs, Croats, and Slovenes and soon developed its own architectural schools, as well as its own identity within the field. A small group of progressive faculty and students at the University of Zagreb achieved international reputations. At the heart of the phenomenon was Viktor Kovacic, the architect most often associated with bringing modernism to Croatia. His most famous structure, the Stock Exchange Building (completed by Hugo Erlich in 1924) in Zagreb, reflects historicist tendencies, although he was one of the first to speak out against the limitations of this trend. In his seminal article "Modern Architecture," published in 1900 in the magazine, *Zivot* (*Life*), Kovacic states that architecture should be "individual and contemporary" while highly functional and practical. In 1923, Kovacic became a professor at the Technical High School in Zagreb where he went on to influence generations of younger architects, including Alfred Albini, Drago Ibler, and Stjepan Planic. Kovacic won many competitions for major projects, most of which, unfortunately, were never built. He designed several residential buildings in Zagreb, including the apartment house in which he occupied an attic flat that has been preserved and converted into a small museum dedicated to the architect. Although Kovacic's designs are admired, he is best known for bringing a modern aesthetic to Croatian architecture.

Many of the buildings constructed between the two world wars have since been modified, or in some cases destroyed, but enough have survived to reflect the clean, simple, and harmonious lines of the early days of modernist architecture in Croatia. These include a tower originally meant to function as a cultural center (1936–1940), located in the suburb of Susak, near the city of Rijeka. The structure is a 14-story skyscraper, designed by Alfred Albini, that fits into a steep corner between two streets. A protégé of Kovacic, Albini established his own practice in 1927. Both Albini and his contemporary Ibler were considered modernists, although they both included a degree of ornamentation in their designs so that their buildings blended into the existing traditional environment. Aside from some villas on the island of Korcula, Ibler's greatest architectural accomplishments in Croatia are the apartment buildings occupying the residential blocks near the center of Zagreb on Martićeva, Smiciklasova, and Vlaska streets. He is remembered as one of the most influential members of the progressive artists' group called *Zemlja* (Earth Group), whose manifesto was to promote art and architecture reflective of the modern needs of Croatian society.

Zemlja's membership included Stjepan Planic, also a student of Ibler's and a modernist who in the 1930s designed residential buildings in Zagreb known for their simplicity and functionality. Examples include existing buildings on Draskoviceva Street (1932), Marinkoviceva Street (1937), Bogoviceva Street (1937), and Marticeva Street (1938). Planic is remembered for converting the circular Arts Pavilion, originally designed in 1938 by sculptor Ivan Mestrovic to function as an art museum, into a mosque by adding three minarets and renovating the interior to reflect Islamic design. In 1945, only three years after their construction, the minarets were demolished, and Mestrovic's distinctively modern cylindrical structure became a museum dedicated to the Socialist Revolution. Today the building is a concert and exhibition space.

Croatia entered World War II in 1941, and until peace resumed in 1945, little construction occurred other than military structures and small bunkers, the ruins of which can still be found, particularly along the coast. Once the fighting was over, reconstruction began but under a different economic system. The Socialist government appropriated almost every large building, including residential structures. Wealthy individuals who had commissioned villas and apartment buildings before the war were disenfranchised and architectural patronage now came primarily from the government. Rather than designing individual buildings, the emphasis shifted toward planned communities, including large apartment complexes and other public structures. The migration of workers from rural to urban areas because of postwar industrialization created a growing demand for housing that required significant planning and new construction.

By the mid-1950s, large housing complexes were designed and built to accommodate new arrivals to the cities. Many of these complexes consisted of two- or three-story masonry structures, sometimes extending across an entire city block. Complete planned communities with multiple reinforced concrete apartment towers, sometimes more than 10 stories high, were also built along with schools, shopping centers, and community and recreational facilities. The goal was to create well-planned urban centers to supplement the traditional, often much older, city centers that were home to most cultural institutions, but whose narrow streets and patchwork of buildings, some hundreds of years old, were not well suited to automobiles and or other aspects of modern life.

Unfortunately, few of these complexes met their full potential, as exemplified in the case of Split 3, a megacomplex designed in the late 1960s to house more than 40,000 residents only a few miles from the center of Split. The well-intentioned plans to build cultural and recreational facilities were never realized.[12] Budget constraints usually were blamed for the delayed construction of a youth center and library that were not constructed either. Instead came shopping centers and other businesses that produced more immediate revenues. As a result, complexes like Split 3 are primarily residential centers with some shopping malls and the inevitable elementary school, minus the galleries, museums, or libraries that were part of the original design.

Nonetheless, this type construction continued through the 1970s and 1980s, with an unfortunate emphasis on inexpensive materials and small budgets for upkeep. Many poorly maintained postwar buildings still dominate the landscape on the suburban fringes of cities like Zagreb and Split and house thousands of residents. Under the Socialist Yugoslav government, public areas suffered from a lack of basic repairs and maintenance, landscaping was minimal, facades were rarely painted or repaired, and graffiti was ignored. Into the 21st century, a majority of large urban housing complexes appear dilapidated, at least externally.

On the inside, the situation usually was better. Although the corridors of large apartment buildings were poorly lit and generally unwelcoming, the apartments themselves, in contrast, were well maintained. Whether residents owned their homes or rented, families tended not to move unless they had to. As a result, they took good care of the apartments that they viewed as their long-term homes. The external appearance of these buildings is slowly improving since the Homeland War, as government-owned apartments were sold to tenants who, as owners, took a greater interest in the overall maintenance of their buildings.

The large hotels constructed along the Dalmatian coast are among the most interesting structures built in Croatia during the 1960s and 1970s. Tourism was growing, and the Yugoslav government saw an opportunity to attract an international clientele. Hotel construction was a natural extension of this thinking. Generally large, overtly modern complexes, the hotels of this era reflected the prevailing structuralist philosophy in architecture, producing designs in which functions of various architectural forms are obvious. For example, one could tell the point at which a beam carried weight and where it was just decorative. Because structuralism leads architects to create designs in which the relationships between components of a building are apparent, these hotels often had a complexity to their appearance making them far more interesting than typical box-like postwar modernist architecture. Finally, the hotels built along the coast at this time were the product of highly controlled and planned development. The government rarely allowed private companies to build resorts, and as a result, construction was limited and the Dalmatian coast remained largely unspoiled.

RESTORATION EFFORTS AND THE HOMELAND WAR

Along with a substantial loss of life, the Homeland War of the 1990s resulted in the destruction of many buildings, including a large number of homes, churches, and historic monuments. A total of 317 towns and villages endured some degree of damage and of these 76 were completely burned down.[13] One of the most extreme examples of destruction was the town of Vukovar, near the Serbian border. The historic baroque town center was completely demolished by Serbian forces in the fall of 1991. After continuous bombing for three months, not a single structure remained standing. The atrocities committed against the citizens of Vukovar and the great loss of human life associated with the siege of that city was particularly brutal and shocking, and significant cultural treasures were lost.

The targeting of cultural and religious monuments is forbidden by the Hague Convention, which was ratified in 1954 by 75 countries, including Yugoslavia. Protected monuments in Vukovar and Dubrovnik bore a Hague Convention banner, which, ironically, was used by Serbian forces to identify and target these very buildings.[14] In addition to the destruction of the entire town of Vukovar, approximately 30 percent of the historic center of Dubrovnik was damaged or destroyed, and Sibenik's Cathedral of Saint James was severely damaged. In Zagreb's Gradac section, more than 70 buildings were damaged, including the Governor's Palace and the Mestrovic Workshop. The historic centers of a number of other smaller towns were heavily damaged as well.[15]

Rebuilding began almost immediately after the war. By 1993, UNESCO started repairing damaged sections of Dubrovnik. Experts were brought in to restore the structural integrity of buildings while preserving the city's historic authenticity. For example, many roofs had to be replaced and whenever possible original rafters, some dating back to the 15th century, were strengthened rather than completely replaced. Also when possible, original terracotta tiles were salvaged, but UNESCO experts estimated that 490,000 tiles had to be replaced. Since the tiles came from a local workshop that had closed more than 100 years ago, the task of finding new tiles that matched, made of similar materials using traditional techniques, was nearly impossible. Eventually, Croatian and French firms were commissioned to make replacement tiles that closely resembled the originals.[16] In spite of this, the new roofs stand in bright contrast to the older ones, which have a darker "antique" tint resulting from centuries of exposure to the elements. The view from the elevated fortifications surrounding the city is one of a patchwork of new and old roofs, reminding us of the destruction Dubrovnik recently endured.

Vukovar is being restored and reconstructed. Many of its historic baroque structures have been rebuilt including an 18th-century Franciscan monastery that was almost totally destroyed. In addition, new construction is ongoing to replace housing and public buildings. One of the most distinctive projects is a 24-apartment housing block simply referred to as Block 21A, designed by the Croatian firm of Penezic & Rogina, specifically for the victims of the Homeland War. The structure won the Vladimir Nazor Award for architecture and urbanism in 2001 and exhibits the firm's trademark modernist philosophy. Occupying a prominent site in the center of town facing the ruins of a department store, the residential building has been warmly received by the town's residents as a symbol of the ongoing effort to revitalize Vukovar.

Blending the New with the Old: Challenges for Contemporary Architects

Successful architecture must be functional while also fitting its environment. Because so many older buildings, including historic landmarks, are being used on a day-to-day basis in Croatia, architects are faced with the challenge of creating contemporary structures that blend on an aesthetic level with a variety of historic styles, including traditional old stone churches, homes, and commercial buildings commonly found along the coast.

Both Penezic & Rogina and the Zagreb-based firm simply named 3LHD took into account traditional elements with respect to both building materials and environment when designing their most challenging high-profile projects. Penezic & Rogina's design for a new church for the parish of Saint Michael's in Dubrovnik involved placing a large, and unapologetically modern, church right next to an older Romanesque one. To avoid dwarfing the older structure, the new church was located perpendicular to the original building. Although the Romanesque church is made of stone and the modern church of concrete, a harmonious relationship is created by the architects' attention to scale. The newer church is the slightly taller of the two, but both buildings' pitched roofs are the same size. In addition, the architects broke up the volume of the new church by using a series of stone-covered walls to create a greater sense of intimacy and connection to the smaller structure nearby.

The 3LHD team of architects faced a similar challenge in designing a sports hall in the small town of Bale whose origins date back to Roman times. Located on the Istrian Peninsula, many of Bale's medieval structures are still standing and in use by the town's 1,000 residents. The environment, while rich in culture and tradition, does not seem like the sort of place into which a modern structure could easily fit. Yet, 3LHD's modern sports hall not only blended into Bale's Old World ambience but also won first prize in the sports category at the 2008 World Architecture Festival, beating the famous Watercube designed for the Beijing Olympics. The architects cite a traditional structure called the *kazun*, which is little more than a stone hut constructed by placing one stone atop another without the use of mortar, as their inspiration. Once used as a shelter for shepherds or workers tending olive groves and

Historic structures in Bale that typify the stone architecture found in many older coastal towns. (Courtesy of the author.)

vineyards, the *kazun* can still be seen in some rural areas. Because the structure functions as a reminder of a pre-industrial age, this sort of stone hut is the perfect vehicle to inform the design of a modern building in an Old World environment. For example, the *kazun* provided inspiration for the surfacing of the exterior walls of the sports hall, which feature an asymmetrical pattern of stones, not quite interlocking, much like those of the typical *kazun*.

The sports hall is a relatively small but versatile building, housing a basketball court, saunas, and a fitness center. It also functions as a public place for town meetings, trade shows, and the like. But for all of its architectural recognition, the sports hall still has one major shortcoming: it cannot be used extensively in the summer because the building does not have air conditioning.

HOUSING: POSTWAR REFUGEE AND RECONSTRUCTION ISSUES

According to European Union–sponsored research,[17] Croatia, along with the rest of the former Yugoslavia, suffered from housing shortages in urban areas before the Homeland War. The population shift away from the countryside and into the cities had been under way since World War II, resulting in a shortage of apartments in larger urban areas such as Zagreb, Split, and Rijeka. The war exacerbated the problem greatly. Approximately 1 million housing units were severely damaged or destroyed across the former Yugoslavia. During the war years, building came to a halt and, by 2001, the rate of new construction reached only one-third of its prewar level. At the same time, the physical maintenance of public apartment buildings was neglected. Finally, the war devastated the economy and created conditions under which, according to European Union estimates, only approximately 70 percent of the population of the former Yugoslavia would have been able to pay market prices for housing in 2001.

The transition from a planned, heavily regulated economy under Yugoslavia to Croatia's market-based economy required new far-reaching policies and institutional changes that Croatia did not have time to make. Croatia's housing problems were complicated by rules quickly established after the war, which allowed for the immediate, and rather messy, privatization of a large number of residential units. Many of these apartments were sold, at very low prices, to the people living in them. Sometimes the buyers were not the owners or the long-term tenants of the homes who held legal rights (referred to as tenancy rights) to the property, but rather people who moved in after the original residents temporarily left during the war.[18] By 2009, many of the disputes that resulted when legal residents tried to reclaim property had made their way through the courts, although anecdotal evidence suggests that a portion of these cases were settled through a combination of intimidation and private financial incentives, that is, owners of homes paying illegal occupants to leave.

During the years following the war, Croatia made substantial efforts to find housing for refugees and internally displaced persons (that is, people who lost their homes during the war). Funds were established for reconstruction efforts and, according to the European Union's *Croatia 2008 Progress Report,*[19] approximately 2,700 units were reconstructed in 2007 and 2008. Another 1,500 will be reconstructed in 2009, leaving an estimated 2,500 housing units yet to be restored depending on the outcome of the 8,700 legal appeals. These are mostly claims for reconstruction funds that were rejected at least once. Many of these claims have been pending for at least four years, although some form of housing assistance has been offered to most of the applicants.

In spite of these positive developments, the European Union's *Croatia 2008 Progress Report* states that the main obstacle to the return of Croatian Serb refugees is still housing, particularly for former tenancy rights holders whose homes were illegally occupied. To appreciate the scope of the issues surrounding the return of Serbian refugees, one must remember that before the war the Croatian state within Yugoslavia was a more ethnically diverse place than it is in 2010. According to the Republic of Croatia's Bureau of Statistics, Serbs accounted for approximately 12 percent of the population in 1991 as opposed to only about 4.5 percent in 2008.

Implementation of the Croatian government's housing program for former tenancy rights holders wanting to return to Croatia continues to be slow, although the system appears to be picking up speed. According to the report, more than 2,100 refugees and 1,100 displaced persons returned to their place of origin in Croatia in 2007, bringing the total number of Croatian Serbs (the largest ethnic refugee group) registered as returnees to Croatia to almost 143,000, although the report states that the number who have permanently returned could be less than 60 percent of this figure. In the meantime, the program to reestablish public infrastructure in villages heavily damaged during the war, and whose populations became refugees, is ongoing. Steps such as building roads to connect the geographically remote villages that were devastated during the Homeland War are critical to repopulation and economic survival.

The construction of new housing is important in urban centers such as Zagreb, as the war resulted in even more migration from rural to urban areas. Private real estate developers have moved into this market and consulting firms have published up-to-date assessments of the housing stock in Croatia. BuildInfoConsult, one such firm doing extensive research in Croatia, divides the housing market into two segments, high end and low end. In Zagreb, the country's fastest growing residential housing market, prices for homes have risen about 15 percent over the last several years, with demand for higher end homes exceeding supply. In contrast, the market for lower cost housing is saturated; supply has exceeded demand because of the combination of the ongoing economic crisis that began in 2008 and excessive building, including 25,000 new units constructed in 2007.[20] The real estate market was stagnant as of the later half of 2009. Developers do not want to incur losses, so they are not reducing prices greatly. Meanwhile, buyers are waiting, expecting prices to drop, and as a result, sales have decreased significantly and probably will remain low until the overall national economy improves.

Many Croatians own houses and land that have been in the family for generations. A large number of these homes are located outside of major cities as much of the economy used to be agrarian. Because of the migration to urban areas over the past several decades, these familial homes have become part-time residences or vacation houses. Sometimes they are sold, although an agreement must be reached among all owners for a sale to be finalized. This can be a complicated process because a family home is traditionally handed down from generation to generation, so it can belong to a dozen descendants, some of whom may not even live in Croatia. Sometimes these houses are simply abandoned because a sale cannot be negotiated to everyone's satisfaction, and the family members do not have the money or the motivation to maintain the property. One can see severely neglected properties in the countryside and in sparsely populated coastal villages a few miles from the beach. However, as Croatia's popularity as a tourist destination grows, developers are making unprecedented efforts to acquire abandoned homes and their adjacent tracts of land. In order to prevent over-development of the most desirable and pristine coastal areas, the government has limited construction to sites where a structure was previously built. Such legislation has protected the environment while escalating the value of even the most decrepit buildings along the coast of Dalmatia and Istria.

NOTES

1. Paul Daniel, "Croatia's Stone Industry Is Expanding," Istria on the Internet—Crafts and Trades–Masonry, 2004, Publicaciones Litos S.L., Spain, October 8, 2008, http://www.istrianet.org/istria/crafts-trades/masonry/white-house.htm (retrieved October 8, 2008).

2. Kosta Rakic, *Treasures of Yugoslavia: An Encyclopedic Touring Guide* (Belgrade: Yugoslaviapublic, 1980).

3. Radovan Ivanicevic, *Art Treasures of Croatia* (Belgrade: Iro Motvun, 1986), 120.

4. *Grove Art Online*, s.v. "Zagreb" (by Paul Tvrtkovic), Oxford Art Online, http://www.oxfordartonline.com/subscriber/article/grove/art/T093151 (retrieved March 27, 2009).

5. Ivanicevic, *Art Treasures of Croatia,* 88.

6. Ibid., 100.

7. Ibid., 199.

8. Ibid., 152.

9. "Church of St. Blaise," Adriatic UNESCO Sites, http://www.sitiunescoadriatico
.org/index.php?pg=1503 (retrieved April 2, 2009).

10. Ibid.

11. Ivanicevic, *Art Treasures of Croatia,* 181.

12. Darovan Tusek, "Polyfunctionality of Split 3, or the Unbearable Lightness of
Giving Up," *Oris Magazine for Architecture and Culture* 57 (2009): 124–135.

13. Ivan Zaknic, "The Pain of Ruins: Croatian Architecture under Siege," *Journal
of Architectural Education* 46, no. 2 (November 1992): 115–124.

14. Ibid., 119.

15. Ibid., 123.

16. Maja Nodari, "Dubrovnik Reborn," *UNESCO Courier,* February 2000, http://
www.unesco.org/courier/2000_02/uk/signes/intro.htm (retrieved April 2, 2009).

17. Stability Pact for South Eastern Europe, *Housing Programme Development Study:
Bosnia Herzegovina, Croatia, Federal Republic of Yugoslavia, Stage 1 Report,* Brussels,
December 2001.

18. Ibid.

19. European Union: European Commission, *Commission Staff Working Document:
Croatia 2008 Progress Report,* Brussels, November 5, 2008, SEC(2008) 2694.

20. "Croatian Construction Growth: A Story to Be Continued?" BuildInfoConsult,
http://www.buildinfoconsult.com/Default.aspx?PageNode=808&PageID=10126
(retrieved August 26, 2009).

Selected Bibliography

CHAPTER 1: GEOGRAPHY AND HISTORY

Bartlett, William. *Croatia: Between Europe and the Balkans*. London and New York: Routledge, 2003.

Central Bureau of Statistics of Republic of Croatia. "Statistical Yearbook for 2005: Geographical and Meteorological Data. http://www.dzs.hr/Hrv_Eng/ljetopis/2005/01-tab.pdf.

Encyclopædia Britannica. "Croatia." Encyclopædia Britannica Online. http://search.eb.com/eb/article-9110562.

Eterovich, Francis H., and Christopher Spalatin, eds. *Croatia: Land, People and Culture*. Vol.1 (1964) and Vol. 2 (1970). Toronto: University of Toronto Press.

Goldstein, Ivo, and Nikolina Jovanovic. *Croatia: A History*. London: C. Hurst and Co. Ltd., 1999.

Magas, Branka. *Croatia Through History: The Making of a European State*. London: Saqi Books, 2007.

Tanner, Marcus. *Croatia: A Nation Forged in War*. 2nd ed. New Haven, CT: Yale Nota Bene, 2001.

United Nations Development Programme. "A Climate for Change: Climate Change and Its Impacts on Society and Economy in Croatia." *Human Development Report, Croatia, 2008*. http://europeandcis.undp.org/home/show/A006D9DC-F203-1EE9-B2EDE14ABB69E2E9 (retrieved April 18, 2009).

Chapter 2: Religion

Bjelajac, Branko. "Serbia: Religious Freedom Survey, August 2004," *World Wide Religious News,* "Forum 18," August 5, 2004, http://www.wwrn.org/article (retrieved February 17, 2010).

Bremer, Thomas. "The Catholic Church and its Role in Politics and Society." In *Croatia since Independence: War, Politics, Society, Foreign Relations,* ed. Sabrina P. Ramet, Konrad Clewing, and Reneo Lukic, 251–268. Munchen: R. Oldenbourg Verlag, 2008.

Eterovich, Francis H., and Christopher Spalatin, eds. *Croatia: Land, People and Culture,* Vol.1. Toronto: University of Toronto Press, 1964.

Goldstein, Ivo, and Nikolina Jovanovic. *Croatia: A History.* London: C. Hurst and Co. Ltd., 1999.

Hofman, Nila Ginger. *Renewed Survival: Jewish Community Life in Croatia.* Lanham, MD: Lexington Books, 2005.

Jambrek, Stanko. "The Great Commission in the Context of the Evangelical Churches of Croatia in the Second Part of the Twentieth Century." *Kairos: Evangelical Journal of Theology* 2, no. 2 (2008): 153–179.

U.S. Commission for the Preservation of America's Heritage Abroad. *Jewish Heritage Sites in Croatia: Preliminarily Report, 2006.* http://www.heritageabroad.gov/reports/doc/CROATIA_Report_2006.pdf (retrieved February 17, 2010).

World Trade Press. "Croatia Religion, 2007." http://www.bestcountryreports.com.

Chapter 3: Civic Values and Political Thought

European Union: European Commission. *Commission Staff Working Document: Croatia 2009 Progress Report,* October 14, 2009. SEC(2009) 1333. http://www.unhcr.org/refworld/docid/4adc274a2.html (retrieved October 20, 2009).

Magas, Branka. *Croatia Through History: The Making of a European State.* London: Saqi Books, 2007.

Ramet, Sabrina P., Konrad Clewing, and Reneo Lukic, eds. *Croatia since Independence: War, Politics, Society, Foreign Relations.* Munich: R. Oldenbourg Verlag, 2008.

Ramet, Sabrina P., and Davorka Matic, eds. *Democratic Transition in Croatia: Value Transformation, Education & Media.* College Station: Texas A&M University Press, 2007.

U.S. Department of State, *2008 Country Reports on Human Rights Practices—Croatia,* February 25, 2009, http://www.unhcr.org/refworld/docid/49a8f198c.html (retrieved September 15, 2009).

Chapter 4: Marriage and Family, Gender Issues, and Education

Enawa (European and North American Women Action). "The Status of Women's Rights in Croatia." http://www.enawa.org/NGO/Croatia1.htm (retrieved June 2, 2010).

Shiffman, Jeremy, Marina Skrabalo, and Jelena Subotic. "Reproductive Rights and the State in Serbia and Croatia." *Social Science & Medicine* 54, no. 4 (2002): 625–642.

Sikiae, Lynette. "Gendered Values and Attitudes among Rural Women in Croatia." *Journal of Comparative Family Studies* 38, no. 3 (2007): 459–479. ProQuest Research Library. http://www.proquest.com/en-US/catalogs/databases/detail/pq_research_library.shtml. (retrieved March 11, 2008)

Vuletic, Dean. "Gay Men and Lesbians." In *Croatia since Independence: War, Politics, Society, Foreign Relations*, eds. Sabrina P. Ramet, Konrad Clewing, and Reneo Lukic. Munich: R. Oldenbourg Verlag, 2008, 293–320.

CHAPTER 5: HOLIDAYS AND LEISURE ACTIVITIES

Ban, Irina. *Culture Smart! Croatia.* London: Kuperard, 2008.

Jakimenko, Boris. "Croatian Basketball and Its Young Players." *FIBA Assist Magazine* (December 2005): 9–11.

Monti, James. "Croatian Christmas Traditions." *The Magnificat Advent* (December/January 2006): 2–5. http://www.croatia.org/crown/articles/8874/1/Croatian-Christmas-Traditions-by-James-Monti-published-in-The-Magnificat-Advent-2006/Advent-2006.html (retrieved February 17, 2010).

CHAPTER 6: CUISINE AND FASHION

Babic, Frances. "Patterns of Meaning: Croatian Folk Life Traditions." Essay in association with exhibition at Ohio Arts Council's Riffe Gallery, 1997. http://www.oac.state.oh.us/riffe/exhibitions/1997/patterns/patterns_pr.asp (retrieved May 24, 2010).

Evenden, Karen. *A Taste of Croatia.* Ojai, CA: New Oak Press, 2007.

Muraj, Aleksandra. "The Stance of the Citizenry in the Towns towards Folk Costume and Peasant Textile Skills" (abstract in English, article in Croatian). *Narodna Umjetnost: Croatian Journal of Ethnology and Folklore Research* 43, no. 2 (December 2006): 7–40.

Pavicic, Lilliana, and Gordana Pirker-Mosher. *The Best of Croatian Cooking.* New York: Hippocrene Books, 2000.

CHAPTER 7: LITERATURE

Culic Nisula, Dasha. "Jure Kastelan." *South Slavic Writers before World War II*, ed. Vasa D. Mihailovich, 75–78. Vol. 147 of *Dictionary of Literary Biography*. Detroit: Gale Research, 1995.

Culic Nisula, Dasha. "Vesna Parun (April 10, 1922–)." In *South Slavic Writers since World War II*, ed. Vasa D. Mihailovich, 210–214. Vol. 181 of *Dictionary of Literary Biography.* Detroit: Gale Research, 1997.

Eekman, Thomas. "Ivan Gundulic." In *South Slavic Writers before World War II*, ed. Vasa D. Mihailovich, 61–67. Vol. 147 of *Dictionary of Literary Biography*. Detroit: Gale Research, 1995.

Encyclopaedia Britannica Online, s.v. "Gundulic, Ivan," http://www.britannica.com/EBchecked/topic/249421/Ivan-Gundulic (retrieved November 12, 2009).

Encyclopaedia Britannica Online, s.v. "Hektorovic, Petar." http://search.eb.com/eb/article-9039863 (retrieved November 6, 2009).

Hawkesworth, Celia. *Zagreb: A Cultural History (Cityscapes)*. New York: Oxford University Press, 2007.

Juraga, Dubravka. "Augustin ('Tin') Ujevic." In *South Slavic Writers before World War II*, ed. Vasa D. Mihailovich, 241–247. Vol. 147 of *Dictionary of Literary Biography*. Detroit: Gale Research, 1995.

Kadic, Ante. "Miroslav Krleza." In *South Slavic Writers before World War II*, ed. Vasa D. Mihailovich, 112–121. Vol. 147 of *Dictionary of Literary Biography*. Detroit: Gale Research, 1995.

Malby, Maria B. "August Senoa." In *South Slavic Writers before World War II*, ed. Vasa D. Mihailovich, 215–221. Vol. 147 of *Dictionary of Literary Biography*. Detroit: Gale Research, 1995.

Matejic, Mateja. "Elements of Folklore in Ivo Andric's *Na drini cupria*." *Canadian Slavonic Papers: An Interdisciplinary Quarterly Devoted to the Soviet Union* 20 (1978): 348–357.

Niseteo, Anthony. "The First Press in Croatia." The Library Quarterly 30, no. 3 (July 1960): 209–212.

Rakic, Bogdan. "Subverted Epic Oral Tradition in South Slavic Written Literatures, 16th–19th Centuries." University of Chicago, Project Muse. http://muse.jhu.edu/journals/serbian_studies/v001/1.1.rakic01.pdf (retrieved December 30, 2008).

Tanner, Marcus. *Croatia: A Nation Forged in War*. New Haven, CT: Yale Nota Bene, 2001.

Witalec, Janet, ed. "Ivo Andric, (1892–1975)." In *Twentieth-Century Literary Criticism*, 1–109. Vol. 135. Detroit: Gale Research, 2003.

CHAPTER 8: MEDIA AND CINEMA

Freedom House. "Nations in Transit: Croatia." http://www.unchr.org/refworld/docid/ (retrieved June 30, 2009).

Horton, Andrew J. "Avant-Garde Film and Video in Croatia." *Central Europe Review*, no. 6 (November 1998). http://www.ce-review.org/kinoeye/kinoeye6old.html (retrieved April 22, 2010).

Human Rights Watch. "Croatia: Events of 2009." http://www.hrw.org/en/world-report-2010/croatia (retrieved June 30, 2009).

Joch Robinson, Gertrude. *Tito's Maverick Media: The Politics of Mass Communications in Yugoslavia*. Urbana: University of Illinois Press, 1977.

Malovic, Stjepan, and Gary W. Selnow. *The People, Press and Politics of Croatia*. Westport, CT: Praeger Publishers, 2001.

"Media Landscape: Croatia." In *European Media Governance: National and Regional Dimensions*. Georgios Terzis, ed. Bristol, UK: Intellect Books, 2008. http://www.intellectbooks.com. Cited by European Journalism Center. http://www.ejc.net/media_landscape/article/croatia.

Pavicic, Jurica. "Moving into the Frame: Croatian Film in the 1990s," *Central Europe Review* 2, no. 9 (May 15, 2000). http://www.ce-review.org/00/19/kinoeye19_pavicic.html.

Peck, L. "Nationalism, News Media and Tolerance in Croatia." *Journal of Interdisciplinary Studies* 20, nos.1/2 (2008): 105–119.

Perusko, Zrinjka. "Media and Civic Values," in *Democratic Transition in Croatia: Value Transformation, Education & Media*. Sabrina P. Ramet and Davorka Matic, eds. College Station: Texas A&M University Press, 2007.

Perusko, Zrinjka, and Kresimir Jurlin. *Croatian Media Markets: Regulation and Concentration Trends*. Zagreb: Institute for International Relations, 2006. http://www.imo.hr/files/Media-Markets-in-Croatia.pdf.

Petkovic, Vladan. "Serbia vs. Croatia: 2008 in Film, Vladan Petkovic Surveys the Scene." Neil Young's Film Lounge. http://www.jigsawlounge.co.uk/film/reviews/serbia-vs-croatia-2008-in-film-vladan-petkovic-surveys-the-scene (retrieved April 22, 2010).

Ramet, Sabrina P., and Davorka Matic, eds. *Democratic Transition in Croatia: Value Transformation, Education & Media*. College Station: Texas A&M University Press, 2007.

Skrabalo, Ivo. "Young Croatian Film," *Central Europe Review* 1, no. 18 (October 25, 1999). http://www.ce-review.org/99/18/kinoeye18_skrabalo.html (retrieved April 22, 2010).

CHAPTER 9: MUSIC AND PERFORMING ARTS

Caleta, Josko. "Klapa Singing: A Traditional Folk Phenomenon of Dalmatia." *Nar, Umjet* 34, no. 1 (1997): 127–145. https://circle.ubc.ca/bitstream/handle/2429/5244/ubc_1994-0320.pdf?sequence=1 (retrieved May 11, 2010).

Djokic, Dejdan. "Ex-Yu rock," openDemocracy.net, August 6, 2002, http://www.opendemocracy.net/arts-festival/article_546.jsp (retrieved May 20, 2010).

Everett, William A. "Contemporary Music in Croatia: Traditions and Innovations." *Central European Review* 2, no. 19 (2000). http://www.ce-review.org/00/19/everett19.html (retrieved May 17, 2010).

Grove Music Online, s.v. "Croatia" (by Stanislav Tuksar and Grozdana Marosevic), Oxford Music Online, http://www.oxfordmusiconline.com/subscriber/article/grove/music/40473 (retrieved May 4, 2010).

Kruth, John. "Miroslav and Gordana Evacic: Drava River Blues." *Singout* 52, no. 4 (March/April/May 2009): 45–47.

Petrovic, Ankica. "Ganga: A Form of Traditional Rural Singing in Yugoslavia." PhD diss., Queen's University of Belfast, 1977. http://www.imota.net/html/ankica_petroviae.html.

Statemaster.com Encyclopedia, s.v. "SFR Yugoslav Pop and Rock Scene," http://www
.statemaster.com/encyclopedia/SFR-Yugoslav-Pop-and-Rock-scene#1960s.
(retirieved May 17, 2010).

Chapter 10: Painting and Sculpture

Djuric, Dubravka, and Misko Suvskovic, eds. *Impossible Histories: Historical Avant-
gardes, Neo-avant-gardes and Post-avant-gardes in Yugoslavia, 1918–1991.*
Cambridge, MA: MIT Press, 2003.
Dzamonja, Fedor, ed. *Dzamonja; Sculpture, Drawings, Projects.* Zagreb: Kaligraph,
2001.
Generalic, Ivan. *The Magic World of Ivan Generalic,* John Shepley, trans. from Italian.
Introduction by *Nebojsa Tomasevic.* New York: Rizzoli, 1976.
Grove Art Online, s.v. "Bukovac, Vlaho" (by Zdenko Rus), Oxford Art Online, http://
www.oxfordartonline.com/subscriber/article/grove/art/T012172 (accessed
September 20, 2010).
Grove Art Online, s.v. "Exat-51" (by Jure Mikuz), Oxford Art Online, http://www
.oxfordartonline.com/subscriber/article/grove/art/T027116 (accessed September
20, 2010).
Grove Art Online, s.v. "Generalic, Ivan" (by Jure Mikuz), Oxford Art Online, http://
www.oxfordartonline.com/subscriber/article/grove/art/T031291 (accessed
September 20, 2010).
Grove Art Online, s.v. "Hegedusic, Krsto" (by Jure Mikuz), Oxford Art Online, http://
www.oxfordartonline.com/subscriber/article/grove/art/T037195 (accessed
September 20, 2010).
Hawksworth, Celia. *Zagreb: A Cultural History.* New York: Oxford University Press,
2008.
Hoptman, Laura, and Tomas Pospiszyl, eds. *Primary Documents: A Sourcebook for
Eastern and Central European Art since the 1950s.* New York: Museum of
Modern Art, 2002.
IRWIN, eds. *East Art Map: Contemporary Art and Eastern Europe.* London: Central
Saint Martins College of Art and Design, University of the Arts, 2006.
Ivancevic, Radovan. *Art Treasures of Croatia.* Belgrade, Yugoslavia: Iro Motovun,
1986.
Mestrovic, Maria, and Marcus Tanner, eds. *Ivan Mestrovic: The Making of a Master.*
London: Stacey International Publishers, 2008.
"Symbolism Lost in Translation: Jan Kempenaers, the Monuments of Former
Yugoslavia." *Monthly Magazine of the Croatian Architects' Association*, nos. 5/6
(2009): 62–67.

Chapter 11: Architecture and Housing

Djuric, Dubravka, and Misko Suvskovic, eds. *Impossible Histories: Historical Avant-
gardes, Neo-avant-gardes and Post-avant-gardes in Yugoslavia, 1918–1991.*
Cambridge, MA: MIT Press, 2003.

European Union Stability Pact for South Eastern Europe. *Housing Programme Development Study, Bosnia Herzegovina, Croatia, Federal Republic of Yugoslavia; Stage 1 Report.* Geneva: European Union/URBACT, 2001.

Ivanicevic, Radovan. *Art Treasures of Croatia.* Belgrade, Yugoslavia: Iro Motvun, 1986.

Grove Art Online, s.v. "Bollé, Hermann" (by Frank Arneil Walker), Oxford Art Online, http://www.oxfordartonline.com/subscriber/article/grove/art/T009720 (accessed September 20, 2010).

Grove Art Online, s.v. "Croatia" (by Paul Tvrtkovic et al.), Oxford Art Online, http://www.oxfordartonline.com/subscriber/article/grove/art/T020328 (accessed September 20, 2010).

Grove Art Online, s.v. "Felbinger, Bartol" (by Paul Tvrtkovic), Oxford Art Online, http://www.oxfordartonline.com/subscriber/article/grove/art/T027788 (accessed September 20, 2010).

Grove Art Online, s.v. "Ibler, Drago" (by Paul Tvrtkovic), Oxford Art Online, http://www.oxfordartonline.com/subscriber/article/grove/art/T039746 (accessed September 20, 2010).

Grove Art Online, s.v. "Kovacic, Viktor." (by Paul Tvrtkovic), Oxford Art Online, http://www.oxfordartonline.com/subscriber/article/grove/art/T047795 (accessed September 20, 2010).

Grove Art Online, s.v. "Planic, Stjepan" (by Paul Tvrtkovic), Oxford Art Online, http://www.oxfordartonline.com/subscriber/article/grove/art/T068028 (accessed September 20, 2010).

Grove Art Online, s.v. "Split" (by Margaret Lyttleton), Oxford Art Online, http://www.oxfordartonline.com/subscriber/article/grove/art/T020328 (accessed September 20, 2010).

Grove Art Online, s.v. "Zagreb" (by Paul Tvrtkovic), Oxford Art Online, http://www.oxfordartonline.com/subscriber/article/grove/art/T093151 (accessed September 20, 2010).

Treasures of Yugoslavia: An Encyclopedic Touring Guide. Belgrade, Yugoslavia: Yugoslaviapublic, 1980.

Zaknic, Ivan. "The Pain of Ruins: Croatian Architecture under Siege." *Journal of Architectural Education* 46, no. 2 (November 1992): 115–124.

Index

About the Author

MARILYN CVITANIC is an adjunct faculty member in the Department of Fine Arts at Manhattan College and the College of Mount Saint Vincent, both located in Riverdale, New York. She is also a painter whose work has been exhibited in New York City, Chicago, Los Angeles, and Croatia.